NATO ENTERS THE
21st CENTURY

Of Related Interest

NATO ENTERS THE 21ST CENTURY

Editor

TED GALEN CARPENTER
(Cato Institute, Washington DC)

FRANK CASS
LONDON • PORTLAND, OR

First Published in 2001 in Great Britain by
FRANK CASS PUBLISHERS
Newbury House, 900 Eastern Avenue
London, IG2 7HH

and in the United States of America by
FRANK CASS PUBLISHERS
c/o ISBS, 5824 N.E. Hassalo Street
Portland, Oregon, 97213-3644

Website: www.frankcass.com

British Library Cataloguing in Publication Data

NATO enters the 21st century
1. North Atlantic Treaty Organization
I. Carpenter, Ted Galen
355'.031'091821

ISBN 0-7146-5058-7 (cloth)
ISBN 0-7146-8109-1 (paper)

Library of Congress Cataloging-in-Publication Data

NATO enters the 21st century / editor Ted Galen Carpenter
   p. cm.
   Includes bibliographical references and index.
   ISBN 0-7146-5058-7 (cloth) – ISBN 0-7146-8109-1 (pbk.)
   1. North Atlantic Treaty Organization. I. Carpenter, Ted Galen.
UA646.3 .N24252 2000
355'.031091821'0905 –dc21

                                                00-063920

This group of studies first appeared in a Special Issue on
'NATO Enters the 21st Century'
of *The Journal of Strategic Studies* (ISSN 0140 2390) 23/3 (September 2000)
published by Frank Cass.

Printed in Great Britain by Antony Rowe Ltd., Chippenham, Wiltshire

Contents

Introduction: NATO's Prospects at the Dawn of the 21st Century

TED GALEN CARPENTER

NATO's 50th anniversary summit in April 1999 was supposed to be a grand and glorious celebration. Not only was the event designed to mark a half-century of success in preserving the peace of Europe, it was to underscore the alliance's continuing indispensable role in the approaching twenty-first century. In its next 50 years, NATO would be able to bring the blessings of peace and democracy to all of Europe, not merely the western half of the Continent as during the Cold War.

The summit proved to be a far more somber proceeding than planned. Just four weeks earlier, NATO had launched air strikes against Yugoslavia to compel the Belgrade government to relinquish control of its restive, predominantly Albanian province of Kosovo to a NATO-led international peacekeeping force. Western leaders evidently assumed that a brief 'demonstration' bombing campaign would cause Yugoslavian president Slobodan Milošević to capitulate, and that the armed conflict would be long over before the NATO meeting convened in Washington in late April. Instead, the war raged on with no end in sight, casting a pall over the gathering. Michael Mandelbaum, a professor at Johns Hopkins University's Paul Nitze School for Advanced International Studies, caustically termed the summit a funeral masquerading as a birthday party.

Mandelbaum's assessment may have been unduly harsh, but there was a palpable atmosphere of uneasiness and apprehension among the NATO dignitaries. The governments of at least four members – Italy, Greece, Hungary and the Czech Republic – were critical of the alliance's use of force against Yugoslavia (although they reluctantly went along with that policy to avoid a public schism), and the publics in those countries were even more negative. Public opinion in NATO's leading member, the United

States, was also bitterly divided, and the US House of Representatives had refused to approve legislation backing the Clinton administration's policy.

The summit survived all of the disharmony and celebrated the alliance's 50th birthday, albeit in a decidedly more subdued manner than originally planned. Alliance leaders even approved a detailed new Strategic Concept to guide NATO in the twenty-first century. Nevertheless, uneasiness about NATO's future persists in many quarters on both sides of the Atlantic. Major disagreements about the alliance's strategy – even about its very purpose – simply will not go away. Indeed, in the months since the 50th anniversary summit, some of those disagreements appear to have intensified rather than diminished.

There are sharp disputes about whether NATO should continue to regard collective territorial defense under Article 5 of the Washington Treaty as its core mission. Advocates of maintaining that focus argue that departing from the traditional mission risks a loss of consensus and even a breach in alliance ranks. The intra-alliance tensions over the 1999 Balkan war, they warn, were an omen of what will befall NATO if it ventures beyond its original purpose. Their opponents respond that most of the problems that have troubled Europe's peace since the end of the Cold War have occurred outside the territory of NATO's members, and that if the alliance refuses to venture out-of-area, it risks becoming irrelevant.

Yet even within the ranks of proponents of out-of-area missions there are sometimes fierce disagreements. The Clinton administration and some other American supporters of NATO suggest that the alliance become an institutional mechanism for defending Western interests wherever they are threatened – even if that task takes NATO outside of Europe entirely. That approach is strongly resisted by NATO's European members, who fear that they might be dragged into disputes that have little relevance to Europe's security interests.

Disputes have also flared about burden sharing and the proper relationship between NATO and the embryonic European Security and Defense Identity (ESDI). US officials complain that the United States had to bear a grotesquely disproportionate share of the military burden during the air war against Yugoslavia. Americans seethe as they witness already low European defense budgets continue their downward slide. Indeed, US military leaders warn that the gap in capabilities between the American military and its NATO counterparts is growing so large that coordination for major operations in the future will become difficult, if not problematic.

In addition to the latest round in the burden-sharing controversy, Americans increasingly wonder whether the European members of NATO are merely engaging in empty rhetoric about building a strong ESDI. The Europeans respond that Washington's professed support for ESDI often appears to be insincere. Indeed, some European leaders note that every time they move closer to making ESDI a reality, the United States voices new caveats designed to preserve NATO's primacy in Euro-Atlantic security. Many Europeans wonder if the various 'conditions' being raised by Washington are not attempts to sabotage any attempt to create an effective European security organization. To some capitals on the Continent, US policy seems designed to perpetuate America's dominance of the transatlantic relationship at all costs.

Finally, there are bitter disagreements about Washington's emerging decision to deploy a national anti-ballistic missile system. European members of NATO fear that the deployment of a US National Missile Defense (NMD) system may reignite a strategic arms race with Russia (and possibly China as well), thereby making Europe less secure. They also worry about decoupling American and European security interests if the United States has reliable protection against missile attacks and Washington's European allies do not. That opposition both puzzles and annoys American leaders. They emphasize that an NMD system is designed to protect the United States from attacks (or more likely, blackmail) by such 'rogue states' as North Korea, Iran or Iraq. The missile capabilities of such states are growing, US officials warn, and the deployment of an effective NMD may be essential if the United States is to continue defending allies and clients without undue risk to its homeland.

Those internal disputes raise new questions about NATO's effectiveness, perhaps even its viability. The studies in this collection examine various aspects of the alliance as it enters the new century. In the first essay, I look at NATO's new Strategic Concept and conclude that it is a document that attempts to placate competing factions on several major issues. Indeed, the carefully crafted language barely conceals the depth of the discord on such matters as NATO's commitment to out-of-area missions or the functional relationship between the alliance and the ESDI. As a political and public relations document, the Strategic Concept has been a solid success in preserving at least the façade of alliance unity. Yet the underlying substantive disagreements continue to roil. Thus, as a coherent strategic blueprint the Concept is not, and likely will not be, terribly relevant.

Alan Tonelson examines the long-standing burden-sharing controversies within NATO. He documents numerous promises by the European members of the alliance – from the 1950s to the present time – to bear a greater share of the defense burden and to build an effective 'European pillar'. All of those promises ultimately went unfulfilled, and as recently as the 1999 war in the Balkans, US planes flew a majority of the missions. Although Tonelson blames the European countries for free-riding on the United States, he reserves his harshest criticism for two generations of American officials who have allowed the allies to get away with such behavior. The underlying problem, Tonelson contends, is that US leaders persist in sending mixed messages. They periodically insist that the Europeans must do more and pay more for transatlantic defense efforts, yet (sometimes in the same speeches) those officials stress how vital Europe is to America's security and that Washington will never de-emphasize the transatlantic link. The second half of the message, in Tonelson's view, lets the other NATO governments and publics know that they can safely ignore the first half of the message demanding greater burden sharing.

Christopher Layne shares Tonelson's conclusion that NATO is hardly an alliance of equals, but he identifies a very different cause. According to Layne, Washington has deliberately fostered European dependency to preserve American hegemony in Europe. Applying offensive realist theory, Layne argues that US behavior since the end of the Cold War has been entirely consistent with the features of that theory – especially its explanation of the behavior of hegemonic powers. He notes that, following the demise of America's principal strategic rival, the Soviet Union, Bush and Clinton administration policymakers did not contemplate a retrenched US role in Europe. Instead, just as offensive realist theory would predict, they expanded both their definition of America's European interests and the possible threats to those interests. They also moved to expand Washington's principal strategic institution, NATO, into the sphere of influence recently vacated by the rival great power.

Finally, US leaders have sought to discourage their European allies from developing an alternative security institution that could become a competitor to a US-dominated NATO. All of this has been astute behavior by a hegemon, Layne contends, but the emerging strategic realities – including an increasingly prosperous and capable European Union – mean that the strategy is likely to fail over the long term.

Alton Frye scrutinizes one important aspect of NATO's policy in the post-Cold War era, the alliance's relationship with Russia, and finds the record troubling. He concludes that the decision to enlarge NATO's membership to include Hungary, Poland and the Czech Republic was short-sighted and aborted what had been a promising partnership with Russia. NATO's military interventions in the Balkans, especially the war over Kosovo, did even more damage. Frye warns that further actions, such a second round of expansion that would incorporate the Baltic republics, risks returning the West's relationship with Russia to the chill environment of the Cold War era. He urges NATO policymakers to take Russia more seriously as a major power and a constructive security partner, pursue opportunities for further arms control agreements, and seek ways to bring Russia into the network of Western institutions. The alternative to such an approach, Frye warns, could be most unpleasant.

In her essay, Kori Schake examines the tensions within the alliance concerning the proper response to such issues as proliferation of weapons of mass destruction, arms control initiatives, and the development of a US national missile defense system. She urges NATO to address the proliferation issue more seriously than it has to date, indeed to make it a policy priority. Schake also warns that the transatlantic relationship will collapse if America's allies try to prevent the United States from deploying NMD. At the same time, she urges US leaders to appreciate European worries about the possible decoupling implications of NMD, and to recognize that the active cooperation of some European allies (who must provide radar data) is essential if NMD is to become operational.

To prevent an intra-alliance crisis, Schake urges a redoubled US effort to gain Russia's acceptance of its NMD initiative by renegotiating the Anti-Ballistic Missile (ABM) Treaty. That action, in turn, would help soothe European worries that Washington's focus on missile defense might re-ignite an offensive strategic arms race. Failure to adopt a common approach to this critical set of issues, Schake warns, could jeopardize the cohesion of the alliance.

Amos Perlmutter's article notes the shift of NATO's focus in the post-Cold War period from territorial defense of limited membership to an expansion of membership and an emphasis on conflict prevention and out-of-area missions. That shift was most unfortunate, in his view. He warns that by expanding both its membership and principal mission into Central and Eastern Europe, NATO has already experienced several undesirable consequences. NATO's move east has entangled the alliance with an assortment of ethnic factions possessing parochial – and not very savory – agendas. The dubious relationship with the Kosovo Liberation Army is only the most graphic example, according to Perlmutter.

NATO's move east has also damaged relations with Russia and, even worse, caused Russia to seek strategic partnerships with other powers, most notably China and Iran. That development, Perlmutter warns, could be extremely detrimental to Western – especially US – interests in the future.

The final essay by Richard Rupp questions whether there is need at all for a 'new NATO' with an expanded membership and a focus on out-of-area missions. The traditional NATO, he argues, still serves useful purposes: as an insurance policy against a revanchist Russia, as a reassurance to the smaller European countries that they will not be vulnerable to either a hegemonic Germany or a Europe dominated by a handful of major EU powers, and as a mechanism to preserve the transatlantic security link. NATO's venture into the Balkans – and the alliance's flirtation with expanding its membership into the Baltic region – threaten to undermine those far more vital purposes. Indeed, Rupp fears that the new NATO might ultimately destroy the cohesion necessary to preserve the traditional NATO.

The essays in this collection are presented in the hope that they will become the basis for a searching debate about the future of Europe's security and the future of the transatlantic relationship. Observations about disarray in NATO, and predictions of the alliance's imminent demise, have become clichés over the decades. Yet it is also true that this time the discord among the members appears to be both wider and deeper. The range of issues about which there is significant disagreement is exceptionally broad, and the animosity of the rhetoric coming from policy circles on both sides of the Atlantic is extremely bitter.

Moreover, this time there is no looming Soviet threat to impose a measure of unity on fractious alliance members. Only time will tell whether the current crisis in NATO is merely the latest in a long series of squabbles, or whether this time the situation is terminal. The authors in *NATO Enters the 21st Century* focus badly needed attention on the crucial issues facing the alliance.

2

NATO's New Strategic Concept: Coherent Blueprint or Conceptual Muddle?

TED GALEN CARPENTER

NATO's new Strategic Concept, approved at the alliance's 50th anniversary summit in April 1999, reflected an uneasy compromise among a variety of competing objectives. It sought to satisfy traditionalists who believe that the core of NATO's purpose remains Article 5, which proclaims that an attack on one member shall be considered an attack on all. At the same time, the new Concept was designed to meet the demands of those who believe that Article 5 collective defense is increasingly marginal, if not irrelevant, in a post-Cold War strategic setting and that NATO must move beyond its traditional commitment to territorial defense. That school of thought holds that the alliance must expand its membership rapidly into Central and Eastern Europe to provide the political framework for stability there, and that NATO must emphasize 'out-of area' missions to prevent brush-fire wars and other indirect threats to members of the alliance.

In addition to bridging the gap on those issues, the final version of the Concept had to accommodate serious differences about the geographic scope of out-of-area missions. Most member governments wanted such missions confined to the European theater. The United States, and to a lesser extent Britain, wanted NATO to commit itself to defend 'Western interests' wherever they might be imperiled. Finally, the Concept had to satisfy the members who insisted that NATO must remain the centerpiece of Europe's security arrangements as well as those members (led by France) who pressed for a strong European-led defense capability under the auspices of the European Union.

With regard to all three areas of contention, the authors of the Concept managed to find language that placated, if not fully satisfied, all parties. The result, however, is something less than a monument to clarity. It also intensifies the suspicion that the alliance is vainly attempting to be all things to all people merely to perpetuate its existence as a security institution. In any case, adoption of the Concept did not end the struggle over NATO's course. Acrimonious disputes continue to erupt about whether the alliance should undertake future Kosovo-style missions, whether additional new members should be admitted anytime soon, and to what extent NATO should remain the dominant security organization in twenty-first century Europe.

THREE FACTIONS DISAGREE ABOUT NATO'S MISSION

On the related issues of NATO's primary mission and the geographic scope of the alliance's security concerns, three identifiable factions had emerged in the years between the adoption of NATO's previous Strategic Concept in 1991 and the 50th anniversary summit.

One faction, the Article 5 traditionalists, still sees NATO's purpose largely in territorial collective defense terms. To people of that persuasion, the 'guts' of the treaty, as Secretary of State Dean Acheson put it in 1949, remain Article 5, which declares that an attack on one member is an attack on all and pledges support for the ally attacked. Put another way, the article 5 traditionalists believe that the primary purpose of NATO in the post-Cold War era is to be an insurance policy in the event that Russia recovers its economic and military power and again turns expansionist. The alliance also serves as an important institutional expression of the transatlantic security relationship, preventing a retreat by the United States into 'isolationism'. Former Secretary of State Henry Kissinger is perhaps the most vocal and prominent member of the Article 5 traditionalist camp.

There were sharp internal disagreements in that faction concerning the initial round of NATO's expansion. Some, such as Johns Hopkins University professor Michael Mandelbaum; William Hyland, former editor of *Foreign Affairs*; and Susan Eisenhower, chairman of the Center for Political and Strategic Studies, criticized even the initial round of expansion. They argued that enlargement would not only poison NATO's relations with Russia, but, equally significant, would also dangerously dilute the strategic purpose of the alliance.[1]

Other Article 5 traditionalists, including Kissinger and Dimitri Simes, president of the Nixon Center, cautiously endorsed the first round of expansion. Bringing Poland, Hungary, and the Czech Republic into the alliance made sense to Kissinger, Simes and those who shared their perspective because it pushed the frontiers of the alliance eastward and gave

NATO the strategic depth that it lacked during the Cold War when Soviet divisions were perched on the Elbe River. Although having a united Germany in the alliance had already moved the defensive frontier from the Elbe to the Oder-Neisse line, adding Poland meant that any future Russian expansionist ambitions would be blocked at the River Bug, some 350 miles further east.

But even those Article 5 traditionalists who backed the initial round of expansion have shown little enthusiasm for additional rounds. Adding members in the Baltics and the Balkans, in their view, would so blur the alliance's strategic mission that the organization would be in danger of becoming simply a slightly more robust version of the Organization for Security and Cooperation in Europe. At that point, NATO would be a political talk shop more than an effective, integrated collective defense organization. They pointed out that the alliance has always operated by consensus, which was difficult enough with 15 members during most of the Cold War and 16 members (with the addition of Spain) in the final years of that era. Even adding the three Central European countries was likely to multiply the difficulties in achieving consensus on some issues. The prospect of having to deal with two dozen or more NATO members, perhaps including some less than predictable east European regimes, made Article 5 traditionalists extremely nervous.

They were even more uneasy about NATO's venture into out-of-area missions in the Balkans or elsewhere. 'Is NATO to be the home for a whole series of Balkan NATO protectorates?' Kissinger asked on the eve of the air strikes against Yugoslavia. He also pointed to a significant gap between America's interests and those of the European members of the alliance. 'Kosovo is no more a threat to America than Haiti was to Europe – and we never asked for NATO support there.'[2]

Columnist Charles Krauthammer was even more caustic about the increasing focus of the 'new NATO' on out-of-area missions, asking rhetorically: 'What was wrong with the old NATO?' Citing Lord Ismay's pithy summary of NATO's purpose (to keep the Russians out, the Americans in, and the Germans down), Krauthammer argued that 'all three missions survive', albeit in altered and more subtle form. 'For the clever young thinkers of [the Clinton] administration, however, this is all too boring.' He accused them of suffering from 'Acheson envy', and saw them as determined to completely refashion NATO as 'a robust, restless alliance ready to throw its weight around outside its own borders to impose order and goodness'. A 'lovely, heartwarming theory', Krauthammer sneered, 'so unfortunately exploded in its first reality test, Kosovo.' That intervention, he argued, 'reveals just how unsuited' NATO is to its new extraterritorial tasks.[3]

Competing with the Article 5 traditionalists were the advocates of geographically limited out-of-area missions for NATO. (Most members of that faction were also supporters of expanding NATO's membership into Central and Eastern Europe, although they sometimes differed among themselves about the pace and scope of enlargement.) Some American scholars and political leaders favored the limited out-of-area option, but it was the policy preferred by most European members of the alliance.[4] Proponents of such missions believe that a narrow adherence to the traditional territorial collective defense rationale will sooner or later render NATO obsolete in Europe's post-Cold War security equation.

The vast majority of European security problems that have emerged since the end of the Cold War are on Europe's periphery – most notably in the Balkans. Most of those developments do not pose a threat to the independence, freedom, or territorial integrity of NATO's members. Nevertheless, turbulence on the periphery can create – and indeed has created – a variety of annoying or worrisome indirect effects. For example, the armed conflicts in the former Yugoslavia have led to large refugee flows into Germany and other NATO states. If NATO is unable to prevent or solve such conflicts, the argument goes, it is failing to address the real security issues of post-Cold War Europe, and is focusing instead on the highly improbable danger of a direct attack on a NATO member that would bring Article 5 into play.

Proponents of out-of-area missions on Europe's periphery are also sensitive to the public relations aspect in both Western Europe and the United States. They worry that Western publics, especially the American public, will not forever support a NATO that seems to be a fossilized alliance concentrating on obsolete Cold War-era threats. That was the thrust of Senator Richard Lugar's warning in 1993 that NATO would have to go out of area or 'it will soon go out of business'.[5]

For advocates of out-of-area missions (even geographically limited ones), the ability of NATO to deal effectively with the various crises in the former Yugoslavia is a crucial test case.[6] In a candid conversation with *New York Times* columnist Thomas L. Friedman, a NATO official, who clearly favored a focus on out-of-area missions, stressed the alliance's bureaucratic stake in being willing and able to address Balkan security problems. 'In order to survive, an international organization can't just have a conceptual mission', the official emphasized. 'Organizations seek out action. They need to do things. That's why NATO needs the Balkans as much as the Balkans need NATO.'[7]

A third faction, though, favored an even broader concept of out-of-area missions. Former Secretary of State Warren Christopher and former Secretary of Defense William Perry advocated that the alliance become an instrument for the projection of force anywhere the West's 'collective interests' are threatened. Their list of threats to those interests – 'the proliferation of weapons of mass destruction, disruption of the flow of oil, genocidal violence, and wars of aggression *in other regions*' – suggested that they did not wish to confine the scope of the alliance's activities to the European theater – even broadly defined.[8] The Clinton administration clearly wished to breach such geographic restraints. In a moment of exuberance, Madeleine Albright stated that NATO should become a force for peace 'from the Middle East to Central Africa'.[9]

The administration especially pressed its NATO colleagues to make blocking the proliferation of weapons of mass destruction a prominent alliance mission. As in the case of the Christopher-Perry proposal, the goal appeared to be to prevent the spread of nuclear, chemical, and biological weapons wherever that problem might emerge.[10]

But little enthusiasm emerged for that or other broad out-of-area missions among European political elites – or among members of the American policy community who want NATO to confine itself to European security issues. One high-level European official noted that 'the Americans have put a program on the table that calls for NATO to play a major role in controlling and countering weapons of mass destruction'. He added that 'we worry that America may be creating a new "threat perception" that scares our populations ... while allowing NATO to become a global organization.'[11] Because the Persian Gulf region, South Asia, and Northeast Asia are the most likely arenas for proliferation, the administration's proposed mission implied that NATO's security role would have no discernible geographic limits.

From the perspective of the European members of NATO, such a mandate would be, at best, a worrisome distraction. Even British Foreign Secretary Robin Cook cautioned against 'a purely open-ended commitment'.[12] Coming from an official of Washington's most loyal ally, that statement indicated the extent of West European opposition to the US initiative. French Foreign Minister Hubert Védrine warned against a 'too elastic interpretation of the new common interests'.[13] He voiced the underlying apprehension of most of his colleagues, fearing that if NATO broadened its mission excessively, 'we would run the risk of diluting the alliance and dividing the allies'.[14]

Some American advocates of geographically limited out-of-area missions made that argument as well. Andrew J. Pierre, Jennings Randolph

Fellow at the US Institute of Peace, emphasized that there is little support for 'globalizing' NATO or for emphasizing alleged 'common interests' outside the European theater. He concluded that NATO should focus on the Euro-Atlantic area and its periphery, act on a case-specific basis, and create 'coalitions of the willing' for non-Article 5 interventions. Anything more ambitious, he warned, risks fracturing the alliance.[15]

Most European supporters of the alliance were even more insistent than Pierre about limiting the geographic scope of NATO's out-of-area ventures. The alliance's great appeal to Europeans is, as it has always been, that it provides a security link to American power and ensures that the United States will never abandon Europe to a predatory enemy.[16] Even in the current benign security environment, marked by the absence of a strong expansionist power on the Continent, NATO is a convenient and (for European taxpayers at least) inexpensive insurance policy should the strategic environment turn malevolent. But the prospect of US-led NATO crusades in the Middle East, the Persian Gulf, central and south Asia, or elsewhere hardly seems to be in Europe's interest. Spanish Foreign Minister Abel Matutes made that point, noting that what happens '8,000 kilometers from us – in Korea, for example … cannot be considered a threat to our security'. NATO is 'the North Atlantic Treaty Organization, and not the North Pacific', echoed Vedrine.[17]

The virulence of the European opposition to Washington's globalist trial balloon both before and during the NATO foreign ministers meeting in December 1998 caused Albright to beat a rhetorical retreat, insisting that her government did not see NATO 'as going global'.[18] Nevertheless, the Clinton administration tenaciously resisted any effort to put even a vague geographic restriction in the language of the forthcoming Strategic Concept.

In addition to the fear that a broad out-of-area mandate might blur the focus of the alliance and entangle the European states in quarrels not relevant to their security, many European publics and governments flatly disagree with the substance of Washington's policies on a variety of issues outside the region. Such issues as the Arab–Israeli conflict, dealing with Iraq, and sanctions against Iran found the United States and its West European allies at odds. There is an understandable wariness in Europe about NATO's becoming a vehicle for implementing US rather than transatlantic policy objectives.

THE STRATEGIC CONCEPT AND NATO'S MISSION

The new Strategic Concept sought to bridge the growing fissures concerning the proper mission of the alliance in the post-Cold War era.

Language in the document proclaimed the continuing relevance of collective territorial defense under Article 5, emphasizing that 'NATO's essential and enduring purpose, set out in the Washington Treaty, is to safeguard the freedom and security of all its members by political and military means.'[19] Elsewhere in the document, there was another explicit recognition of a continuing Article 5 commitment.

> The maintenance of an adequate military capability and clear preparedness to act collectively in the common defence remain central to the Alliance's security objectives. Such a capability, together with political solidarity, remains at the core of the Alliance's ability to prevent any attempt at coercion or intimidation, and to guarantee that military aggression directed against the Alliance can never be perceived as an option with any prospect of success.[20]

Despite such references to NATO's traditional core function, there was an unmistakable shift of emphasis toward the new missions of crisis management and out-of-area interventions. The section on security challenges and risks, for example, began with the admission that 'large-scale conventional aggression against the Alliance is highly unlikely', although a future threat might conceivably emerge.[21]

The absence of a large-scale conventional threat did not mean that NATO faces no security difficulties, according to the authors of the Strategic Concept. 'The security of the Alliance remains subject to wide variety of military and nonmilitary risks, which are multi-directional and often difficult to predict.' As if that notion of security threats were not vague enough, the document goes on to describe the nature of such 'threats' in an expansive manner.

> These risks include uncertainty and instability in and around the Euro-Atlantic area and the possibility of regional crises at the periphery of the Alliance, which could evolve rapidly. Some countries in and around the Euro-Atlantic area face serious economic, social and political difficulties. Ethnic and religious rivalries, territorial disputes, inadequate or failed efforts at reform, the abuse of human rights, and the dissolution of states can lead to local and even regional instability. The resulting tensions could lead to crises affecting Euro-Atlantic stability, to human suffering, and to armed conflicts. Such conflicts could effect the security of the Alliance by spilling over into neighbouring countries, including NATO countries, or in other ways, and could also affect the security of other states.[22]

Two things are notable about that passage. First, the phrase 'in and around the Euro-Atlantic area' is never defined; indeed, it is not defined anywhere else in the document. Without a definition, the term is so vague that it could apply not only to developments anywhere in Europe, but also to events in North Africa, the Middle East and even Central Asia. That lack of precision is in marked contrast to the language in Article 6 of the Washington Treaty adopted in 1949. 'For the purpose of Article 5 an armed attack on one or more of the Parties is deemed to include an armed attack on the territory of any of the parties in Europe or North America... on the occupation forces of any Party in Europe, on the islands under the jurisdiction of any Party in the North Atlantic area north of the Tropic of Cancer or on the vessels or aircraft in the area of the parties.'[23]

The omission of any geographic restriction in the new Strategic Concept was at least a partial victory for the Clinton administration and other advocates of a broad mandate for out-of-area missions. A similar implicit endorsement of that position could be found in a passage on nuclear and other Weapons of Mass Destruction (WMD) proliferation threats. Asserting that the proliferation of nuclear, biological and chemical (NBC) weapons was 'a matter of serious concern', the Concept warned that some states, 'including on NATO's periphery *and in other regions*, sell or acquire or try to acquire NBC weapons and delivery means'.[24]

It is significant, however, that the Strategic Concept did not explicitly endorse the notion of defending Western interests anywhere they might be threatened. Thus, the result appears to be a compromise that implies a substantial but as yet undefined expansion of NATO's territorial coverage. The struggle between the two expansionist factions was, therefore, not resolved but merely postponed.

The second significant feature of the passage on the nature of out-of-area menaces to the alliance is that the concept of a security threat is so elastic that it now arguably applies to everything from a slowdown in economic reforms in (unnamed) countries to (undefined) human rights abuses. The daisy-chain reasoning is breathtaking: 'tensions' could lead to 'crises' that 'might affect' neighboring countries or cause problems 'in other ways' that might then adversely affect the security of NATO members or 'other states'. One would be hard pressed to find any unpleasant development within several thousand kilometers of a NATO member that could not arguably be considered a potential security issue for the alliance under those criteria.

On the other issue that causes Article 5 traditionalists significant apprehension (further enlargement of the alliance's membership), the Strategic Concept was also less than reassuring.

The Alliance remains open to new members under Article 10 of the Washington Treaty. It expects to extend further invitations in the coming years to nations willing and able to assume the obligations of membership, and as NATO determines that the inclusion of these nations would serve the overall political and strategic interests of the Alliance, strengthen its effectiveness and cohesion, and enhance overall European security and stability.

If that language were not troubling enough to Article 5 traditionalists, the document adds: 'No European democratic country whose admission would fulfill the objectives of the Treaty will be excluded from consideration.'[25] That was a clear victory, at least on the rhetorical level, for Secretary of State Albright and others who want to bring the Baltic republics and other East European states into NATO.

FINESSING THE EUROPEAN SECURITY AND DEFENSE IDENTITY (ESDI)

The delicate balancing act in the language of the new Strategic Concept was more evident on the issue of a distinctly European security role. The key paragraph fairly oozed with language that sought to satisfy both the NATO primacists and their opponents. The paragraph begins by emphasizing that the alliance is 'the foundation of collective defence of its members and *through which common security objectives will be pursued whenever possible...*' Yet it was also 'committed to a balanced and dynamic transatlantic partnership'.[26] The paragraph praised the European allies for having made decisions 'to enable them to assume greater responsibilities in the security and defense field', but stressed that the European Security and Defense Identity would be developed 'within NATO'.

Finally, there was a convoluted passage that sought to balance every conceivable objective of both camps. ESDI would 'reinforce the transatlantic partnership'; yet it would also enable the European allies 'to act by themselves...' But they could act by themselves only 'as required through the readiness of the Alliance, on a case-by-case basis and by consensus, to make its [NATO's] assets and capabilities available for operations in which the Alliance is not engaged militarily...'[27]

In other words, the European members of NATO were given approval to take greater responsibility for dealing with security problems in their region through the Western European Union, or a new security mechanism under the auspices of the European Union, as long as their military initiatives remained clearly subordinate to NATO's control. The implication was that NATO would have a 'first right of refusal' to intervene in a conflict, and only if the alliance considered the problem beneath its notice would the ESDI be given the authorization to take action. Although the language offered cover to both factions, in terms of the substantive implications, it represented a victory for the NATO-centric camp.

CONTINUING TURMOIL OVER NATO'S SCOPE AND MISSION

Even though the Article 5 traditionalists may have lost the battle over language in the Strategic Concept on the enlargement issue, it was significant that no new membership invitations were issued at the 50th anniversary summit. Following the admission of the first round of applicants the previous year, it had been widely expected that invitations would be extended to Slovenia and possibly Romania. In the intervening months, however, there appeared to be growing sentiment in several West European governments – as well as in the US Congress – that NATO should fully integrate the three new members before even contemplating another round of enlargement. The Albright State Department attempted to regain the initiative and push the candidacies of the Baltic republics and other countries in late 1999 and early 2000, but that reluctance seems to have become stronger and more pervasive.[28]

Although the brakes appear to have been applied to further enlargement of NATO's membership, the same is not true of the flirtation with geographically expansive out-of-area missions. Ominously, at the NATO summit meeting itself, the alliance took two actions that suggested a rapidly expanding scope of concerns. One was a pledge to defend Serbia's neighbors against any aggression emanating from Belgrade.[29] In essence, that gave the Balkan states a *de facto* Article 5 security guarantee without any corresponding obligation on their part. Indeed, in a response to a reporter's question about an earlier version of the commitment made at a ministerial meeting of the North Atlantic Council on 12 April 1999, NATO Secretary General Javier Solana conceded as much:

> Patricia Kelly, CNN: Secretary General, on your security guarantees for the surrounding countries … are those security guarantees NATO is offering the same as NATO nations enjoy under Article 5 … ?
>
> Secretary General: On the first question, of course the security guarantee will not be exactly the same as the guarantee that the NATO countries do have but the difference will be very slight.[30]

Such expansion of the alliance's security obligations – an action taken without modifying the treaty or requesting ratification of the change by the legislatures of the existing NATO members – infuriated critics in the United States. One influential Senate staff member caustically described the measure as 'a stealth expansion of NATO'.[31]

An unusual 'informal' meeting of NATO foreign ministers during the summit produced statements on another issue that were equally worrisome. The ministers expressed the alliance's concern about the continuing violence in the Caucasus and urged Georgia, Armenia, and Azerbaijan to settle their various problems.[32] That was a less than subtle indication that the Caucasus, like the Balkans before it, might become a region in which NATO asserts an interest, if not outright jurisdiction.

Actions taken since the summit have tended to confirm such impressions. Alliance leaders have repeatedly warned the Belgrade government not to attempt any coercive measures against Montenegro, Serbia's sister republic in what remains of the Yugoslav federation.[33] A significant NATO presence continues in Macedonia, and an already extensive network of military and intelligence ties exists between the alliance and Albania.[34] There is more than a little irony in that development. KFOR, the NATO peacekeeping force in Kosovo, is encountering more and more challenges and difficulties. Indeed, alliance officials now speak openly of the mission lasting years, perhaps even a decade, and the prospect grows that serious fighting may erupt between KFOR and Albanian Kosovars – the very people NATO sought to help with its bombing campaign in 1999.[35] Yet, even as the situation in Kosovo becomes increasingly grim, the alliance's role elsewhere in the Balkans appears to be expanding, not shrinking.[36]

The level of interest in the Caucasus is also on the rise. For example, NATO could not resist the temptation to lecture, criticize, and cajole Russia about its brutal counterinsurgency campaign in Chechnya in late 1999 and early 2000. Granted, there was little prospect that the alliance would be so reckless as to intervene militarily as it did in Kosovo in response to similar tactics by the Serbian government. Russia's nuclear arsenal effectively precluded that option. (Indeed, NATO's new Secretary General, Lord Robertson, summarily rejected calls from some ardent human-rights activists for a military response: 'I have not met anyone in their right mind who suggests that we take military action against Russia for what they are doing in Chechnya.')[37]

Nevertheless, NATO repeatedly criticized Moscow for its conduct of the war and sought to pressure the Russian government to enter into peace negotiations or even accept international mediation.[38] Such hectoring further damaged Russian-NATO relations that had already been frayed by NATO's eastward expansion and, even more, by the alliance's military intervention in the Balkans.[39] Russian leaders did not react well to NATO's nagging on Chechnya. Responding to a December 1999 statement from NATO's council of foreign ministers criticizing Russia for its conduct of the war, the Russian Foreign Ministry used blistering language: 'The latest outpouring of crocodile tears in Brussels over human rights strikes one as flagrant cynicism.' The Ministry rebuttal added, 'The statement from the NATO Council is pointless in its contents, unacceptable in its essence, and immoral as far as its authorship is concerned.' Lest anyone have the slightest doubt, 'Russia's domestic policy issues are not, cannot, and will not be the subject of international dialogue, especially with NATO.'[40]

In addition to the frictions caused by intrusive diplomacy pursued by NATO as a whole, actions by the alliance's leading member, the United States, also exacerbated tensions with Russia. For example, the Albright State Department held meetings with Chechnya's so-called foreign minister when he visited Washington in February 2000. Predictably, Russia objected strongly to Washington's willingness to confer legitimacy on an 'official' of a government which no nation recognized and which Moscow considered nothing more than a gang of terrorists. The Clinton administration's contemptuous dismissal of the Russian objections did nothing to ameliorate the situation.[41]

One cannot fully comprehend the depth of Moscow's anger without taking into account the context in which the US action occurred. The Kremlin was already deeply suspicious that the United States and its NATO allies were pursuing a multifaceted strategy to establish a sphere of influence on Russia's southern flank.[42] Pertinent measures include: Washington's attempt to mediate the territorial dispute between Armenia and Azerbaijan over Nagorno-Karabakh; the US-Turkish insistence that the recently discovered oil riches of the Caspian Basin be transported through a new pipeline that would run from Baku in Azerbaijan, to Ceyhan in Turkey (thereby bypassing Russia); trial balloons in the Western press about possibly establishing a US military base in Azerbaijan; and statements from officials in Azerbaijan and Georgia that their countries would like to join NATO. All of those developments were viewed with growing annoyance and alarm in Moscow.[43]

Russians also note that the usual crowd of Russophobes, such as former National Security Advisor Zbigniew Brzezinski and *New York Times* columnist William Safire, seized on the Chechnya episode to push for

Western 'support' for Russia's neighbors in the Caucasus and NATO membership for the Baltic republics.[44]

Advocates of out-of-area missions for NATO have quietly but effectively steered NATO toward an expanded (and long-term) presence in the Balkans and the initial stages of involvement in the Caucasus. These actions – especially the burgeoning Balkan role – have not gone unopposed by those who want NATO to return to a more traditional mission, however. In addition to criticism by academics of that policy drift, two prominent US senators, Kay Bailey Hutchison (Republican, Texas) and Robert Byrd (Democrat, West Virginia), have urged that responsibility for dealing with Balkan problems be transferred from the United States and NATO to the European powers. Hutchison stated bluntly, 'Any NATO member can patrol the Balkans. But only the United States can defend NATO.'[45] Byrd recommended that Congress give the Clinton administration a mere three months to craft a plan to turn Kosovo peacekeeping responsibilities over to 'an all-European peacekeeping force'.[46] Their lack of enthusiasm for Kosovo-style missions was palpable. Opposition to involvement in the Caucasus is not nearly as visible or vocal, but, then, neither is NATO's role as yet. One anticipates that if NATO's activity in that region escalates, so too will the criticism expressed by Article 5 traditionalists and other critics.

CONTINUING TENSIONS OVER THE EUROPEAN SECURITY AND DEFENCE IDENTITY (ESDI)

Of all the differences that adoption of the new Strategic Concept failed to resolve, the disagreements between the United States and its European allies over ESDI have become the most acute. The United States, as it has so often in the past, continues to exhibit a profound ambivalence about the prospect of a serious, substantive European defense initiative. On the eve of the meeting of NATO's defense ministers in early December 1999, Secretary of Defense William Cohen delivered a speech to German military commanders in Hamburg criticizing Germany for cutting its already modest military budget. 'The decisions Germany makes in the next few months and years will have a profound and lasting impact on the capabilities, not only of this nation, but of the alliance as a whole', he warned.[47] In a high-profile article in the *Washington Post* upon his return from the defense ministers meeting, Cohen broadened his criticism, insisting that not just Germany but all European members of NATO would have to spend more on defense.[48]

Cohen's criticisms reflected a long-standing American annoyance with the European allies for making rhetorical commitments to a strong

'European pillar' in NATO while invariably failing to create the substance – in the form of military outlays – needed for such a pillar. That annoyance had been recently exacerbated by the disproportionate burden borne by the United States in the air war against Yugoslavia. US planes flew more than half of the combat missions and more than two-thirds of the support sorties. 'Kosovo revealed a huge disparity between the United States and our NATO allies', Cohen stated bluntly.[49]

Yet even as he expressed irritation at the European members of NATO in general, and Germany in particular, for not bearing their fair share of the defense load, Cohen's comments epitomized official Washington's own ambivalence about the prospect of a strong European defense capability. Although he expressed understanding for the desire of the Europeans to continue their quest for a defense identity 'somewhat separate and apart from NATO', he insisted that NATO must remain the dominant security organization. 'The reality is that there can be no separation', he stated. Making explicit what had been implied in the new Strategic Concept, Cohen emphasized 'that NATO should have what I call a first option on any action that would be taken in the way of a military operation'.[50] A sentence in his *Washington Post* article encapsulated Washington's repeated habit of sending mixed messages on the issue. The Secretary stated that the allies had to spend more on defense if they were to 'establish a European Security and Defense Identity that is separable but not separate from NATO'.[51]

To many Europeans, the implicit meaning of such comments was that the European nations should do more and pay more to carry out policies of a US-dominated NATO. They were also aware that a major portion of America's political and policy elite was openly unenthusiastic about ESDI, fearing that it would automatically become a competitor to NATO and dilute Washington's influence in the overall transatlantic relationship. Former Assistant Secretary of State John Bolton was only a little more candid than like-minded colleagues when he stated, 'Many in Europe and America believe that creating a European Security and Defence Identity will not weaken NATO. Sadly for transatlantic relations, they are wrong both about ESDI's role and about its impact on the alliance.'[52]

US inconsistency, if not hypocrisy, on the ESDI issue began to raise European emotions to the boiling point in early 2000. Even German Chancellor Gerhard Schroeder began to express sentiments that Americans were more accustomed to hear coming from Paris – especially during the days of Charles de Gaulle. Europe needed to act as virtually a single country if it wanted to escape political and economic dominance by the United States, Schroeder opined. Asked in a television interview whether the

United States lacked consideration for its allies, Schroeder replied, 'Yes, that certainly is so.' He added, 'Whining about US dominance doesn't help. We have to act.'[53]

European leaders professed to be baffled by Washington's lukewarm (at best) response to the plan adopted by the EU governments at Helsinki in December 1999 to develop the ability by 2003 to deploy up to 60,000 troops within 60 days and sustain that force up to a year. They noted Madeleine Albright's explicit caveats (the so-called 'three D's') that ESDI must not 'decouple' the United States from Europe, must not 'duplicate' NATO's structures and capabilities, and must not 'discriminate' against NATO members that do not belong to the EU (primarily Turkey and the three new central European members).[54] 'We seemed to be damned if we do and damned if we don't by our American friends', concluded former NATO Secretary General, and now EU Commissioner in charge of foreign and security policy, Javier Solana.[55] Even Solana's successor as NATO Secretary General, Lord Robertson, expressed exasperation at US criticism. 'The United States suffers from a sort of schizophrenia', Robertson concluded. 'On the one hand, the Americans say, 'You Europeans have got to carry more of the burden.' And then when Europeans say, "Okay, we will carry more of the burden", the Americans say, "Well, wait a minute, are you trying to tell us to go home?"'[56]

There continues to be posturing and less than candid actions on both sides of the Atlantic. US skeptics contend that the Europeans are no more serious about ESDI than they were about previous plans to build a distinctive defense capability. Americans recall similar grandiose schemes going back to the abortive European Defence Community in the early 1950s. All of them collapsed as soon as the West European powers realized that they would have to appropriate money to build the necessary forces. Such critics note that the defense budgets of the European members continue their downward trajectory. Indeed, despite Secretary Cohen's admonitions in his December 1999 Hamburg speech, four months later an independent defense panel chaired by former German President Richard von Wiezsaecker recommended that Germany cut its armed forces by *another* 100,000 troops.[57] General Klaus Naumann, the former head of NATO's military committee, believes that the EU plan for a 60,000-strong crisis response force by 2003 is utterly unrealistic. It would take more like ten years to develop such a force, he concludes.[58]

US suspicions of EU posturing may be justified, but American policymakers are also disingenuous when they contend that they want to see a strong ESDI develop. That result would, in reality, be Washington's worst nightmare. Even if European leaders did not seek to make a robust ESDI a competitor to NATO, the dynamics of international politics would ultimately lead to that result. That is especially true if NATO (or more accurately, the United States) did not have the option to preempt ESDI and take control of a military mission. An explicit or implicit division of labor in which a European security organization would be responsible for dealing with future Bosnia or Kosovo-type contingencies while NATO remained responsible for responding to a major security threat would gradually but inexorably marginalize the alliance.

That is because the security problems that may bedevil Europe from time to time in the first decades of the twenty-first century are likely to be small-scale. Indeed, the only semi-plausible large-scale threat would be a revanchist Russia. But even that possibility would require a series of unlikely adverse developments: the emergence of a virulently anti-Western regime in Moscow; an economic recovery sufficient to rebuild a powerful Russian military; the actual creation of such a first-class military force; and the adoption of an expansionist agenda. Even then, a truncated Russia would have to operate without allies or satellites (with the exception of Belarus), in contrast to the Cold War era when a much larger Soviet Union had the Warsaw Pact and forward-deployed forces in Central Europe. In a worst-case scenario, an aggressive Russia might menace its small neighbors in the Caucasus and the Baltics, but it requires a scenario verging on a paranoid fantasy to posit a Russia that would pose a credible Article 5 threat to NATO's current membership.

That means that a substantive ESDI would become the organization called upon to deal with Europe's real security concerns. NATO would become little more than a standby 'insurance policy' against a highly improbable threat. Such a development would mean the inevitable dilution of US influence in the transatlantic security relationship, since the relationship itself would be increasingly irrelevant. At some level, US policymakers (and most members of the American foreign policy community) perceive that outcome, and that is why they regard even the possibility of a successful ESDI as unsettling.

THE NEW STRATEGIC CONCEPT:
A VAIN ATTEMPT TO CONCEAL WIDENING FISSURES

The continuing disagreements about NATO's mission and the proper division of labor between the alliance and a European security entity raise a possibility that NATO partisans understandably do not want to confront:

perhaps the alliance is in fact irrelevant to the security environment of post-Cold War Europe. It is theoretically possible that an institution created to deal with one set of strategic conditions is, by happy coincidence, the optimal institution for managing a very different set. It is more logical, however, that new institutions and arrangements, designed to reflect the realities of a post-Cold War context, need to be created. The campaign to preserve a NATO-centered security policy may be a vain effort to postpone a terminal crisis of relevance.

The tensions over ESDI and the transatlantic sniping about responsibility for the deteriorating conditions in Kosovo are combining to expose and widen serious policy fissures in the alliance. Complacent members of the 'NATO-forever' crowd will, predictably, respond that the fracturing of the alliance has been predicted periodically for nearly four decades, and yet NATO remains intact at the start of the twenty-first century. One scholar has even suggested that the term 'disarray' should be used to describe NATO's permanent condition. Both points have some validity. But on this occasion one very important factor is different from all previous crises that the alliance successfully weathered. The Soviet threat, the primary factor that promoted cohesion in the alliance throughout most of its history, has been gone for nearly a decade. When intra-alliance disputes surfaced in the past, all members understood that allowing those disputes to get out of hand might prove fatal to them all. At the dawn of the new millennium, there is no looming common threat, and, therefore, no such constraint.

Even the most ardent advocates of a NATO-centric policy ought to consider that NATO may be following (albeit belatedly) the pattern of other alliances that dissolved once the common threat that brought the members together no longer existed. If NATO has entered its twilight years – and that is a possibility that can no longer be dismissed – the members would be better advised to use their talents and energy to devise successor security arrangements instead of remaining in a state of denial. There is clear evidence of a growing divergence of both interests and policy preferences between the United States and its European allies. It is not yet certain that such a divergence will be sufficient to ultimately fracture the alliance, but the odds are growing that it will.

At the very least, the United States and the European members of NATO ought to adopt more realistic approaches and make the substance of their policy correspond to the underlying strategic realities. That means the United States should move beyond its crabbed, highly conditional (and ultimately insincere) 'support' for ESDI and enthusiastically embrace the concept. Washington should accept the fact that a functional ESDI would gradually displace NATO as Europe's primary security organization. That would, of course, mean a great diminution in Washington's dominance of the transatlantic relationship, but such an outcome is probably inevitable over the long term no matter what policy the United States pursues. Washington's preeminence began in the context of a Western Europe that was devastated and demoralized by World War II and had to face a potentially lethal security threat. It is unrealistic to believe that, more than half a century later, a prosperous, capable and confident European Union will forever defer to the United States. The wonder is that the arrangement managed to last this long, not that it may finally be coming to an end.

Moreover, there are significant offsetting benefits to the United States if it accepts and encourages the development of a robust ESDI. No longer would the United States be expected to participate in – much less lead – interventions to deal with parochial problems such as those in the Balkans. A Europeans-only security organization would have that responsibility, as it should. America has no interests at stake in the Balkans or other peripheral regions that warrant the costs and risks it is incurring as the leader of a NATO increasingly devoted to out-of-area missions. Off-loading such security responsibilities onto the EU would be a wise move for the United States.

But if Washington needs to adopt a more sensible and honest policy, so too must the European members of NATO. The Europeans may talk all they wish about no longer wanting to be dominated by the United States, and they may spin grand schemes about a capable ESDI and an effective rapid reaction force. Those plans will remain nothing more than paper fantasies, however, unless the governments of the major EU states are willing to spend the money needed to build credible military forces. Rhetoric about developing a capable European defense entity while already anemic military budgets are cut further is just that: empty rhetoric. The United States was unwise to encourage such pervasive dependency, and to create incentives for cynical free-riding on the US security guarantee, throughout NATO's history. But only the Europeans can decide if they at last have the fortitude to break their addictive dependency on the United States. And that must be shown by actions, not words.

A dose of realism is badly needed on both sides of the Atlantic. The widening fissures in the transatlantic security relationship cannot be concealed – much less repaired – by language (however clever) in the New Strategic Concept. Indeed, the primary problem with the Strategic Concept is that it is not really a document about NATO's future strategy at all. It is a purely political and public relations document designed to satisfy all parties. Like most such efforts that are divorced from the underlying realities, it will ultimately fail.

NOTES

1. Michael Mandelbaum, *The Dawn of Peace in Europe* (NY: Twentieth Century Fund Press, 1996) pp.45–65; M. Mandelbaum, 'NATO Expansion: A Bridge to the Nineteenth Century', Center for Political and Strategic Studies, June 1997; William Hyland, 'NATO's Incredible Shrinking Defense', in , Ted Galen Carpenter and Barbara Conry (eds.) *NATO Enlargement: Illusions and Reality* (Washington DC: Cato Institute 1998) pp.31–40; and Susan Eisenhower, 'The Perils of Victory', in *NATO Enlargement*, pp.103–19. For other examples, see Michael E. Brown, 'The Flawed Logic of NATO Expansion', *Survival* 18/2 (Spring 1995): 34–52; and Fred C. Ikle, 'How to Ruin NATO', *New York Times*, 11 Jan. 1995, p.A21.
2. Henry Kissinger, 'No US Ground Forces for Kosovo', *Washington Post*, 22 Feb. 1999, p.A15.
3. Charles Krauthammer, 'Floundering in Vainglory', *Washington Post*, 16 April 1999, p.A29.
4. Author's conversations with French, German, Italian, Danish, and Greek foreign ministry and defense ministry officials, August 1998–June 1999.
5. Richard G. Lugar, 'NATO: Out of Area or Out of Business: A Call for US Leadership to Revive and Redefine the Alliance', Remarks delivered to the Open Forum of the US Department of State, 2 Aug. 1993, p.7.
6. See, for example, Gregory L. Schulte, 'Former Yugoslavia and the New NATO', *Survival* 39/1 (Spring 1997) pp.19–42; David Buchan, 'In the Line of Fire', *Financial Times*, 26 March 1999, p.21; Anthony Lewis, 'In Credibility Gulch', *New York Times*, 20 March 1999, p.A27; and Helle Bering, 'NATO Meets the Beast', *Washington Times*, 31 March 1999, p.A21. Article 5 traditionalists also saw the Kosovo intervention as a crucial event – but in a disturbing and negative sense. According to Henry Kissinger, 'The various allied leaders are correct in treating Kosovo as a watershed. The Alliance abandoned its historical definition of itself as a strictly defensive coalition and insisted on the right to occupy a province of a state with which it was not at war.' Henry Kissinger, 'The End of NATO as We Know It?' *Washington Post*, 15 Aug. 1999, p.C7.
7. Quoted in Thomas L. Friedman, 'NATO or BATO?' *New York Times*, 15 June 1999, p.A31.
8. Warren Christopher and William J. Perry, 'NATO's True Mission', *New York Times*, 21 Oct. 1997, p.A27. Emphasis added.
9. Quoted in William Drozdiak, 'European Allies Balk at Expanded Role for NATO', *Washington Post*, 22 Feb. 1998, p.A27.
10. Steven Erlanger, 'Call to NATO: Widen Purpose to Deter Arms', *New York Times*, 7 Dec. 1998, p.A1.
11. Quoted in Roger Cohen, 'A Policy Struggle Stirs Within NATO', *New York Times*, 28 Nov. 1998, p.A1.
12. Quoted in Toby Helm, 'Allies Oppose U.S. Proposal to Give NATO Global Role.' *Daily Telegraph*, 9 Dec. 1998, p.14.
13. Quoted in David Buchan, 'Bonn Doubts Over NATO N-Weapons', *Financial Times*, 9 Dec. 1998, p.3.
14. Quoted in Craig R. Whitney, 'Europe Looks Quizzically at US Proposal for NATO Strategy', *New York Times*, 9 Dec. 1998, p.A9.
15. Andrew J. Pierre, 'NATO at Fifty: New Challenges, Future Uncertainties', United States Institute of Peace Special Report, 22 March 1999.
16. For a discussion of European motives regarding NATO, see Ted Galen Carpenter, 'Conflicting Agendas and the Future of NATO', *Journal of Strategic Studies* 17/4 (Dec. 1994) pp.143–64.

17. Quoted in John-Thor Dahlburg, 'NATO Ponders New Role as It Nears 50', *Los Angeles Times*, 9 Dec. 1998, p.A8.

18. Office of the Spokesman, Office of the Dept. of State, Secretary of State Madeleine K. Albright, Press Conference at NATO Headquarters, Brussels, 8 Dec. 1998, p.3. http://secretary.state.gov/www/statements/1998/981208b.html.

19. The Alliance's Strategic Concept, Approved by the Heads of State and Government participating in the meeting of the North Atlantic Council in Washington DC, 23–24 April 1999, Press Release NAC-S (99)65, 24 April 1999. http://www.nato.int/docu/pr/1999/p99-065e.h, para. 6.

20. Ibid. para. 28.

21. Ibid. para. 20.

22. Ibid.

23. Article 6, North Atlantic Treaty, signed at Washington DC, 4 April 1949.

24. The Alliance's Strategic Concept, para. 22. Emphasis added.

25. Ibid. para. 39.

26. Ibid. para. 30. Emphasis added.

27. Ibid.

28. Christopher Lockwood and Tim Butcher, 'NATO Plans for Eastward Enlargement Put on Hold', *Daily Telegraph* (London), 3 April 2000. For examples of the comments by Deputy Secretary of State Strobe Talbott and other administration officials, see Michael Tarm, 'Talbott Reassures Baltics on NATO', Associated Press, 24 Jan. 2000; Alistair Holloway, 'U.S. Says Baltics Must Join EU, NATO for Security', Reuters, 24 Jan. 2000; and 'More NATO Expansion', *Washington Times*, 21 March 2000, p.A14. Even some American policy experts who pushed hard for the first round of enlargement have sounded a note of caution about rushing into a second round. At the very least, they seem more sensitive to Russia's likely opposition. See Hans Binnendijk and Richard L. Kugler, 'Open NATO's Door Carefully', *Washington Quarterly* 22/2 (Spring 1999) pp.125–38; and Robert Hunter, 'Solving Russia: The Final Piece in NATO's Puzzle', *Washington Quarterly* 23/1 (Winter 2000) pp.115–34.

29. Chairman's Summary, Meeting of the North Atlantic Council at the level of Heads of State and Government with Countries in the Region of the Federal Republic of Yugoslavia, 25 April 1999, para. 5, http://www.nato.int/docu/pr/1999/p99-070e.h.

30. Press Conference by NATO Secretary General, Javier Solana, 12 April 1999, p.4, http://www.nato.int/docu/speech/a999/s990412a.h

31. Confidential conversation with author, 28 April 1999.

32. Carol Giacomo, 'NATO Urges Caucasus to Avoid Kosovo-Like Violence', Reuters, 25 April 1999; and untitled news story, Agence France Presse, 25 April 1999.

33. 'U.S. Tells Serbia to Keep Out of Montenegro', Reuters, 14 Jan. 2000; 'Montenegro "Very Tense", Clark Says', Reuters, 20 Feb. 2000; and Anatoly Verbin, 'NATO Warns Belgrade It Is Watching Montenegro', Reuters, 13 March 2000.

34. As of late Feb. 2000, there were some 4,100 NATO troops in Macedonia and another 1,400 in Albania: 'Numbers of KFOR Forces Deployed', Agence France Presse, 24 Feb. 2000. Those numbers do not include the increasingly hectic shuttle of US military (and probably intelligence) personnel not officially connected with KFOR in and out of Albania and Macedonia.

35. Matthew Cox and John Omicinski, 'No End in Sight for Balkan Missions', *Army Times*, 14 Feb. 2000, p.15; R. Jeffrey Smith, 'Kosovo Rebels' Serbian Designs Concern NATO', *Washington Post*, 28 Feb. 2000, p.A9; Carlotta Gall, 'NATO Chief Fears a Cross-Border Insurgency', *New York Times*, 11 March 2000, p.A3; Jane Perlez, 'Kosovo's Unquenched Violence Dividing U.S. and NATO Allies', *New York Times*, 12 March 2000, p.A1; 'NATO Urges Allies to Reinforce Kosovo Troops', Reuters, 15 March 2000; Jane Perlez, 'Peacekeepers Are Overwhelmed in Kosovo, Pentagon Envoy Says', *New York Times*, 15 March 2000, p.A12; Yann Tessier, 'Interview: KFOR Chief Sees Long-Haul Kosovo Role', Reuters, 17 March 2000; and Jeffrey Ulbrich, 'NATO May Be Stuck in Kosovo', Associated Press, 22 March 2000. For a concise analysis of what has gone wrong in Kosovo and why, see Nikolaos Stavrou, 'Milestone…with Creep?' *Washington Times*, 14 March 2000, p.A16.

36. Merita Dhimgjoka, 'Albright Warns Albania on Expansion', Associated Press, 19 Feb. 2000. Albright warned an audience in Tirana, Albania, that NATO and the international community would no more countenance a 'Greater Albania' than they would a 'Greater Serbia'.
37. Quoted in James Clark, 'NATO Warns of More Chaos in Kosovo', *The Times* (London), 19 Dec. 1999.
38. 'NATO Urges Moscow to Seek Peace with Chechnya', Reuters, 28 Jan. 2000; 'NATO Chief Urges Moscow to End Chechen Campaign', Reuters, 11 Feb. 2000; and Elif Kaban, 'Robinson Says Russia Should Open-Up Chechen Camps', Reuters, 21 Feb. 2000.
39. For a discussion, see Ted Galen Carpenter, 'Damage to Relations with Russia and China', in idem (ed.) *NATO's Empty Victory: A Postmortem on the Balkan War* (Washington DC: Cato Institute 2000) pp.77–91.
40. Quoted in 'Russia Dismisses NATO Criticism', Associated Press, 16 Dec. 1999. For the text of the NATO statement, see Final Communiqué, Ministerial Meeting of the North Atlantic Council held at NATO Headquarters, Brussels, 15 Dec. 1999, para. 31, http://www.nato.int/docu/pr/1999/p99-166e.h
41. Barry Schweid, 'U.S. Defends Meeting with Chechens', Associated Press, 17 Feb. 2000; and 'U.S. Dismisses Russian Anger at Chechen Meeting', Reuters, 17 Feb. 2000.
42. One widely circulated journalistic analysis even charged that 'NATO is seeking to gain control of the Caucasus and to turn that area into its bridgehead for war.' Moreover, if 'NATO comes to the Caucasus to protect the interests of the Georgian and Azerbaijani populations there, it is quite clear that the Abkhazians and the Armenians are not the only ones who will suffer in the intervention.' Dmitry Gornostayev and Mekhman Gafarly, 'Starting From the Balkans, the U.S. Will Proceed to CIS States', *Nezavisimaya Gazeta*, 23 April 1999, p.1
43. For a Russian perspective on the various Caucasus disputes and concern that the West, especially the United States, is meddling in those disputes, see Sergo A. Mikoyan, 'Russia, the United States, and Regional Conflict in Eurasia', *Survival* 40/3 (Autumn 1998) pp.112–26. Also see 'NATO's Kosovo Campaign Touches Nerve in the Caucasus', Agence France Presse, 6 July 1999; Stephen Kinzer, 'Azerbaijan Asks United States to Establish Military Base', *New York Times*, 31 Jan. 1999; 'Shevardnadze Sees Latest Events in Kosovo as Model for Conflict Settlement', BBC Worldwide Monitoring, 9 June 1999; and James Gerstanzang and Richard C. Paddock, 'U.S.-Backed Caspian Oil Project to Skirt Russia', *Los Angeles Times*, 18 Nov. 1999, p.A1. For a skeptical view of the strategy being pursued by Washington and its allies, see Anatol Lieven, 'The (Not So) Great Game', *National Interest* 58 (Winter 1999–2000) pp.69–80.
44. Zbigniew Brzezinski, 'Russia Would Gain by Losing Chechnya', *New York Times*, 19 Nov. 1999, p.A31; and William Safire, 'G-8 Minus One', *New York Times*, 25 Nov. 1999, p.A29. For a scholarly argument that 'Western assertiveness' in the Balkans, the Caucasus, and elsewhere is likely to make Russia less rather than more aggressive, see Paul Kubicek, 'Russian Foreign Policy and the West', *Political Science Quarterly* 114/4 (Winter 1999–2000) pp.547–68.
45. Kay Bailey Hutchison, 'Chasing a Balkan Mirage', *Washington Post*, 26 March 2000, p.B7.
46. Robert C. Byrd, 'Europe's Turn to Keep the Peace', *New York Times*, 20 March 2000, p.A25.
47. Bundeswehr Commanders' Conference, Remarks as Delivered by Secretary of Defense William S. Cohen, Hamburg, Germany, 1 Dec. 1999, transcript, p.4, http://www.defenselink.mil/cgi-bin/dppr. For an account of some of the implications of Cohen's remarks and probable German actions on defense, see William Drozdiak, 'Cohen Criticizes German Arms Cuts', *Washington Post*, 2 Dec. 1999, p.A29.
48. William S. Cohen, 'Europe Must Spend More on Defense', *Washington Post*, 6 Dec. 1999, p.A27.
49. Ibid.
50. Quoted in Drozdiak (note 47).
51. Cohen (note 48).
52. John Bolton, 'The European Threat to NATO's Future', *Financial Times*, 11 Feb. 2000, p.11.
53. Quoted in 'Schroeder to Europe: Unite Vs. U.S.', Associated Press, 28 Dec. 1999.
54. White House, Office of the Press Secretary, Secretary of State Madeleine K. Albright,

Secretary of Defense William S. Cohen, and National Security Advisor Sandy Berger, Press Briefing at End of NATO Summit, Washington DC, 25 April 1999, transcript, p.2, http://secretary.state.gov/www/statements/1999/990425.htm.

55. Quoted in William Drozdiak, 'U.S. Tepid on European Defense Plan', *Washington Post*, 7 March 2000, p.A1.
56. Quoted in ibid.
57. 'German Panel Calls for Troop Cuts of 100,000', Reuters, 16 March 2000.
58. 'Long Wait Seen for EU Crisis Force', Reuters, 30 March 2000.

3

NATO Burden-Sharing: Promises, Promises

ALAN TONELSON

Fool me once, shame on you; fool me twice, shame on me, the old adage goes. What, then, should be made of the US record on NATO burden-sharing, in which Washington has consistently been fooled for a span of half a century?

America's failure to convince its European allies to assume significantly more defense responsibilities in the post-Cold War period is especially puzzling and disturbing. During the East–West confrontation, after all, the unwillingness of NATO's increasingly wealthy European members to provide adequately for their own defense arguably was balanced – and even dwarfed – by major strategic benefits. Granted, coddling the Europeans directly threatened US security by increasing NATO's reliance on the US nuclear deterrent – and thereby raising the odds that a Soviet attack on Western Europe would escalate into a full-blown nuclear war engulfing the American homeland. But tolerating Europe's foot-dragging at least helped to maintain alliance solidarity. In turn, deterrence in Europe was undoubtedly strengthened, making a Soviet conventional attack less likely in the first place – although the added increment of deterrence is unknowable. As a result, Washington believed that other significant benefits from the Atlantic Alliance could be preserved, ranging from maintaining the freedom of Europe and keeping its military-industrial potential from Soviet domination to profitable transatlantic economic relations.

Today, however, US indulgence is much less justifiable from an American standpoint. The danger of domination of the Continent by an expansionist power has vanished for the foreseeable future, as have the related political and economic dangers. At the same time, the danger of the

United States becoming embroiled in (an admittedly limited) European conflict remains needlessly high. Indeed, this danger has at least three sources in the post-Cold War world.

First, US forces could become involved in European conflicts simply because fighting breaks out in countries where they are stationed. Such forces could even be attacked directly – especially by terrorist or irregular forces. NATO's continuing expansion into Eastern Europe has significantly increased this danger.

Second, US forces could become involved because they are stationed close enough to the fighting to make their use a tempting option for interventionist presidents.

Finally, American forces could be involved in post-Cold War European conflicts out of a perceived need to strengthen NATO's credibility. Significantly, that rationale figured prominently in America's Bosnia and Kosovo interventions.[1]

The crises that triggered those interventions are openly recognized by US policymakers as posing no direct threats to significant US national interests. Indeed, as will be discussed below, they are now referred to as 'non-Article 5 operations', meaning that they are not serious enough to trigger the alliance's automatic collective security provision. None the less, US involvement in today's European conflicts has already entailed major financial costs and always presents the risk of American casualties. Such costs and prospective risks would be greatly reduced if NATO's European members had the capabilities to deal with these problems on their own. Yet 50 years after NATO's creation, and despite the alliance's recognition that the Soviet Union's demise permits the defense of Western interests with considerably smaller, less ready forces, the European countries cannot even handle small-scale wars with local pipsqueaks, much less whatever threat a revitalized Russia might pose.

Compelling questions have been raised about whether Washington truly desires significantly improved NATO burden-sharing.[2] After all, a Europe that shared fully the alliance's burdens would win a claim to share fully the alliance's decision-making power, and it is clear that Washington is exceedingly comfortable in the driver's seat. Although American leaders have no interest in surrendering control over NATO, however, abundant evidence shows that they have vigorously sought greater European military and economic contributions.

They have been motivated by political considerations – in particular, concern that Congress and the American people would eventually balk at defending wealthy allies who free-rode excessively.

They have been motivated by economic considerations – most often the drain created by overseas military expenditures on America's international balance of payments. They have been motivated by the aforementioned nuclear considerations – the determination to reduce or limit (though not to eliminate) the nuclear risks of the NATO commitment. And they have been motivated by global strategic considerations – an awareness that because the US military budget has shrunk in inflation-adjusted terms, during various post-World War II periods, Washington would need more help from its allies in carrying out an increasingly ambitious agenda. As President George Bush and other NATO leaders stated in 1989, 'We recognize that our common tasks transcend the resources of either Europe or North America alone.'[3]

Indeed, the Pentagon has declared that 'the cornerstone of effective alliance relationships is the fair and equitable sharing of mutual security responsibilities and the proper balancing of costs and benefits'.[4] By this standard, America's burden-sharing efforts – and in fact much of its entire alliance policy – have been a dismal failure, exposing the nation to needless dangers and incurring excessive costs. Unfortunately, significant burden-sharing progress will not be possible until the United States fundamentally transforms its security relationship with Europe, and in the process the basic structure of NATO.

EARLY BURDEN-SHARING TENSIONS

Another sign of how seriously American leaders have taken the burden-sharing issue is how early it came up in alliance relations. In 1947, two years before NATO's creation, the Marshall Plan designated the West European countries as major recipients of US foreign economic aid. As of 1950, the first full year of NATO's existence, the US economy was more than three times the size of the combined economies of six other NATO members – the United Kingdom, France, Belgium, Canada, the Netherlands, and Italy.[5] Nevertheless, the alliance's division of labor had already become a contentious issue.

Although the Truman administration had decided that America's tremendous post-1950 military buildup could be financed sustainably through high levels of deficit spending, US officials recognized that the United States could not defend Western Europe singlehandedly.[6] Despite their economic weakness, the west Europeans would have to make a significant contribution and, quite understandably, US and European leaders devoted considerable time to sorting out defense responsibilities. The

Truman administration also worried that Congress might not adequately fund common defense efforts unless Europe played a substantial role. In fact, in 1951, General Dwight D. Eisenhower, the Supreme Allied Commander in Europe, traveled throughout the Continent warning the allies that 'the maintenance of the equivalent of six US divisions was an emergency measure only, and would be maintained only until the effects of the Marshall Plan could take hold... .'[7]

Eisenhower was not freelancing in issuing such a warning. In NSC-82, the Truman administration formalized the decision to bolster Europe's defense with American divisions and to bring NATO forces under US command. But the document also stated:

> The United States should make it clear that it is now squarely up to the European signatories of the North Atlantic Treaty to provide the balance of forces required for the initial defense. Firm programs for the development of such forces should represent a prerequisite for the fulfillment of the above commitments on the part of the United States.[8]

The allies' decision to create a European Defence Community (EDC), complete with an integrated European army containing German forces, indicated that American prodding was working.[9]

US burden-sharing pressure intensified during Eisenhower's presidency, which overturned Truman's policy of heavy deficit spending. Yet French fears of the German rearmament needed for meaningful European defense torpedoed the EDC. And although Eisenhower decided to fill the deterrence gap caused by the collapse of the proposed EDC through greater reliance on US nuclear weapons, Washington's resentment of alleged European shirking smoldered throughout the decade. Two growing, related problems annoyed US leaders.

First, America's international financial position had deteriorated so that the nation ran its first post-World War II balance of payments deficit in 1958.

Second, partly responsible for that problem was growing European trade competition – competition that Eisenhower blamed directly on 'our heavy defense expenditures at home, which come to a total of...over 10 per cent of our GNP'.[10]

Both the military risks and the economic costs of NATO continued to rise for the United States during the 1960s. After the Cuban Missile Crisis, the Soviet Union launched a major military buildup aimed at achieving strategic nuclear parity – and, many observers believed, superiority. By offsetting the nuclear edge long enjoyed by the United States, Moscow forced US defense planners to focus again on the conventional military balance in Central Europe, where the Soviets had always held the upper hand. As a result, not only was the United States compelled to rely heavily for Europe's defense on a possibly suicidal threat to use nuclear weapons, but the conventional defense of Europe depended significantly on more than 300,000 American troops (as well as their families) who were likely to be overwhelmed by the Warsaw Pact if nuclear weapons were not used.

In addition, US balance of payments grew worse, and pressure therefore mounted on the dollar-based international monetary system of fixed exchange rates. Among the policies weakening America's international financial position was the continued heavy spending on forward-based forces in Europe (and elsewhere) and on foreign aid. The Vietnam War became a major new drain on American resources. And the traditional American surpluses in trade continued to shrink in the face of sharper global competition – much of it from military allies in Europe and Asia.

Both the military and financial strains on US alliance policy could have been significantly eased by Europe's assumption of greater alliance defense responsibilities. During the 1960s, the European countries, especially West Germany, did increase various forms of compensation they paid Washington for its global labors. But those actions – their stepped up purchases of US military equipment, their higher host-nation support payments, and their willingness to hold on to their dollars despite their steadily declining real worth – could not come close to correcting Americaca's international deficit.[11]

THE LATE COLD WAR DECADES

At the start of the 1970s, these pressures produced major shocks in Washington's security and economic relations around the world, not merely in Europe. In 1971 President Richard Nixon unilaterally ended the dollar's convertibility into gold at $35 per ounce, devalued the currency, and slapped a ten per cent surcharge on imports. Nixon also enunciated a new foreign policy doctrine declaring that the United States would no longer assume most of the primary conventional defense responsibilities for its treaty allies. Since the West had not closed the conventional military gap in Europe, in particular, the obvious NATO-related implication was that the Europeans would have to do considerably more. Indeed, Nixon not only pressed the Europeans harder on burden-sharing, he also changed the focus of America's demands. Rather than continue increasing their offsets and financing more of the local basing costs of US forces, the Europeans were asked to make improvements in their own forces.[12]

Congress turned up the heat on Western Europe as well. Many legislators were increasingly frustrated by the stalemate in Vietnam and by the soaring costs of the war and the rest of US foreign policy; many were also angered by the Europeans' refusal to lend a hand in Southeast Asia and by their insistence on trading with North Vietnam. Consequently, support grew for a series of resolutions introduced by Senate Majority Leader Mike Mansfield (Democrat-Montana) calling for unilateral US troop withdrawals from Western Europe. In May 1971 Mansfield's efforts culminated in binding legislation that would have cut the US military force in Europe by 50 per cent by the end of the year. The Mansfield Amendment lost by a 61–36 vote – largely because of an all-out administration lobbying campaign and because of the Soviet Union's stunning announcement at the height of the Senate debate of its willingness to begin talks on mutual East–West force reductions in Europe.[13]

Despite that defeat, congressional burden-sharing efforts continued through the early 1970s. In late 1973 the Nixon administration actually signed the Jackson-Nunn Amendment, which gave the Europeans only two years to start offsetting most of the costs for forward-deployed US forces before the president would begin withdrawing these forces. The administration seems to have agreed to the Jackson-Nunn measure largely because that spring it had decided to change its burden-sharing focus back to financial compensation, and because this ultimatum from Congress might help prod the allies.[14]

By several measures, relative Western defense burdens did shift during the Nixon-Ford years. In 1969 – at the height of the Vietnam War, to be sure – the United States spent three and one half times as much on defense as its NATO allies (who by then numbered 14 countries) combined. A decade later, US spending on its NATO forces had fallen to 42 per cent of NATO's total military spending. And as of 1975, total US defense spending as a percentage of Gross National Product had fallen to six per cent – still one of the alliance's highest levels, but no longer in a class by itself.[15] More important, however, this burden-shifting failed to close the military gap in Central Europe. The allies' growing relative efforts, in other words, were too meager to enhance their own security significantly.

By the early 1980s, burden-sharing quarrels were back with a vengeance. The Soviet invasion of Afghanistan triggered a reversal of the decade-long decline in US military spending, and Ronald Reagan's election as president shifted a new buildup into high gear. The Reagan military buildup and the onset of 'Cold War II' drove a wedge between the United States and Western Europe over security policy, with the NATO allies and their neighbors generally struggling to preserve detente with the Soviet Union and the United States adopting a more confrontational approach.

Economic tensions roiled the alliance as well. Washington and Bonn in particular had been feuding over macroeconomic policy priorities since the late 1970s, with the Bundesbank's insistence on fighting inflation clashing with President Jimmy Carter's attempts to reflate the US economy back to health. At the same time, continuing European trade barriers and faltering American competitiveness had produced ever deeper US payments deficits. The Reaganomics combination of tight money and record peacetime federal deficits during the 1980s produced exchange-rate misalignments that helped push the Western economies increasingly out of synch.

Nuclear issues, moreover, put a special edge on transatlantic disputes. Throughout the 1970s, NATO's continuing weakness in conventional forces had kept the burden of deterrence in Europe squarely on American strategic nuclear forces. This strategy was growing ever riskier for the United States given the Soviet Union's achievement of strategic parity, and even superiority in certain respects, and also given a Soviet buildup in intermediate-range or theater nuclear forces (INFs or TNFs in arms control parlance) whose range was confined to Europe. An allied conventional buildup in Europe would have raised the nuclear threshold, but such a change threatened to create an unacceptable situation for the allies. An East–West conflict that did not quickly become nuclear and strike the superpowers' homelands would have wreaked massive destruction on Western Europe with conventional weapons for weeks or longer.

The Carter administration's decision to deploy American INFs in Europe was widely portrayed as a simple response to the new Soviet weapons – a response that would deny Moscow escalation dominance on the Continent. Yet it was also an American attempt to shift military risks back to Europe – by raising the odds that an East–West war (even a nuclear war) would be confined to the Continent and spare the American homeland.[16]

President Carter also pushed a major initiative to rebuild NATO's conventional military strength by committing member governments to boost inflation-adjusted defense spending by three per cent annually between 1979 and 1984. During this period, however, the United States maintained no meaningful burden-sharing pressure on its allies – or even pressure to keep their military budget commitments. Partly owing to Western Europe's economic weakness and partly owing to mounting transatlantic disputes over dealing with the Soviets, Reagan administration officials seem to have concluded that simply preserving the burden-sharing *status quo* would be difficult enough. Through 1986, even oblique references to burden-sharing all but vanished from the NATO communiqués that American leaders were signing. By mid-1985, moreover, the three per cent pledge – which had been extended even though no US allies had kept their promise – had been watered down to 'general guidance'.[17]

Congress, however, was determined not to let the issue drop. The legislative branch required the Defense Department to begin reporting on allied contributions to the common defense, and the House of Representatives authorized a special study of the issue. In addition, Congress passed legislation placing a numerical cap on American force levels in Europe.[18]

Largely as a result of the congressional initiatives, the Reagan administration finally began pressuring the allies. A NATO Defence Planning Committee meeting in May 1987 resolved that members would 'make every effort to avoid reductions in their defence contributions' unless they were made 'within the Alliance planning framework'. The defense ministers' report added, 'Solidarity and the willingness to share equitably the risks and burdens as well as the benefits of defence has always been a fundamental principle of Alliance policy; it must remain so.'[19] Three months later, the Defence Planning Committee members commissioned a burden-sharing report, while once again emphasizing 'the need for Alliance members to share equitably the roles, risks and responsibilities, as well as benefits, of collective defence...'.[20]

And in October 1987 a North Atlantic Council ministerial meeting endorsed the Western European Union's efforts to develop 'a positive identity in the field of European security within the framework of the Atlantic Alliance...'.[21]

At the March 1988 NATO summit in Brussels, the alliance heads of state and government affirmed that endorsement, with each leader also promising to play his part in 'maintaining Alliance defences, reaffirming our willingness to share fairly the risks, burdens, and responsibilities of our common efforts'. Later that year, the burden-sharing report was published. It found that 'major contributions [are] being made by both the European and North American pillars of the Alliance', but conceded that 'there are significant variations among countries in the scale and nature of their contributions...'.[22]

Despite all the reports and promises, the relative and absolute importance of America's contribution to Western Europe's defense remained essentially undiminished. Indeed, within a few years of NATO's 'three per cent decision', the US contribution loomed as large as ever, due mainly to the Reagan buildup. By 1986, when that buildup peaked, US defense spending hit 6.3 per cent of Gross Domestic Product. The figure for NATO's European members was 3.4 per cent – and had already begun to fall.[23]

True, the West European economies were not growing as rapidly as America's economy for much of this period, making decisions to increase or even maintain defense spending levels difficult. Between 1976 and 1980, both the US and the European Community economies expanded at an average annual rate of 3.2 per cent. From 1981 to 1985, however, the US figure shrunk to 2.5 per cent while western Europe's plummeted to 1.5 per cent.[24] But the European allies' sagging defense contribution also reflected deliberate political choice. Europe's NATO members were devoting an average of 9.8 per cent of their central government spending to defense by 1975; the US figure was 26.2 per cent. Ten years later, the European level had fallen to 8.8 per cent while the American had risen to 26.5 per cent. America's European allies clearly were not strapped for public funds. They simply chose not to spend them on defense.[25]

Those trends continued through the end of the Cold War. By 1990 American military expenditures had declined to 5.3 per cent of national economic output and 23.5 per cent of federal spending. The NATO-Europe figures had fallen to 3 per cent and 7.8 per cent, respectively. Europe's relative defense contribution was shrinking by other measures, too. The United States spent $1,408 per American on defense, and US military personnel made up 8.7 per cent of the total population. NATO-Europe's military expenditures per capita were only $541, although thanks largely to the retention of the draft throughout Europe, military personnel still represented 8.8 per cent of these countries' total populations.[26]

Many other burden-sharing measures fleshed out this by now familiar story. From 1981 to 1990 military spending as a share of central government expenditures was virtually unchanged in the United States. For NATO's European members, it dropped by 10.3 per cent. US military personnel as a share of the total American population fell by 7.4 per cent from 1981 to 1990, but Western Europe's share fell even faster – by 10.2 per cent. Total US military personnel rose 3.8 per cent during this period while the corresponding NATO-Europe figure decreased by 2.1 per cent. NATO-Europe's military spending per capita did rise by 13.7 per cent from 1981 to 1990, but the US increase was twice as fast from a base more than twice as large. Consequently, as of 1989, the US military still made up 36 per cent of NATO's total armed forces and the United States accounted for 64.7 per cent of the alliance's total military spending.[27]

Although most European forces and resources were devoted to NATO missions – unlike the US military with its worldwide commitments – that disparity was hardly surprising. The Continent is, after all, the homeland of NATO's European members. If anything, their share of the security burden should have been rising, since whatever European security threats remained from the East–West confrontation would clearly affect them more – and more immediately – than they would the United States.

Most important, European defense contributions were falling short by the paramount burden-sharing measure – how they helped NATO stack up against the Warsaw Pact. Despite the Reagan military buildup, and repeated promises by the allies (solemnly accepted by Washington), at the decade's end, NATO defense ministers stated that, even after a series of major troop cuts pledged by the Soviet bloc was completed, those countries 'will retain well-equipped forces which substantially outnumber those of the West'.[28] In fact, as Cato Institute analyst Rosemary Fiscarelli observed in a 1990 study, Europe's NATO members had embarked on a campaign of 'burden-shedding…with a view to reaping a peace dividend in this new era of lowered tensions'.[29]

WHY DID COLD WAR BURDEN-SHARING FAIL?

America's Cold War burden-sharing efforts failed for many reasons. But the main explanation is that US leaders never gave the Europeans sufficient incentive to assume greater relative military responsibilities. The incentive was lacking, in turn, because Washington never believed it could afford to walk away from NATO, or even reduce its role, if the allies stood firm. Worse, US leaders repeatedly telegraphed that message to the Europeans – often in the midst of burden-sharing controversies.

Of course, Washington has often claimed that burden-sharing either has succeeded, is succeeding, or will soon succeed. In early 1971, for example, Secretary of State William Rogers stated that 'The United States is gratified with the way our allies are responding toward increasing their share of the burdens of the common defense.' More than ten years later, former Under Secretary Defense Robert Komer testified to Congress that 'the record shows that our European allies began increasing real defense spending during the early 1970s while US spending ex-Vietnam was going down'.[30] And as the Reagan buildup was peaking, Secretary of Defense Caspar Weinberger announced that the allies 'as a group are bearing roughly their fair share of the NATO defense burden'.[31]

The main fact used to support Weinberger's claim was that the European allies provided the vast bulk of NATO military forces stationed on the continent in peacetime – some 90 per cent of the manpower, 95 per cent of the divisions, 85 per cent of the tanks, 95 per cent of the artillery, and 80 per cent of the combat aircraft, according to one 1986 study.[32] Many US leaders and analysts have also noted that most European countries kept the military draft long after the United States dropped conscription, and thus supposedly realized personnel cost savings without sacrificing manpower.[33] Finally, American leaders have spotlighted a series of nonmilitary contributions to free world security allegedly made by West European countries (and other allies) that never show up in most burden-sharing tallies. For example, Washington has emphasized the continuing host nation support for US forces, as well as the relatively greater foreign aid expenditures of the European governments. Komer even credited the Europeans with providing 'the battlefield in wartime – an unquantifiable but inestimable contribution to burden-sharing' – as if geography gave the allies any choice in the matter.[34]

Such arguments, however, show how far from common sense American leaders let the burden-sharing debate drift. In particular, the arguments reflected the apparent belief that the main standard for assessing the allies' defense efforts was how they stacked up compared to the US force commitment in Europe. That comparison obviously sounded plausible on both sides of the Atlantic. But aside from the pleasingly symmetrical picture it formed, a neat split of all responsibilities right down the middle offered no advantages from the American standpoint. Even ignoring the obviously central issue of how Western defense efforts measured up against Warsaw Pact forces, it would have been far more sensible to divide Western responsibilities according to the interests of the alliance partners in European stability and security. And however great America's stake, the West Europeans' stake was unquestionably far greater. The only remaining reason for valuing the even split so highly was clearly a political one – convincing Congress and the American people that the allies were indeed pulling their weight.

If, by contrast, the main purpose of European defense contributions was to maximize European security, then the main standard for judging Western Europe's effort should have been how it helped NATO stack up against Soviet forces – as the alliance's defense ministers themselves made clear in late 1988.[35] During the Cold War, the levels of US forces stationed in Europe and NATO's heavy reliance on US conventional re-enforcements and US nuclear weapons demonstrated that West European militaries were inadequate to fight the Warsaw Pact and even to deter an attack. The most important NATO burden-sharing reality when the Cold War ended was that, if the United States had to risk its territorial security and spend more than

$100 billion annually to protect the largest economic region in the world, then that region's defense efforts were sorely lacking.

America's Cold War burden-sharing efforts did face numerous built-in obstacles. For example, during NATO's early years, the United States was so economically predominant and the allies so economically fragile that Europe could not hope to match America's military performance. In addition, the Eisenhower administration's partly budget-driven decision to rely for deterrence largely on US nuclear forces, combined with America's then-formidable nuclear edge, probably undercut Washington's burden-sharing message during the 1950s. But by far the biggest obstacles to burden-sharing efforts have been (a) America's determination to preserve NATO at literally all costs – even if burden-sharing had to be sacrificed and (b) American leaders' equally strong insistence on letting the European allies know that the US commitment to NATO overrode all other considerations. The high priority Washington assigned to NATO during the Cold War was perfectly understandable – if not beyond criticism. The penchant repeatedly shown by American negotiators for shooting themselves in the foot was not.

US ineptitude at burden-sharing diplomacy became apparent almost as soon as burden-sharing controversies began. In 1953, for example, Secretary of State John Foster Dulles threatened to begin an 'agonizing reappraisal' of America's entire foreign policy, including NATO, if the allies refused to create a viable European Defence Community that included German forces. But throughout early 1954, American policymakers also labored mightily to assure the Europeans that America's NATO commitment remained firm – that is, that no major reappraisal would take place.[36] Eisenhower's own ambivalence was summed up neatly at a December 1958 meeting. The President specified to his top national security aides that 'he has no intention of running away from our commitments…but we should ask the European governments to what extent they intend to continue leaning on the US'.[37]

US diplomatic incoherence was apparent during the Nixon years as well. Shortly before one of President Nixon's most important articulations of his burden-sharing 'Nixon Doctrine' in February 1970, Under Secretary of State Elliot Richardson addressed the issue in a Chicago speech. 'The United States believes that our European allies can and should do more', he said. 'We have told them often that if they increase their own efforts, it would help us to maintain ours.' Yet Richardson also insisted that 'the security of the United States is directly linked to the security of Western Europe'. He went on to warn that 'any sudden or dramatic reduction in the

US military presence in Europe' would endanger 'the entire structure of world order which we have helped erect since the war'.[38]

On a September 1970 trip to Europe, Nixon announced that US burden-sharing efforts would emphasize building up European military forces rather than securing more cash subsidies from the allies. But on the same trip, the President declared that the United States 'will, under no circumstances, reduce, unilaterally, its commitment to NATO'.[39] Several months later, Nixon appeared to place burden-sharing conditions on America's NATO policy when he told a North Atlantic Council meeting in a message:

> We have agreed that NATO's conventional forces must not only be maintained, but in certain key areas strengthened. *Given a similar approach by our Allies* [emphasis added], the United States will maintain and improve its forces in Europe and will not reduce them unless there is reciprocal action from our adversaries.

Yet at the same meeting Secretary of State William Rogers told the allies, 'President Nixon has made clear that our own commitment has not diminished.'[40]

The attitude that doomed the Carter administration's burden-sharing efforts was displayed by then Under Secretary of Defense Komer in his 1982 congressional testimony. Komer noted that 'US threats…such as recurrent warnings that we'll pull our troops out of Europe, never seem to work very well. The Europeans know that we need them as much as they need us.'[41] The main reason the European governments 'knew' that, of course, was because of the repeated assurances given by Komer and other US officials.

Despite a modest escalation of burden-sharing pressure, the Reagan and Bush administrations, too, repeatedly bungled opportunities to make progress. For example, in the May 1987 NATO Defence Planning Committee meeting that urged alliance members not to make unilateral defense cuts, the United States also agreed that European and American defense are 'indivisible', and that the continued presence of Canadian and United States forces at existing levels in Europe played an irreplaceable role in the defence *of North America* [emphasis added] as well as Europe.[42]

A typical speech by Deputy Secretary of Defense William H. Taft IV in 1988 revealed similar problems. Noting that budget, trade, and political pressures were making burden-sharing a hot-button domestic political issue, Taft told a London audience that 'our allies are prosperous enough to do more than they do now' and that 'Alliance members must be prepared to

id more on their defenses.' But Taft also hastened to declare that 'Our
rity partnership with Europe is vital to our overall national security –
whatever other interests we may have acquired or expect to acquire.'[43] Taft,
like Komer, Dulles, and so many others, might as well have worn an 'Ignore
Me' sign.

EARLY POST-COLD WAR BURDEN-SHARING

As described above, the winding down of the Cold War led all NATO
members to accelerate a reduction in military spending that had begun in the
mid-1980s. Yet not only did the gap among relative US and West European
defense burdens continue to widen, but a new burden-sharing controversy
opened up – over the allies' respective responsibilities in the Persian Gulf
and other non-European regions where events could have major European
and global repercussions.

Since the Soviet invasion of Afghanistan in late 1979, NATO has
officially recognized that 'events outside NATO boundaries can bear
directly on the security of alliance member states'. In December 1980 the
Defence Planning Committee 'took note' of Washington's plans for sending
a Rapid Deployment Force to southwest Asia and agreed that NATO
members would need to 'prepare against the eventuality of a diversion of
NATO-allocated forces the United States and other countries might be
compelled to make' to protect NATO's interests in areas such as the Persian
Gulf. But NATO members without long-range power projection capabilities
(meaning all members other than the United States and possibly Britain and
France) were simply obliged to provide enough host nation support for the
re-enforcement of units temporarily sent outside Europe. NATO's smaller,
weaker members were not asked to participate in out-of-area combat, or
even to develop such capabilities.[44]

Two years later, the alliance's Defence Planning Committee added some
urgency to this formulation, not only acknowledging that 'developments
beyond the NATO area might threaten the *vital* [emphasis added] interests
of members of the alliance', but also agreeing to 'take full account of the
effect of such developments on NATO security, defence capabilities, and the
national interests of member countries...'[45] The Committee supported
continuing to give 'due attention to fair burden-sharing and developing
areas of practical co-operation', and specified that 'the efforts by European
members of the Alliance to maintain and improve their defence capabilities'
were 'essential'. But only a very limited vision was sketched out for burden-
sharing 'out of area'.

Indeed, the only important change announced in NATO policy was a new burden on the United States: to consult more with its allies. NATO defense ministers 'stated that those countries, such as the United States, which have the means to take action outside the treaty area to deter threats to the vital interests of the West, should do so in timely consultation with other allies…'. Other NATO countries would simply 'make an important contribution to the security of the Alliance by making available facilities to assist such deployments'.[46]

Perhaps not surprisingly – given the clear determination of all NATO members to paper over new burden-sharing problems – by the eve of the 1991 Persian Gulf War, references to out-of-area contingencies had dropped out of NATO policy and planning documents entirely. Even the landmark declaration of the July 1990 London NATO summit on a transformed North Atlantic Alliance lacked any reference to southwest Asia or any region of the developing world. Instead, the focus was on NATO's relations with the Soviet Union and the former Warsaw Pact countries.[47]

None the less, Iraq's invasion of Kuwait in August 1990 refocused NATO's attention, and the heavy dependence of NATO's European members (as well as Japan) on Persian Gulf oil placed burden-sharing issues back in the spotlight. By most reasonable standards, the allies flunked the test, and their performance was even less impressive considering that it came after more than three decades of burden-sharing promises – and frequent praise on the issue from Washington. Even as staunch a defender of the allies' general burden-sharing record as Robert Komer acknowledged that in the Gulf, 'our allies have indubitably fallen short'.[48]

When the ground war began in February 1991, a total of 844,650 coalition troops (including air and naval personnel) had been deployed to the Gulf. Of these, 532,000 were American, and many of the rest came from allied Arab countries, not NATO-Europe. The coalition also deployed 2,614 total aircraft, of which 1,990, or 76.1 per cent, were American. A grand total of 175, or 6.7 per cent, came from the NATO-Europe countries.[49]

Since the air war comprised the bulk of Operation 'Desert Storm' combat operations, it is worth examining in detail this phase of the conflict. According to the US Air Force's Gulf War Air Power Survey, a total of 118,661 total sorties were flown over a 43-day period during the Gulf War. US aircraft flew 58 per cent (69,406) of these sorties. The total sorties can be broken down into strike sorties (45 per cent of the total, or 53,075) and sorties of other types, such as reconnaissance missions. Fully 62 per cent (32,834) of the strike sorties were flown by US aircraft.[50]

Because it became so clear so early during the Operation 'Desert Shield' military buildup that the US military role was overwhelmingly disproportionate, and because American public and congressional criticisms of free-riding allies were intensifying, the Bush administration began to press NATO members and other US allies to contribute non-military support for the looming war effort. The US 'responsibility sharing' campaign began in early September 1990 when senior US officials traveled to the United Kingdom, France, Germany, Italy, Japan, South Korea, and Arab countries such as Saudi Arabia to discuss and coordinate prospective contributions. Once it became clear that the confrontation with Iraq would extend into 1991, those efforts resumed and intensified.

The responsibility-sharing campaign achieved impressive results. Of the $61 billion worth of incremental costs incurred by the US military during operations 'Desert Shield' and 'Desert Storm', America's allies reimbursed nearly $54 billion. These contributions came in three main forms: cash, in-kind airlift, and in-kind sealift. But the responsibility-sharing campaign was hardly a triumph of *NATO* burden-sharing. Roughly two-thirds of these commitments came from the Gulf states directly in Iraq's line of fire. Non-NATO member Japan contributed much of the rest. Germany was the only NATO member to make a significant contribution – just under $6.5 billion, including $5.5 billion in cash.[51] Just as important, NATO never endorsed a coordinated alliance-wide response to the Gulf crisis. Rebuffing Secretary of State James Baker's efforts, the allies decided to provide support for the war as individual countries.[52]

Nevertheless, responsibility sharing blunted some of the sharpest American criticisms of allied military efforts and burden-sharing. Official NATO pronouncements of the period congratulated the alliance for its superb joint performance, and Washington's endorsement of these positions, plus the Pentagon's official Gulf War report, indicated that US leaders were indeed pleased with the burden-sharing *status quo*, too.

As early as December 1990, NATO's Defense Planning Committee and Nuclear Planning Group praised alliance members whose 'contributions have enabled a more rapid and formidable international response to the crisis than any single nation could have achieved through its own devices'. In May 1991 these organizations stated, 'We warmly welcome the success of the international coalition forces in the recent Gulf War. We note with satisfaction the effectiveness of the prompt action taken by the Alliance in deploying naval and air forces to its Southern region to deter any possible attacks on its members.'[53] No mention was made of the preponderant American role.

Similar complacent sentiments were expressed by Under Secretary of Defense Paul Wolfowitz in the Pentagon's Gulf War report to Congress:

> [The contributions of our allies] would rank, by a considerable margin, as the world's third largest defense budget... Few would have imagined this level of foreign participation. There will no doubt be those who will focus attention on whether a particular country paid as much as it might have or as promptly, but these concerns – valid as they are – should not overshadow all that has been accomplished.[54]

None the less, NATO leaders and strategists seemed to sense that something was amiss, for the development of a new alliance Strategic Concept was in the works. Released at the Rome summit in November 1991, that blueprint highlighted and suggested a relationship between two new themes: first, that new kinds of threats to European security were beginning to replace the classical Warsaw Pact invasion of the West; and second, that more progress was needed on militarily strengthening of NATO's 'European pillar'.

Clearly eyeing the increasingly violent breakup of Yugoslavia, the 1991 summiteers declared, 'Risks to Allied security are less likely to result from calculated aggression against the territory of the Allies, but rather from the adverse consequences of instabilities that may arise from the serious social and economic difficulties, including ethnic rivalries and territorial disputes, which are faced by many countries in central and eastern Europe.'[55] The summiteers did not draw a direct, explicit link between these new security challenges and burden-sharing. But a relationship was suggested. According to the new Strategic Concept, the new threats required multi-faceted responses – political as well as military. Consequently, NATO leaders conceded that institutions such as the European Community, the Western European Union (WEU), and the Conference on Security and Cooperation in Europe (CSCE) also had roles to play in European security affairs. In this context the NATO leaders stated, 'The creation of a European identity in security and defence will underline the preparedness of the Europeans to take a greater share of responsibility for their security...'. Assuming a greater role would also 'help to reinforce transatlantic solidarity'.[56]

NATO's new security challenges would require different kinds of forces, the summiteers agreed. In order to 'manage' crises short of war and 'reinforce political actions within a broad approach to security', these forces would require not only 'enhanced flexibility and mobility' but new political characteristics. They would be 'increasingly multinational forces, complementing national commitments to NATO'.[57]

BREAKDOWN IN THE BALKANS

During the early 1990s, the intensifying Balkans crisis seemed to push all of these trends forward vigorously. NATO agreed to a UN Security Council request in June 1992 to support peace operations in Bosnia, and at the end of the year announced that it was prepared to support, 'on a case-by-case basis', other such missions.[58] At the same time, at Washington's insistence, NATO declined to include Yugoslavia in its ongoing purview, seeming, thereby, to rule out a combat role for the alliance. That position largely reflected the Bush administration's belief that the Balkan wars did not affect vital US security interests.[59]

The evidence of US disinterest in a problem at their doorstep further convinced many Europeans that, with the end of the Cold War, America's perceived stakes in Europe's security and stability would indeed lessen. Accordingly, signs began appearing of greater European determination to fill the gap. The imminent completion of the single-market economic integration plan increased confidence that Europe could be a coherent international political and military actor as well as a unified market. In particular, French efforts intensified to bring to life the WEU's goal of a European Security and Defence Identity. And in October 1991 the European Community announced its intention to operate a joint Eurocorps that would enable the Europeans to respond 'to crises such as the Yugoslav civil war'. Luxembourg's foreign minister, Jacques Poos, one of the EC negotiators trying to contain the crisis, went so far as to proclaim 'the hour of Europe has come'.[60]

Yet three towering obstacles quickly became apparent. First, the Europeans were seriously divided on how to handle the Yugoslavia crisis, with NATO members such as France and Germany often supporting different belligerents in the conflicts. Second, even if there had been a European consensus on the Balkans, the European countries lacked the means to carry it out. After years of ostensibly improving burden-sharing efforts, even small brushfire conflicts loomed as huge military challenges to America's European allies. Finally, despite numerous alliance decisions and resolutions, the Bush administration had convinced itself that the French-led Europe-only military cooperation drive could all too easily lead to NATO's breakup and Europe's transformation into an independent great power – and possible competitor or rival.[61] The gravity of the last concern emerged as early as the Rome NATO summit of 1990, when Bush departed from prepared remarks and exclaimed at a press conference, 'If, my friends, your ultimate aim is to provide independently for your defense, the time to tell us is today.' Indeed, the Bush administration seemed to have followed a determined strategy of keeping its allies internationally passive and therefore unthreatening by smothering their independent diplomatic impulses.[62]

Some evidence indicates that President Bush's defeat in 1992 removed one obstacle to more extensive European military involvement in the Balkans. Under Bill Clinton, the United States showed signs of appearing genuinely to welcome European defense efforts that were not only stronger but more independent. These signs ranged from Clinton's clear reluctance early in his presidency – despite belligerent campaign rhetoric – to involve the United States militarily in the Bosnia war to his administration's frequently telegraphed message that US foreign policy was too 'Eurocentric'.[63]

Yet the biggest remaining obstacle – inadequate European military capabilities – remained firmly in place. The end of the Cold War should have represented a golden opportunity for the European allies to narrow – and even close – the security gap between their military forces and their security challenges. But the Europeans continued to respond to the transformed security landscape simply by shrinking their militaries. According to the International Institute for Strategic Studies (IISS), NATO's European members cut their military budgets by 22 per cent in real terms from 1992 to 1998. US military spending shrank even more during the decade – by 40 per cent – but the US base was much larger. At least as important, the new Balkans-style troubles in Europe are greater threats to the European members of NATO than to America.[64]

That observation, however valid, has traditionally been considered the greatest heresy in NATO. The alliance's fundamental tenet is that its members' security is indivisible. Until the mid-1990s only NATO critics contended anything else. But in a little-noticed revolutionary change in NATO doctrine in 1994, the alliance itself conceded that divisibility was an inescapable fact of post-Cold War transatlantic security relations. At their Brussels summit that January, the NATO Heads of State agreed to authorize the European members to develop 'separable but not separate capabilities which could respond to *European* [emphasis added] requirements and contribute to Alliance security'.[65] NATO's reasoning was explained by its Secretary General Javier Solana in a November 1996 speech:

In future crises NATO will continue to be fully capable of undertaking all missions, including non-Article 5 operations. For any major problem, the best and safest choice is NATO. Yet, it is also possible that some operations, which may differ in scale or be local in character, could be launched by the WEU with NATO's help. We want to build that additional option – a European-led, WEU-directed operation – into our new structure... .

The reason is a practical one. We cannot predict all possible contingencies, and we should not tie ourselves to one organisational response...we should not expect the US to lead every action or contribute significantly to every operation. There may be times when a European-led force would be appropriate.[66]

Solana's artful phrasing, however, could not conceal a basic problem raised for NATO by this doctrine of subsidiarity. If European crises were 'local in character', what disciplined doctrine of national self-interest would militate for any US involvement in the first place? If the United States viewed these crises as unimportant enough to justify letting relatively inexperienced European militaries take charge, could not these crises by definition be safely ignored by Washington? Conversely, if, as US officials have maintained sporadically about Bosnia and Kosovo, such conflicts inevitably spread if not snuffed out, why would Washington run the risks entailed in detachment?

The debate would remain largely academic – at least for the NATO allies, if not for the peoples of the Balkans, who suffered the worst consequences of this experimentation. As earlier in the decade, the European NATO members lacked the capability to act in a militarily effective way even in the militarily weak Balkans. Consequently, US forces comprised one-third of the original 60,000-strong Implementation Force (IFOR) force sent to Bosnia in 1995 to enforce the Dayton peace accords. As of spring 1999, more than a fifth of the troops in the Stabilization Force (SFOR, IFOR's less potent successor) were still American.[67] As British Prime Minister Tony Blair sadly noted, 'We [the Europeans] thought we could deal with the Bosnian crisis alone. The guns over Sarajevo destroyed that illusion along with much else. Washington in the end had to get involved to provide the military muscle for our diplomacy.'[68]

Revealingly, the most devastating indictment of America's NATO burden-sharing efforts – not only for the post-Cold War period but also for the alliance's entire history – came in its most recent operation, in Kosovo.

Half a century after NATO's founding the European allies still had not outgrown military pygmy status relative to the United States. Indeed, as even most NATO supporters admitted, in many ways, the military gap between the United States and its allies is as wide as it has ever been since the Vietnam War.

As has often been the case in NATO's history, this latest burden-sharing development was preceded by repeated burden-sharing promises and much hype about progress. In 1994 the Brussels summiteers endorsed the stronger European Security and Defence Identity precisely to 'strengthen the European pillar of the Alliance'. As a result, they predicted, the Europeans would be able 'to take greater responsibility for their common security and defence'.

Two years later, NATO again declared its determination to 'build a European Security and Defence Identity within NATO, which will enable all European Allies to make a more coherent and effective contribution to the missions and activities of the Alliance...'. In particular, the idea was to 'facilitate...the use of separable military capabilities in operations led by the WEU'.[69] And since the standard was military effectiveness in conflicts too small and local to engage the United States significantly, this bar was set rather low.

Meanwhile, the Pentagon's burden-sharing reports continued to highlight the progress and contributions being made by the allies and to soft-pedal or excuse whatever shortcomings the record revealed. For example, the 1999 version, published on the eve of the Kosovo operation (and like its predecessors, covering non-NATO allies as well), concluded, 'As stated in previous reports on this topic, the Department believes country efforts present a mixed but generally positive picture in terms of shouldering responsibility for shared security objectives.' Thanks to US efforts on the burden-sharing issue, moreover, the Pentagon observed 'an increased awareness of our concerns in allied capitals'. Allied efforts won more plaudits at the April 1999 Washington NATO summit. In a new strategic concept paper, NATO leaders reported that 'the European Allies are strengthening their capacity for action, including by increasing their military capabilities.[70]

The inaccuracy of the Defense Department's overall burden-sharing assessment is made all too clear by what the Europeans themselves were saying at the time about their military capabilities. Using language that would undoubtedly get an American diplomat fired, Prime Minister Blair wrote in late 1998, 'If Europe wants America to maintain its commitment to Europe, Europe must share more of the burden of defending the West's security interests.' And according to no less than the Assembly of the WEU, '[W]e now find ourselves in a situation of dependence and imbalance that is extremely disadvantageous to Europe and even to our American interests.'[71]

This dependence and imbalance were precisely what was revealed by the Kosovo intervention. By some measures, the European share of the Kosovo burden was larger than its share in the Gulf War nearly ten years before. In the Gulf, for example, 62 per cent of the air strike sorties – the air war's most hazardous missions – were flown by US planes. In Kosovo this figure declined to 53 per cent. But US aircraft flew 62 per cent of total sorties in Kosovo – up from 58 per cent in 'Desert Storm'. And with 639 total aircraft in theater as of mid-May 1999, one conservative tally pegged the US air deployment as more than double that of its NATO allies combined.[72] In all, according to one estimate, the United States bore between 65 and 75 per cent of the conflict's costs.[73]

But these figures only hint at the gap between the US and allied roles in Kosovo. In the first place, the United States viewed Iraq's invasion of Kuwait as a national security threat of the first order. Most of NATO's European members agreed that Iraqi aggression not only threatened oil resources on which they relied heavily, but also threatened to undermine global norms against cross-border aggression. For all of Bill Clinton's hyperbolic rhetoric, Washington never saw the Kosovo crisis as anything comparable. At worst, the failure to frustrate Serbia's aims would weaken NATO's credibility and call into question its ability to handle other, similarly small-scale contingencies. No direct threats to US national security and prosperity were claimed. Europe's NATO members plainly acted as if Kosovo's fate was not significantly linked to their own. But however modestly they defined their stakes in the conflict, these stakes were clearly much larger than America's. Therefore, the NATO-Europe role in the conflict should have dwarfed that of the United States, not (at least by these criteria) roughly matched it.

In addition, the raw numbers obscure enormous qualitative differences between the US and European contributions, and between US and European military capabilities on the eve of the millennium. Those differences belie the Washington-drawn picture of allies determined to stand on their own. Instead, the Kosovo intervention showed that the allies' military efforts barely met the laugh test. For example, although the NATO allies had some two million military personnel when the Kosovo campaign started, only two to three per cent of these troops could handle such missions, largely because readiness was so poor. In particular, European units were hampered by a shortage of specialists such as engineers and communications and medical staff.[74] German forces were stretched so thin that the *Bundeswehr's* Inspector General reported that 63,000 of its troops had been deployed to the Balkans six times in recent years.[75]

Another reason for the difficulty the European deployments encountered was the almost complete lack of long-range airlift capability. The United States, moreover, deployed more than ten times the number of air-to-air refueling tankers over Kosovo as did the allies.[76]

European air combat capabilities were equally woeful. The United States had to supply the allies with laser-guided bombs. Europe's unmanned aerial vehicles – used for target acquisition and damage assessment – were all in urgent need of upgrading. And several allies lacked secure radio networks for their pilots, who were forced to use open airwaves that could be monitored by the Serbs.[77] Yet at least one ally successfully pressed for decisive influence over the Kosovo air campaign despite its paltry contribution. According to US Lieutenant General Michael Short, commander of the allied forces in southern Europe, France frequently vetoed targeting choices and restricted operations in hopes of limiting collateral damage. Those restrictions, Short charged, 'placed the crew force at increased risk and made us predictable'. And in a direct criticism of the Clinton administration's approach to burden-sharing and alliance leadership, Short stated, 'I felt that the United States was in a position to leverage our position of being the big dog to a degree that we perhaps did not.'[78]

The Kosovo campaign seemed to jolt the Clinton administration out of its burden-sharing complacency. Declared Secretary of Defense William Cohen in Germany in late 1999, 'We cannot afford the disparity of alliance capabilities we witnessed this spring. The disparity of capabilities, if not corrected, could threaten the unity of this alliance.' Cohen has even singled out Germany's shrinking defense budget for explicit criticism.

His British counterpart at the time, George Robertson, was even more blunt about the allies' efforts. At a WEU meeting convened to develop a common defense policy, Robertson stated, 'In Kosovo, we have all come face to face with the European future, and it is frightening.'[79]

Europe's military failure in Kosovo even prompted the 15 leaders of the European Union to meet in June 1999 and approve a concrete plan for giving the organization a military arm that would replace the ineffectual WEU. The EU leaders promised to appoint a single foreign policy and security 'tsar' by late 2000, to create and staff an EU command headquarters, and place the WEU's 60,000-strong Eurocorps at the EU's disposal. That decision was formalized at the EU summit in Helsinki in December 1999.[80]

Yet many reasons for skepticism are still in place. According to the IISS, most European military budgets continued to fall in inflation-adjusted terms in 1999. Even in Britain, whose leaders have so passionately called for greater European military efforts, real defense spending was unchanged between 1998 and 1999. Further cuts are likely in Germany, and Defense Minister Rudolph Scharping has stated that 'where we can make only limited progress in 2000 is in developing the new abilities we need in NATO, the European Union and transforming the Eurocorps into a rapid reaction corps'.[81]

The qualitative picture is no better. The Europeans' military spending is so inefficient, Cohen now charges, that 'NATO countries spend roughly 60 per cent of what the United States does, and they get about 10 per cent of the capability.' The IISS estimates that allied spending on military research and development is only one-fourth of US levels. And European dithering over a new joint transport plane is now in its 16th year. As Lord Robertson admitted in December 1999, 'We could double our capabilities as they stand and still not be able to do very much on our own.'[82]

Perhaps most worrisome, the allies seem to view their new missions more as social work and humanitarian operations than as military efforts. The Netherlands, for example, ended the draft in 1996, arguing that conscription 'no longer fitted with the army's role in a world where peacekeeping has taken over from combat'. And Britain's 1997–98 *Annual Report on Defence Activity* makes clear that London feels the same way. The report is filled with illustrations of British soldiers cradling children in their arms and providing medical care to senior citizens in global hotspots.[83]

CONCLUSION

After 50 years of broken promises, there can be no doubt that significant NATO burden-sharing progress will never be made as long as the United States trumpets how vital Europe's security and stability are to America's and acts as the hammer of first resort whenever unrest breaks out in whatever remote corner of the Continent. Game theory and common sense both make clear why the allies will not act until they have an incentive to do so. Today's relatively benign European security environment provides the perfect opportunity for Washington to change the incentive structure.

NATO doctrine, repeatedly endorsed by Washington, classifies Bosnia and Kosovo-type conflicts as situations in which Article 5 of the North Atlantic Treaty does not apply. The United States, in other words, has absolutely no obligation to become involved. And European endorsement of subsidiarity, plus the noises Europeans periodically make about developing autonomous defense capabilities, indicate that the allies implicitly acknowledge that reality.

Indeed, from time to time, the Europeans have shown that they recognize how the all-important transatlantic balance of interests has changed. As Blair has written, 'The imperatives that drove defense spending in America during the superpower standoff are gone.' Germany's *Die Welt* has observed editorially, 'Europe is closer to the epicentres of the new dangers than the United States.'[84]

US policy, however, still presents two related obstacles. First, although the Clinton administration is on record as supporting 'separable but not separate' European military capabilities, news reports make clear that Washington's private doubts remain considerable.[85] Moreover, statements from senior Republican figures leave little doubt that a Grand Old Party victory in the 2000 presidential election would stiffen US opposition. In the somewhat circular view of John Bolton of the American Enterprise Institute, an Assistant Secretary of State in the Bush years, 'If the EU were really capable of a united security policy...it would undermine the sole remaining argument for an American military presence in Europe, which is that the Europeans cannot handle these critical questions themselves.'[86]

Second, there is no evidence that the Clinton administration, much less any prospective likely Republican successors, would ever adopt the unilateral measures – primarily force reductions – required to prod the allies into taking significant action. US officials and much of the nation's foreign policy establishment still insist that – as Robert Komer insisted more than a decade ago – even in the post-Cold War era, the United States needs Europe at least as much as Europe needs the United States. Until that attitude changes, there is little hope of meaningful progress on the burden-sharing front.

In a rare recent example of bipartisan cooperation, the Republican Congress and the Democratic White House joined forces in 1996 to pass sweeping welfare reform legislation. The new policy reflected a new bipartisan consensus that, without adequate incentives to fend for themselves, even welfare recipients capable of working tend to stay on the dole. As Representative Barney Frank (Democrat-Massachusetts) has argued, America's European allies are threatening to become foreign policy 'welfare recipients', and that, unless compelled to do so, they will never pay their own way.[87] Lamentably, for most American leaders, this common sense insight still stops at the water's edge.

NOTES

The author gratefully acknowledges the research assistance of Kim Gabriel and Ted Galen Carpenter.

1. See, for example, the statement by then National Security Advisor Anthony Lake quoted in Jonathan Clarke, 'Beckoning Quagmires: NATO in Eastern Europe', in Ted Galen Carpenter (ed.) *The Future of NATO* (London and Portland, OR: Frank Cass 1995) p.44.
2. Two representative views of this position are found in Benjamin C. Schwarz, '"Cold War" Continuities: US Economic and Security Strategy Towards Europe', in Carpenter (ed.) (note 1) pp.82–104; and Ted Galen Carpenter, *A Search for Enemies: America's Alliances after the Cold War* (Washington DC: Cato Institute 1992).
3. 'Declaration of the Heads of State and Government participating in the Meeting of the North Atlantic Council', Brussels, 29–30 May 1989, http://www.nato.int/docu/comm/49-95/c890530a.htm p.5.
4. *Report on Allied Contributions to the Common Defense: A Report to the United States Congress by the Secretary of Defense* (Washington DC: US Dept. of Defense, March 1999), p.1-1, http://www.defenselink. mil/pubs/allied_contrib99/rs-chpt1.html.
5. Curtis Everett, 'The Growing, Unequal Burden of Atlantic Defense', *Freedom & Union*, Feb. 1952, p.7.
6. For the economics of US national security policy from the Truman to the Carter administrations, see John Lewis Gaddis, *Strategies of Containment* (NY: Oxford University Press 1982).
7. 'Memorandum of Conference with the President, 12 Dec. 1958 – 2:30 PM', 15 Dec. 1958, *Papers as President, 1953–61* (Ann Whitman File), DDE Diary Series, 13 x.38, 'Staff Notes – Dec. 1958', Dwight D. Eisenhower Library, Abilene, Kansas.
8. Quoted in Carpenter, *A Search for Enemies* (note 2) p.21.
9. For good, concise accounts of the Defence Community's painful creation, see Stanley R. Sloan, 'European Cooperation and the Future of NATO: In Search of a New Transatlantic Bargain'; and William Wallace, 'European Defence Cooperation: The Reopening Debate', both in *Survival* 26/6 (Nov.–Dec. 1984) pp.242–45, 252.
10. 'Memorandum of Conference' (note 7) p.2.
11. For the political economy of alliance relations during the 1960s, see Wallace (note 9); and especially David P. Calleo, *Beyond American Hegemony: The Future of the Western Alliance* (NY: Basic Books 1987).
12. C. Gordon Bare, 'Burden-Sharing in NATO: The Economics of Alliance', *Orbis* 20/2 (Summer 1976) p.421.
13. See Ibid. p.426 ff. for a good summary of these events.
14. Ibid. p.431.
15. See 'If the US Pulls Back From Europe', *US News & World Report*, 16 March 1970, p.79; and 'Carter's Goal: More Sharing of the NATO Load', *Business Week*, 8 Aug. 1977.
16. This analysis of the INF controversy is spelled out in Alan Tonelson and Christopher Layne, 'Divorce, Alliance-Style', *New Republic*, 12 June 1989, pp.23–5.
17. On both points, see, for example, 'Final Communiqué', Defence Planning Committee, Brussels, 22 May 1985, http://www.nato.int/docu/comm/49-95/c850522a.htm, pp.2–3.
18. See Rosemary Fiscarelli, 'NATO in the 1990s: Burden Shedding Replaces Burden-Sharing', Cato Institute Foreign Policy Briefing No. 1, 26 June 1990, http://www.cato.org/pubs/ fpbriefs/fpb-001.html, p.2. For the Congressional troop cap, which maintained in place a

historically large American deployment, see Sloan (note 9) p.246. For other congressional burden-sharing initiatives, see Carpenter (note 2) pp.26–7.

19. 'Final Communique', Defence Planning Committee, Brussels, 26–27 May 1987, http://www.nato.int.docu/comm/49-95/c870527a.htm, pp.2–3.
20. 'Chronology of events: 1988', online version, Oct. 1995, http://www.nato.int/docu/hand book/hb615443.htm, p.1.
21. 'Final Communiqué', North Atlantic Council, Brussels, 11 Dec. 1987, http://www.nato.int/ docu/comm/49-95/c87121a.htm, p.4.
22. 'Declaration of the Heads of State and Government participating in the meeting of the North Atlantic Council', 2–3 March 1988, http://www.nato.int/docu/comm/49-95/c880303a.htm, p.2; and 'Final Communiqué', Defence Planning Committee, Brussels, 1–2 Dec. 1988, www.nato.int/docu/comm/49-95/c881202a.htm, p.2.
23. US Arms Control and Disarmament Agency, *World Military Expenditures and Arms Transfers 1991–1992* (Washington DC: US Government Printing Office, March 1994), 'Table I., Military Expenditures, Armed Forces, GNP, Central Government Expenditures, and Population, 1981–1991', p.48.
24. *Economic Report of the President Transmitted to the Congress February 1992* (Washington DC: US Government Printing Office, Feb. 1992), 'Table B-108.–Growth rates in real gross national product/gross domestic product, 1971–91', p.421.
25. Alan Tonelson, 'The Economics of NATO', in Ted Galen Carpenter (ed.) *NATO at 40: Confronting a Changing World* (Lexington, MA: Lexington Books 1990) p.106.
26. US Arms Control and Disarmament Agency, *World Military Expenditures and Arms Transfers 1996*, http://www.state.gov/www/global/arms/wmeat96.html, Table I. Military Expenditures, Armed Forces, GNP, Central Government Expenditures and Population, 1985–1995, pp.56, 96.
27. Calculated from *World Military Expenditures and Arms Transfers 1996* (note 26).
28. 'Final Communiqué', Defence Planning Committee, Brussels, 28–29 Nov. 1989, http://www.nato.int/docu/comm/49-95/c8911299.htm, p.2.
29. Fiscarelli (note 18) p.1.
30. 'North Atlantic Council Ministerial Meeting Held at Brussels: Secretary Rogers' Arrival Statement December 2', *Department of State Bulletin*, 64, no.1645, 4 Jan. 1971, p.1; 'Prepared Statement of Hon. Robert W. Komer, the RAND Corp.; Former Under Secretary for Policy, Department of Defense', 20 May 1982, presented to *NATO's Future Role: Hearings Before the Subcommittee on Europe and the Middle East of the Committee on Foreign Affairs, House of Representatives*, 97th Congress, 2d Session, 20 May, 8 and 9 June 1982, p.9. Interestingly, Komer's emphasis on non-Vietnam spending seemed to acknowledge implicitly what many Vietnam War critics had claimed – that the war made no meaningful contribution to Western defense.
31. Quoted in Tonelson (note 25) p.105
32. Ibid. p.105.
33. See, for example, 'Prepared Statement of Hon. Robert W. Komer' (note 30) p.7.
34. Washington still emphasizes allied economic contributions to Western security in order to demonstrate burden-sharing progress. See *Report on Allied Contributions to the Common Defense* (note 4) especially Chart I-2, 'Countries Making Substantial Contributions Based on Ability to Contribute;' Chart III-21, 'Share of US Overseas Stationing Costs Paid by Selected Allies, 1997'; Chart III-23, 'Foreign Assistance in Billions of Constant 1988 Dollars'; and Chart III-24, 'Foreign Assistance as a Percentage of GDP, 1997'. Komer's argument is found in 'Prepared Statement of Hon. Robert W. Komer' (note 30) p.8.
35. 'Final Communiqué', 1–2 Dec. 1988 (note 25) p.2.
36. See Sloane (note 9) p.243.
37. 'Memorandum of Conference' (note 7) p.3.
38. 'Excerpts From Richardson Speech on the Troops in Europe', *New York Times*, 21 Jan. 1970.
39. Drew Middleton, 'Nixon Wants NATO to Furnish Troops, Not Cash', *New York Times*, 9 Oct. 1970.

40. 'Message from President Nixon', *Department of State Bulletin*, 64, no.1645, 4 Jan. 1971, p.2; ibid. p.1.
41. 'Prepared Statement of Hon. Robert W. Komer' (note 30) p.10.
42. 'Final Communiqué', May 1987 (note 19) pp.1–2.
43. 'Roles, Risks, and Responsibilities in the Common Defense: Remarks Prepared for Delivery by the Honorable William H. Taft, IV, Deputy Secretary of Defense at Regents College, London, United Kingdom, Wednesday, 4 May 1988', News Release, Office of Assistant Secretary of Defense (Public Affairs), 4 May 1988, pp.3–4.
44. Ibid. p.2; 'Final Communiqué', Defence Planning Committee, Brussels, 9–10 Dec. 1980, http://www.nato.int/docu/comm/49-95/c801209ahtm, p.3.
45. 'Final Communique', Dec. 1980 (note 44) p.3 ff; 'Final Communiqué', Defence Planning Committee, Brussels, 1–2 Dec. 1982, http://www.nato.into/docu/comm/49-95/c821201a.htm, p.3.
46. 'Final Communiqué', 1–2 Dec. 1982, p.3.
47. 'London Declaration On a Transformed North Atlantic Alliance: Issued by the Heads of State and Government participating in the meeting of the North Atlantic Council', London, 5–6 July 1990, http://www.nato.int/docu/comm/49-95/c900706a.htm. See also 'Final Communiqué', North Atlantic Council, Turnberry, United Kingdom, 7–8 June 1990, http://www.nato.int/docu/comm/49-95/c900608a.htm.
48. 'Prepared Statement of Hon. Robert W. Komer' (note 30) p.12.
49. The ground and air force figures come from Richard P. Hallion, *Storm Over Iraq: Air Power and the Gulf War* (Washington DC: Smithsonian Inst. Press 1992) pp.156–8.
50. Figures compiled by Winslow Wheeler, staff member, Senate Budget committee, sent by e-mail to author by Stephen Daggett, Congressional Research Service, US Library of Congress, 3 Aug. 1999.
51. US Department of Defense, *Final Report to Congress: Conduct of the Persian Gulf War*, (Washington DC: US Government Printing Office, April 1992) Appendix P, 'Responsibility Sharing', pp.P-2-P-4.
52. See Carpenter (note 2) p.29.
53. 'Final Communiqué', Defence Planning Committee and Nuclear Planning Group, Brussels, 6–7 Dec. 1990, http://www.nato.int/docu/comm/49-95/c90127a.htm, p.2; 'Final Communiqué', Defence Planning Committee and Nuclear Planning Group, Brussels, 28–29 May 1991, http://www.nato.int/docu/comm/49-95/c910529a.htm, p.2.
54. *Final Report to Congress* (note 51) p.P-1.
55. 'The Alliance's New Strategic Concept, Agreed by the Heads of State and Government Participating in the Meeting of the North Atlantic Council in Rome on 7–8 Nov. 1991', http://www.nato.int/docu/comm/49-95/c911107a.htm, p.3.
56. Ibid. pp.3, 6.
57. Ibid. pp.10, 11, 14.
58. Dick A. Leurdijk, *The United Nations and NATO in Former Yugoslavia: Partners in International Cooperation* (The Hague: Netherlands Atlantic Commission, Netherlands Inst. of Int. Relations 1994) p.8.
59. Susan L. Woodward, *Balkan Tragedy: Chaos and Dissolution after the Cold War* (Washington DC: Brookings 1995), pp.150, 155, 156.
60. See Leurdijk (note 58) p.8; and Woodward (note 59) p.464. The now-infamous Poos quote is cited in Isabel Hilton, 'Books: As the Wall Came Down', *Financial Times*, 12 June 1999.
61. See, for example, Woodward (note 59) p.155.
62. Bush's statement is cited in Carpenter (note 2) p.17. See Schwarz (note 2) p.89, for a brief discussion of the Bush administration defense planning document that called for 'discourag[ing] the advanced industrialized nations from challenging our leadership or even aspiring to a larger global or regional role'.
63. For this view, see, for example, David Garnham, 'Ending Europe's Security Dependence', in *The Future of NATO* (note 1) p.134. Analyses that see little or no difference between the Bush and Clinton policies toward European security initiatives include Daniel Nelson, 'America and Collective Security in Europe', in ibid. pp.105–24, 396.
64. See Alexander Nicoli, 'European Leaders Found Wanting When it Comes to Putting Up

Cash for Defence', *Financial Times*, 22 Oct. 1999; John Hillen, 'The Burdens of Power', *San Diego Union-Tribune*,16 March 1997.
65. Quoted in Garnham (note 63) p.135.
66. 'NATO and the Development of the European Security and Defence Identity', Secretary General's Speech, IEEI Conference, Lisbon, 25 Nov. 1996, http://www.nato.int/docu/speech/1996/s961125a.htm, p.2.
67. *Report on Allied Contributions to the Common Defense* (note 4) p.2.
68. Tony Blair, 'It's Time to Repay America', *New York Times*, 13 Nov. 1998.
69. Quoted in Garnham (note 63) p.135; 'Final Communiqué', Ministerial Meeting of the North Atlantic Council, Berlin, 3 June 1996, http://www.nato.int/docu/pr/1996/p96-063e.htm, p.2.
70. *Report on Allied Contributions* (note 4) p.4; 'The Alliance's Strategic Concept, Approved by the Heads of State and Government participating in the meeting of the North Atlantic Council in Washington DC on 23 and 24 April 1999', http://www.nato.int/docu/pr/1999/p99-65e.htm, p.4.
71. Blair (note 68). The WEU statement appears in 'Defence – Third Report', Select Committee on Defence, House of Commons, http://www.parliament.the-stationery-office.co.uk/pa/cm199899/cmselect/cmdfenc...3916.ht, p.2.
72. Winslow Wheeler data (note 50). Secretary of Defense William S. Cohen roughly corroborated this data in Jim Garamone, 'Germany Must Increase Defense Budget, Cohen Says', American Forces Press Service, 1 Dec. 1999, http://www.defenselink.mil/news/Dec1999/n12011999_9912011.html, p.1. Then British Defence Minister (now NATO Secretary General) George Robertson, however, gave a lower figure – 20 per cent – for European strike sorties in a Sept. 1999 London speech. See 'The Way forward on European Defence', http://www.britainusa.com/bis/fordom/eu/defence/8dec99/stm, p.1. For numbers of aircraft, see Roger Cohen, 'Dependent on US Now, Europe Vows Defense Push', *New York Times*, 12 May 1999. An even wider disparity in aircraft deployments is found in Craig R. Whitney, 'Hey, Allies, Follow Me. I've Got All the New Toys', *New York Times*, 30 May 1999.
73. 'Time for Europeans to Pay Up', *Washington Times*, 17 May 1999.
74. Nicoli (note 64).
75. 'BBC Monitoring International Reports: German Inspector General Advocates Restructuring of Bundeswehr: Text of report by the German news agency ddpADN', 29 Nov. 1999, http://www.globalarchive.ft.com/search-components/index.jsp.
76. See Cohen, 'Dependent on US Now' (note 72); and Nicoli (note 64).
77. See Elizabeth Becker, 'European Allies to Spend More on Weapons', *New York Times*, 22 Sept. 1999; and Nicoli (note 64).
78. Stephen Fidler, 'France Under Fire over Kosovo Curbs', *Financial Times*, 22 Oct. 1999.
79. See Garamone (note 72); Craig R. Whitney, 'Europe Says Its Strike Force Won't Impair Role of NATO', *New York Times*, 2 Dec. 1999; and Cohen, 'Dependent on US Now' (note 72).
80. Craig R. Whitney, 'European Union Vows to Become Military Power', *New York Times*, 4 June 1999; and Anne Swardson, 'EU to Form European Military Force', *Washington Post*, 12 Dec. 1999.
81. Nicoli (note 64); and Ralph Atkins and Haig Simonian, 'Efforts in Berlin to Balance an Austerity Package with Increased International Commitments in Kosovo', *Financial Times*, 1 Nov. 1999.
82. Becker, 'European Allies to Spend More' (note 77); Nicoli (note 64); Atkins and Simonian' (note 81); and 'NATO Chief: US Has Role in Europe', Associated Press, 7 Dec. 1999. The IISS estimate of military R&D spending was roughly corroborated by former senior NATO military commander Gen. Klaus Naumann in Whitney, 'Hey Allies' (note 72).
83. France has recently dropped conscription as well, and Spain is scheduled to do so by the end of 2002. Neither country, however, has advanced this new-age rationale. See Hillen (note 64); *Annual Report on Defence Activity* http://www.mod.uk/policy/ ar97-98/p4htm; and Craig R. Whitney, 'As the Battlegrounds Shift, the Draft Fades in Europe', *New York Times*, 31 Oct. 1999.
84. Blair (note 68); and 'BBC Monitoring International Reports: German Daily Says Europe

Closer to New Dangers than USA', http://www.globalarchive.ft.com/search-components/
index.jsp.
85. See, for example, Whitney (note 79); Andrew Borowiec, 'Paris, London Tell US Corps No
Threat to NATO', *Washington Times*, 22 Dec. 1999.
86. See, John Bolton, 'The Next President and NATO', *Washington Times*, 21 July 1999. For
other examples, see Henry A. Kissinger, 'The End of NATO as We Know It?' *Washington
Post*, 15 Aug. 1999; and Sen. John McCain cited in 'EU to Form European Military Force'
(note 80).
87. Quoted in 'Time for Europeans to Pay Up' (note 73).

4

US Hegemony and the Perpetuation of NATO

CHRISTOPHER LAYNE

Both history and neorealist alliance theory would seem to predict that once the Cold War ended, NATO would have unraveled. This, of course has not happened. The alliance has not only survived but expanded. And the United States continues to be the preponderant power in European security affairs. The most compelling explanation for both developments is furnished by offensive realist theory. Offensive realism not only accounts for the post-Cold War extension of America's European security interests, it also explains the seamless continuity that is the hallmark of Washington's European grand strategy during and after the Cold War. Since 1945, the United States has always aspired to hegemony (and, indeed, during the Cold War, the United States was hegemonic in the non-Soviet world). The Soviet Union's demise simply removed the one impediment to the realization of America's hegemonic ambitions. Ironically, however, in the long run Washington's hegemonic post-Cold War grand strategy is unlikely to save either NATO or the US position in Europe.

Questions about the future of America's European commitment, and NATO, are especially salient in the wake of the spring 1999 Kosovo war. US involvement in that conflict cannot be explained by the grand strategic concerns that are commonly thought to have been the motive for America's European grand strategy during most of the twentieth century. Historically, US policy toward Europe has been 'counter-hegemonic': Washington feared that America's security would be jeopardized if a single great power succeeded in dominating the Continent and harnessing its resources.[1] When it became problematic that the European balance of power could operate successfully to prevent the emergence of a continental hegemon, the United

States intervened in both world wars to block Germany from achieving mastery over Europe.

America's military engagement in Europe during the Cold War similarly was characterized as counterhegemonic. The bipolar superpower confrontation defined America's interests and role. The United States, as the only great power in the non-Soviet sphere, assumed the political, military, and economic leadership of an anti-Soviet coalition. The Atlantic Alliance – which ostensibly was created to contain the expansion of Soviet power, and to protect the territorial security of its members – was the preeminent instrument of America's Cold War grand strategy.

During the Cold War, the American-led alliance kept the Soviet Union in check, and maintained the post-World War II peace in Europe, without ever firing a shot in anger. Yet, in the spring of 1999, the United States and its European allies were at war in Europe against a sovereign state for the first time since 1945. Rather than opposing a challenger for European hegemony, or defending the borders of the alliance from external aggression, the United States, and NATO, were fighting an offensive war against a small, economically run-down nation – Yugoslavia – which had not committed external aggression, but rather was waging a bitter counterinsurgency campaign on its sovereign territory against ethnic Albanian separatist rebels in Kosovo.

If we assume that America's post-World War II European commitment was animated by counterhegemonic considerations, the fact that NATO is still in business ten years after the Soviet Union's demise is surprising. After all, as neorealist theory tells us, alliances are temporary, not permanent, arrangements formed when two or more states believe their security is menaced by a common foe. The existence of an alliance does not mean that the members' interests are completely congruent. To the contrary, allies typically have many interests that conflict, but these are subordinated to the immediate imperative of collaborating to provide security against the adversary that threatens them. When the threat to the allies' security dissipates, however, the glue holding an alliance together dissolves and the suppressed tensions among the allies resurface, causing the alliance to break up.[2] Unsurprisingly, when the Cold War ended, neorealist scholars predicted – and still predict – that NATO would not long survive the conflict that gave it life.[3]

NATO TENSIONS AT THE END OF THE COLD WAR

Quite apart from the expectations generated by neorealist theory, the alliance's post-Cold War durability seems even more surprising when one remembers that during the mid and late 1980s – *before* the Cold War ended – NATO's cohesion was challenged severely. Tension between the United States and the West Europeans stemmed primarily from two salient issues: the meaning of, and proper response to, Mikhail Gorbachev's reforms of Soviet domestic and foreign policies; and the widespread belief that the United States was in the throes of a serious decline in its relative economic power.

Although the US security commitment to Western Europe was the keystone of America's Cold War grand strategy, it is commonplace that, as Henry Kissinger put it, NATO was a 'troubled partnership'. This was never more true than in the mid-1980s, when Gorbachev came to power. Throughout the 1970s, the Atlantic Alliance's cohesion had been eroded by transatlantic differences over detente with Moscow and how to respond to Soviet advances in the Third World. From 1979 to 1983, moreover, NATO was subjected to acute stress as a result of its decision to deploy intermediate range Pershing II and cruise missiles (INFs) to counter Moscow's deployment of intermediate range SS-20 missiles.

Because NATO succeeded in deploying the INFs in the face of both Soviet diplomatic pressure and strong opposition among West European – especially West German – public opinion, the conventional wisdom was that the INF crisis ended in a victory for the alliance.[4] In fact, however, by crucially weakening the central US-West German relationship, 'the battle of the Euro-missiles' was a serious defeat for the Alliance.[5] The INF controversy exposed the fundamental contradictions in NATO's 'flexible response' strategy, and thereby contributed both to reviving the dormant 'German Question' and to pushing West Germany to seek accommodation with the Soviet Union as the best means of resolving its 'security dilemma'.[6]

The transatlantic rift between Washington and Bonn was widened further by Gorbachev's 'new thinking' in foreign policy – specifically, his vision of a 'common European home'.[7] In the United States, policymakers and analysts debated whether Gorbachev's initiatives presaged a real change in Soviet policy, or whether Moscow was merely seeking a 'breathing spell' in the Cold War, during which it would use access to Western technology and financial assistance to modernize its economy so that it could compete more effectively against the United States in the military arena.[8] Although near the end of his term President Ronald Reagan declared the Cold War to be over, the incoming Bush administration was much more skeptical about Gorbachev's intentions.[9]

Washington's caution exacerbated tensions with Western Europe, especially with West Germany. Sensing that Gorbachev's policies offered the hope for ending the continent's – and perforce Germany's – Cold War division, West German Foreign Minister Hans Dietrich Genscher declared in February 1987 that Gorbachev should be taken at his word: 'If...there could be a turning point in East-West relations, it would be a mistake of historic dimensions for the West to let this chance slip just because it cannot escape from a way of thinking which invariably expects the worst from the Soviet Union.'[10] Conflicting American and West German perceptions of Gorbachev's foreign policy posed a serious problem for the incoming Bush administration: Washington was under pressure 'to get moving, to match him with offers of our own'.[11] Both the administration and the broader foreign policy community felt a palpable urgency to formulate 'bold' initiatives to regain the diplomatic momentum from Moscow.[12] As the Bush administration realized:

> The Soviet leader was preaching that the Cold War in Europe was over and we should be dismantling its structures (although he said little about the future of Soviet forces in Europe). If we looked as if we were dragging our feet, the Europeans would cease to follow and the Soviets would seize the international agenda. The President agreed that Gorbachev had undermined US leadership, and he wanted to go to the NATO summit in May [1989] with a series of bold proposals that would put us out in front.[13]

The Bush administration proved better at diagnosing the problem than fixing it.

There were scattered calls in the American foreign policy community to trump Gorbachev by coupling mutual superpower disengagement in Central Europe with German reunification.[14] On the whole, however, the foreign policy community's response to Gorbachev was unimaginative. Although analysts such as Harvard University Professor Graham Allison argued that 'American diplomacy must be imaginative and aggressive in proposing bold actions', in practice their proposals manifested a profound intellectual stasis. 'Bold actions' turned out to be nothing more than warmed-over versions of a stale Cold War agenda: initiatives regarding arms control, regional conflicts, and human rights.[15] The Bush administration's policy was equally cautious.[16] The lack of dynamism in American policy was potentially disastrous.

By May 1989, a widening gulf existed between Washington and Bonn on the future of European security. Although he apparently did not realize it, by playing the 'German card' at any time up to that point, Gorbachev might well have splintered NATO and won the Cold War in Europe.[17]

Several months later, events on the ground had changed dramatically in Europe, ensuring that the Cold War in Europe would end on Washington's terms, not Moscow's. But it was, as the Duke of Wellington said of Waterloo, 'a damned near run thing'.

In the mid- and late-1980s, NATO also was frayed by US concerns about 'burden sharing', which reflected deeper worries about America's competitiveness in the international economy. Those fears were symbolized by the nation's mounting national debt and the persistent 'twin' deficits: the federal budget deficit and the trade deficit.[18] At the root of America's economic apprehensions was a growing belief that the United States was being disadvantaged economically as a consequence of the postwar bargains it had made with Western Europe and Japan.[19] By generously aiding their economic recovery, and bearing a disproportionate share of responsibility for the West's security, the United States had made it possible for Western Europe and Japan to becoming prosperous 'trading states'.[20] As the Defense Burdensharing Panel of the US House of Representatives asked in 1988, now that Western Europe was a wealthy and powerful economic rival, why should the United States continue to subsidize the Continent's security?[21]

Paul Kennedy's 1987 book *The Rise and Fall of the Great Powers* crystalized the growing anxieties about America's lagging economic performance, and its causal relationship to US security commitments in Western Europe and East Asia.[22] Kennedy argued that history's dominant great powers had been fatally weakened when they became 'imperially overstretched': that is, when their interests and security commitments expanded to the point where military spending consumed too large a share of national wealth.[23]

Reflecting the concerns Kennedy raised, by the later 1980s an increasing number of analysts questioned the wisdom of a grand strategy that caused the United States to bear heavy costs to protect the very states with which it seemed to be locked in an increasingly intense economic rivalry.[24] Those who found Kennedy's argument persuasive invoked the concept put forth by Walter Lippmann four decades earlier, that of 'strategic solvency'.[25] Making a direct connection between America's economic ills and the perception that the United States was strategically over-extended abroad, they argued that to revitalize its economy and deal with domestic social problems, the United States needed to cut back its overseas commitments and achieve a more equitable distribution of security burdens by 'devolving' to Western Europe and Japan a greater share of the responsibility for their defense.[26]

These arguments for readjusting US grand strategy were being made even before the full implications of Gorbachev's new thinking could be discerned. However, once it became clear that Gorbachev's policies portended the Cold War's end, the case for fundamentally reassessing American grand strategy ought to have become even stronger.

OFFENSIVE REALISM AND US HEGEMONY AFTER THE COLD WAR

The sudden collapse of Soviet power beginning in late 1989 seemingly swept away the foundations upon which America's European grand strategy had been based for more than four decades. Many US foreign policy analysts recognized that the Cold War's dramatic termination meant that, for the first time since the late 1940s, the United States was in a position to reexamine its commitment to Europe, and to NATO, from the ground up.[27] As we know, this did not happen. Doubts that arose in the Cold War's immediate aftermath about whether US alliances could – or should – remain intact quickly vanished.

Instead, policy analysts argued that in the post-Cold War world, NATO should be invested with new missions: preventing power vacuums and instability; providing 'reassurance'; and promoting the spread of democracy and free markets into east central Europe.[28] What explains the continuation of the American commitment to Europe, and the survival of NATO, after the Soviet Union's collapse? Although liberal international relations theorists have advanced their own arguments, 'offensive realism' offers the most compelling explanation.

Offensive realism actually has two distinct, though closely related, variants, which I call Type I and Type II. Type I offensive realism explains why great powers engage in expansionist behavior. Type II offensive realism explains why great powers are impelled to seek hegemony.

Type I offensive realism's main claim is that as a state becomes more powerful, its grand strategic interests expand. That is, as a state becomes more powerful economically, it builds up its military capabilities and becomes more deeply engaged in international politics, and it seeks to expand its influence accordingly.[29] Type I offensive realism advances two explanations for the tendency of rising powers to expand. First, states expand as their power increases because capabilities drive intentions.[30] Simply put, the more a state is able to do in international politics, the more it will want to do; and the more it is able to do, the more it will perceive that it needs to do. Thus an increase in a state's relative power not only causes an expansion of its external interests, but also results in the broadening of the state's *perception* of its interests and security requirements.[31]

Second, states expand because the anarchic nature of international politics makes them insecure, and the best antidote to insecurity is for a state to maximize its relative power.[32] Given the security dilemma that pervades international politics, the most promising route to security is 'for a state to increase its control over that environment through the persistent expansion of its political interests abroad.'[33]

Type II offensive realism posits that attainment of hegemony is – or should be – the ultimate aim of a state's grand strategy. Dominance, or hegemony, is the logical outcome of a grand strategy that seeks to maximize the state's relative power or influence. For Type II offensive realists, there is only one way for a state to be safe: by becoming the most powerful state in the international system.[34] Simply stated, Type II offensive realism holds that the best way for a state to attain security is to eliminate, or overawe, its competition. A state becomes a hegemon either by eliminating its rivals, or by strategies that subjugate or subordinate them.[35]

There are three reasons why hegemony is Type II offensive realism's preferred grand strategy.

First, Type II offensive realism regards multipolar international systems as inherently less peaceful and stable than bipolar or unipolar systems.[36]

Second, a hegemon gains security when the distribution of power is skewed decisively in its favor, because others will be deterred from attacking it.[37]

Third, hegemony also is the best grand strategic response to a state's uncertainty about others' intentions, and about others' present and future capabilities. States strive for superiority, not equality, as a hedge against miscalculating both the present and future distribution of power between them and their rivals.[38]

Even if a state attains hegemony, however, its quest to maximize its relative power does not stop, and it cannot relax its guard. Hegemons cannot be *status quo* powers, because they want to maintain their predominance, and they fear the emergence of new rivals who could challenge their preeminence. Security is never permanent because there is no guarantee that the distribution of power will not change adversely in the future (because of uneven economic growth rates and/or the emergence of counterhegemonic alliances).[39] When its comes to relative power, a hegemon can never afford to relax its efforts to maintain its margin over others. A hegemon must always strive to forestall the emergence of future rivals while simultaneously maintaining its own internal economic growth rates.[40] A paradox of hegemony is that hegemons invariably believe their dominance is tenuous. Hence, the hegemon must constantly increase its power simply to hold on to what it has. As the Athenian leader Alcibiades recognized, the imperatives of security compel a hegemon constantly to seek to expand its power and influence: 'We cannot fix the exact point at which our empire shall stop; we have reached a position in which we must not be content with retaining what we have but must scheme to extend for, if we cease to rule others, we shall be in danger of being ruled ourselves.'[41] For hegemons, the injunction seems to be that they must expand their power or die.

The Soviet Union's collapse caused a drastic increase in America's relative power position in the international system, and specifically in Europe. Given that enhancement of its relative power in Europe, Type I offensive realism would predict the following:

(1) the United States would seek to extend its influence in, and control over, the European security environment;

(2) this extension of US control would be manifested by both the geographical and ideological extension of US interests;

(3) Washington's *perception* of its European security interests would expand.

The Cold War's end also left the United States as the preeminent power globally, and especially in Europe. Type II offensive realism would predict the following:

(1) the United States would seek to prevent the re-emergence of a multipolar system within Europe;

(2) the United States would seek to maintain its hegemony by preventing the emergence of rival great powers, including Germany, a united Europe, or a resurgent Russia.

OFFENSIVE REALISM AND THE PERPETUATION OF NATO

The predictions of offensive realist theory are borne out by the actual course of America's post-Cold War European policy. This became evident as the Berlin Wall fell, and as German reunification emerged as the crucial issue in shaping post-Cold War Europe's security environment. The European security arrangements that emerged as the Cold War ended were not inevitable. For example, there was no *a priori* reason to assume that, as

Soviet power receded from East Central Europe, the United States would retain its military presence in Europe.

Similarly, there was no reason to assume that NATO would survive once the Warsaw Pact began to dissolve. Finally, it was not preordained that, with the end of the superpower rivalry in Europe, a reunited Germany would be tied to an American-led alliance rather than being unaligned.

Prior to 1989, most observers probably would have made exactly the opposite predictions had they been asked to peer into their crystal balls and describe what a post-Cold War Europe would look like. If the Cold War indeed came to an end, there was every reason to assume that the United States would withdraw its military forces from Europe, and that once the conflict that brought them into being faded away, both Cold War alliances would disappear and be replaced by new security structures.

Indeed, before 1989, many observers, especially Europeans, had argued that the dissolution of both blocs was a necessary precondition for ending Europe's division.[42] And, as far as Germany's reunification was concerned, those who envisioned it as a realistic possibility invariably believed that it could happen only if both superpowers militarily disengaged from Central Europe and a unified Germany was aligned with neither Washington nor Moscow.[43]

When the Cold War actually did end, however, American policymakers did not skip a beat. At the highest levels of government, it was unquestioned that America's European grand strategy would remain unchanged not withstanding the geopolitically transforming events of 1989.[44] US policymakers did understand, however, that because the unraveling of the Soviet empire challenged the basis upon which America's post-World War II European commitment had been justified to Congress and the American public, the Cold War's end threatened Washington's preeminent role in European security affairs.[45] President George Bush implicitly admitted that point. When asked in December 1989, immediately after his summit with Gorbachev, if the Cold War was over, he refused to say that because, he said, if he did, questions then would be asked about why US troops still were needed in Europe and whether NATO still was relevant.[46]

American policymakers had no intention of withdrawing US forces from Europe or dismantling NATO. To the contrary, they sought to ensure that the United States would retain its hegemony in Europe notwithstanding the Cold War's end, and that NATO – the instrument through which Washington's continental preeminence was exercised – would remain intact. As Bush administration officials Philip Zelikow and Condoleezza Rice observe:

[The Bush] administration believed strongly that, even if the
immediate military threat from the Soviet Union diminished, the
United States should maintain a significant military presence in
Europe for the foreseeable future...The American troop presence
thus...served as the ante to ensure a central place for the United States
as a player in European politics. The Bush administration placed a
high value on retaining such influence, underscored by Bush's flat
statement that the United States was and would remain 'a European
power'...*The Bush administration was determined to maintain
crucial features of the NATO system for European security even if the
Cold War ended.*[47]

As Bush's National Security Adviser, Brent Scowcroft, has written,
'whatever developed with respect to the Cold War', America 'had to
continue to play a significant role in European security', and 'the vehicle for
that role *must* be NATO'.[48] The United States greeted coldly any suggestions
that, in a post-Cold War Europe, NATO could be replaced by a new
continental security order based on pan-European institutions such as the
Conference for Security and Cooperation in Europe (CSCE).[49] In the post-
Cold War world, NATO was key to the US objectives of controlling
Germany, preventing Russia's resurgence as a great power, and expanding
the geographical and ideological scope of American interests in Europe.

Prior to November 1989, the Bush administration articulated the
American goal of achieving a 'Europe whole and free'. Rhetoric aside,
however, the administration was not prepared to make a serious effort to
push for German reunification, notwithstanding that reknitting Germany
was the logical precondition to ending Europe's post-1945 division. To the
contrary, as Scowcroft observed, from Washington's standpoint, 'The *status
quo* was the basis of postwar stability and peace in Europe. Why disrupt the
situation with unnecessary talk of reunification?'[50] When events thrust the
German reunification issue to the forefront of the international agenda, the
paramount US goal was to ensure that a reunified Germany remained in the
Atlantic Alliance.

Washington wanted to 'anchor' Germany to NATO to ensure that, once
reunified, Germany did not follow an independent foreign or security
policy, and to ensure that it did not acquire nuclear weapons of its own.[51]
The United States made clear to Bonn that support for reunification was
conditioned on Germany's remaining a full NATO member, and
Washington created the so-called 'Two Plus Four' diplomatic process to
ensure that Bonn and Moscow would not be able to cut a separate deal on

reunification that would undermine US objectives.[52] Washington's determination to tether a reunified Germany firmly to NATO reflected America's concerns about Germany's great power revival, and its determination to contain and control German power and ambitions in post-Cold War Europe.[53] The US insistence on keeping Germany tied to NATO also was driven by Washington's determination to use its increased relative power to marginalize Russia as a future player in European security.

By insisting both on a reunified Germany's membership in NATO and on the alliance's continued centrality in post-Cold War Europe, the Bush administration clearly aimed to reduce Moscow's influence drastically. As US policymakers recognized, they were taking advantage of America's vastly increased relative power (the result of Soviet weakness) to achieve 'a fundamental shift in the strategic balance' by compelling Moscow to accept an American-imposed settlement as if it had 'suffered a reversal of fortunes not unlike a catastrophic defeat in a war'.[54] Indeed, the United States was so determined to determined to have its way on German reunification that it was prepared to risk a backlash within the Soviet Union against Gorbachev and his reforms.[55]

To be sure, the United States wanted Moscow 'to accept this result and believe they retained an appropriate, albeit diminished, role in European affairs'.[56] To this end, Washington took the lead in making cosmetic changes in NATO's declaratory policy to make it 'appear' to Moscow that the alliance was no longer a threat to the Soviet Union's security.[57] And the United States tirelessly lectured the Soviets on why *they* would be better off if a reunified Germany were part of NATO. US officials told their Soviet counterparts that unless attached to NATO, a reunified, neutral Germany would become a nuclear-armed loose cannon in post-Cold War Europe.[58]

The Soviets opposed the US position, and argued that a reunified Germany should either belong to both the Warsaw Pact and NATO, or to neither of them.[59] For all the pretense that Washington wanted to make it possible for Moscow to acquiesce gracefully to Germany's reunification, the United States clearly was playing geopolitical hardball and exploiting the Soviet Union's weakness. Washington simply dismissed the possibility of a compromise settlement that would respect Moscow's security interests. As President Bush said:

> The Soviets are not in a position to dictate Germany's relationship to NATO. What worries me is talk that Germany must not stay in NATO. To hell with that! *We prevailed, they didn't.* We can't let the Soviets snatch victory from the jaws of defeat.[60]

Washington's reassurances to Moscow that the United States 'was not forcing Germany into NATO' were disingenuous.[61] In fact, as Scowcroft emphasized in May 1990, the issue of Germany's full NATO membership was 'not negotiable' because the United States had decided in early 1990 that this was the only basis on which Washington would accept reunification.[62] As James Baker told Eduard Shevardnadze: 'If push came to shove, we were going to admit a unified Germany into NATO over Soviet objections.'[63] Washington used its enhanced geostrategic capabilities to reduce Moscow's role in Europe by compelling the Kremlin to accept a very one-sided resolution of the German Question. Subsequently, the Clinton administration took further advantage of Russia's weakness relative to US power by expanding NATO to incorporate the former Soviet satellites of Poland, Hungary, and the Czech Republic.

NATO expansion also illustrates how offensive realist theory accounts for US policy in post-Cold War Europe. Without countervailing Soviet power, there was nothing to prevent the United States from taking advantage of its increased relative power by expanding its influence in Europe both territorially and ideologically. Geographically, the alliance's expansion served to project American power into a region that simultaneously was traditionally within Russia's strategic orbit and far outside the ambit of Washington's previous strategic concerns. Indeed, enlargement moved NATO's power to the very frontiers of the former Soviet Union. The United States pushed for the alliance's enlargement despite Moscow's strenuous objections, and notwithstanding that expansion was a repudiation of assurances that had been given to Russia during the German reunification negotiations.[64]

Although the Clinton administration repeatedly stated that the alliance's enlargement was not directed at Russia, Russian security anxieties were not allayed by US rhetoric.[65] Moscow viewed NATO expansion as a manifestation of America's hegemonic aspirations, a threat to Russia's security, and a betrayal of the promises made by Washington during the German reunification process.[66] NATO's formal enlargement, moreover, was only part of the picture of Washington's territorial extension of its European interests.

Washington's policy, in fact, has been one of 'double enlargement': not only extending NATO eastward, but also broadening its mission beyond the alliance's boundaries.[67] In the post-Cold War era, advocates of new missions for NATO assert that America's, and NATO's, strategic concerns extend to Europe's peripheries, including the Baltic States, Ukraine, the Caucasus and Central Asia, North Africa, and – of course – the Balkans.[68] In post-Cold

War Europe, 'instability' on the periphery is to be stopped before it can 'spill-over' into Europe's core.[69] Thus, as President Clinton put it, the United States is 'building a NATO capable not only of deterring aggression against its own territory, but of meeting challenges to our security beyond its territory...'.[70]

Offensive realist theory also predicts that enhanced material capabilities will lead the United States to seek to broaden its influence on the Continent by imposing its preferred ideology, values, and political institutions beyond its traditional sphere of influence in Europe. As America's power has increased, its definition of its interests has indeed expanded, as has the perception of threats to those interests. As the United States has become a more powerful international actor, the objective of its grand strategy has shifted from the protection of national interests to the defense of 'core values'.

The concept of core values, historian Melvyn P. Leffler observes, links the external and domestic determinants of grand strategy because it fuses 'material self-interest with more fundamental goals like the defense of the state's organizing ideology...the protection of its political institutions, and the safeguarding of its physical base or territorial integrity'.[71] America's post-Cold War European grand strategy is illustrative. As the United States has become relatively more powerful following the collapse of the Soviet Union, the definition of core values has become more extensive, as have the perceived threats to those core values.

Specifically, the United States has sought to expand free market democracy into East Central Europe and the Balkans; defined nondemocratic governments (Serbia for example), as inherent threats to European 'stability'; and proclaimed its right to intervene in the internal affairs of other European states when it deems their policies to jeopardize American values.

Ideologically, NATO expansion has advanced the Clinton administration's aim of 'enlarging the zone of democracy' by helping to consolidate the fledgling free-market democracies of Poland, Hungary, and the Czech Republic. As President Clinton said:

> We want all of Europe to have what America helped build in Western Europe – a community that upholds common standards of human rights, where people have the confidence and security to invest in the future, where nations cooperate to make war unthinkable. That is why I have pushed hard for NATO's enlargement and why we must keep NATO's doors open to new democratic members, so that other nations will have an incentive to deepen their democracies.[72]

Indeed, the retraction of Soviet power that accompanied the Cold War's end presented the United States with the opportunity to build a post-Cold War Europe based on America's liberal political and economic ideals. As Undersecretary of Defense Walter Slocombe put it: 'We have the possibility to build a system in Europe – and indeed the entire world – organized on the model of what we used to call the Free World – that is, liberal market democracies living in peace with their neighbors.'[73]

The post-Cold War expansion of US ideological objectives was manifested not only in the policy of democratic enlargement but also in the assertion of Washington's prerogative to intervene in the internal affairs of states that treated their own citizens in ways that offended America's ideals. The outlines of what subsequently became known as the 'Clinton Doctrine' were in place as early as April 1993, when President Clinton stated:

> During the Cold War our foreign policies largely focused on relations among nations. Our strategies sought a balance of power to keep the peace. Today, our policies must also focus on relations within nations, on a nation's form of governance, on its economic structure, on its ethnic tolerance. These are of concern to us, for they shape how these nations treat their neighbors as well as their own people and whether they are reliable when they give their word.[74]

More recently, in January 2000, Deputy Secretary of State Strobe Talbott declared that 'the way a government treats its own people is not just an "internal matter"; it is the business of the international community because there are issues of both universal values and regional peace at stake and also because true security and stability in Europe can only come when those commodities exists within society as well as between states.'[75] Thus, according to Talbott, the United States and NATO have the right 'to enforce the principle that, in Europe on the eve of the twenty-first century, national leaderships must not be allowed to define national interests or national identity in a way that threatens international peace and leads to crimes against humanity'.[76]

US interventions in Bosnia and the Kosovo war were obvious demonstrations of Washington's willingness to flex its military muscle to further its ideological aspirations. Since the Kosovo war ended, there have been two further examples.

First, the United States is attempting to undermine the regime of Serbian President Slobodan Milošević. Talbott states bluntly, 'We must do everything possible to support the democratic opposition in Serbia until it brings about the democratic transformation of Serbia. That, in turn, can happen only when Yugoslavia is under new management.'[77]

And Washington's condemnation of democratic Austria following the formation of a coalition government that included Jorg Haider's Freedom Party demonstrates concretely America's willingness to use its diplomatic, and military muscle against those states that it views as sources of ideological contagion.[78]

The United States has taken advantage of the collapse of Soviet power to replicate throughout the Continent the security structures it constructed in Western Europe after World War II. As President Clinton has said:

> I came to office convinced that NATO can do for Europe's East what it did for Europe's West: prevent a return to local rivalries, strengthen democracy against future threats, and create the conditions for prosperity to flourish. That's why the United States has taken the lead in an...effort to build a new NATO for a new era.[79]

Through NATO, the United States has taken on the task of becoming Europe's 'stabilizer'. As Europe's stabilizer, the United States is responsible both for preventing the reemergence of new great powers within Europe that could cause European security affairs to become 'renationalized', and for stopping instability from spilling over from the Continent's peripheries and threatening its core.[80]

The US military presence in Europe serves to 'reassure' the Europeans that they need not fear each other, and thereby prevents Europe from relapsing into its bad, old habit of power politics.[81] For the United States, the prospect of renewed security competitions in Europe, or of regional turbulence, could unsettle the 'virtuous circle' of peace, democracy, and prosperity that is the foundation of Washington's European grand strategy.[82]

NATO thus serves to advance several interconnected key objectives of America's post-Cold War European grand strategy: it provides stability for the Continent; it keeps the lid on Europe's latent geopolitical rivalries; it creates the security environment in which economic interdependence can flourish; and it forestalls the rise of European power centers that could challenge US preponderance.[83] That is, NATO is the instrument through which the United States perpetuates its hegemonic role in Europe.

The striking aspect of America's post-Cold War European grand strategy is its familiarity, not its novelty. The United States today is pursuing the same European grand strategy that it pursued from the late 1940s until the Cold War ended.[84] As the political scientist Wolfram Hanreider observed, America's post-World War II strategy was *double* containment – the simultaneous, and mutually reinforcing, containment of both the Soviet Union *and* Germany.[85] The conundrum facing Washington in the early Cold War years was how to revive (West) Germany economically – which was the key to Western Europe's economic recovery – without arousing West European fears that the Continent would again be vulnerable to the political and economic domination of a resurgent Germany.

The United States solved that dilemma by integrating West Germany into a network of American-dominated security and economic arrangements. Through NATO, the United States controlled democratic Germany, assumed responsibility for protecting the West European states from each other, and, by acting as Europe's 'pacifier', thereby provided 'reassurance' to Western Europe.[86] In effect, the American military presence removed both the security dilemma, and the relative gains problem, from the agendas of its Western European allies. Freed from looking over their shoulders, the West Europeans were able to set aside their historical animosities and work together to achieve economic integration.

As they recovered from World War II's devastation, an economically revitalized West Germany and Western Europe were able to contribute to the US policy of containing the Soviet Union. Nevertheless, although the United States helped West Germany and Western Europe rebuild, Washington sought to maintain tight political control over them throughout the Cold War. Washington wanted Western Europe to be strong enough to shoulder some of the burdens of containing the Soviet Union; it did not want Western Europe to become strong enough to challenge American leadership. The United States consistently sought to maintain its geopolitically privileged position *vis-à-vis* Western Europe.

Plus ça change, c'est la même chose. The reason US grand strategists did not reassess America's European grand strategy when the Cold War ended is quite simple: even in the mid- and late 1940s, the driving force behind American policy was more fundamental than the mere containment of the Soviet Union.[87] When World War II ended, hegemony was America's overriding grand strategic objective.[88] As National Security Council-68's principal author, Paul Nitze, put it, US strategy aiming at attaining 'preponderant power'.[89] Although the Soviet Union was the immediate focus of postwar US grand strategy, it was incidental to the overarching policy objectives that America pursued after 1945.

Since the end of World War II, the United States has attempted to prevent the emergence of new geopolitical rivals. In the 1940s, of course, the United States accepted the reality of Soviet power. Short of preventive war (a thought with which some American policymakers flirted), the United

States could not prevent the Soviet Union's ascendance to superpower status.[90]

However, from 1945 on the United States was, and was determined to remain, the sole great power in its own sphere of influence, the non-Soviet world – especially in Europe. As historian Melvyn P. Leffler points out, American policymakers believed that 'neither an integrated Europe nor a united Germany... must be permitted to emerge as third force or a neutral bloc'.[91] The Cold War's end – specifically, the Soviet Union's disappearance – has served to lay bare the hegemonic foundation that has underpinned US grand strategy continuously since 1945.

THE TWILIGHT OF US HEGEMONY IN EUROPE

At the same time, the Cold War's end also raises the question of whether America's hegemonic grand strategy can succeed in the absence of the Soviet threat which caused the West Europeans to accept US predominance in European security affairs in exchange for American protection against the Soviet Union. To return to international relations theory, although offensive realism explains the pressures that drive great powers to expand, and to seek hegemony, it does not furnish compelling reasons to believe that hegemons can be successful, especially over the long term. Indeed, most realists believe that hegemons invariably fail because when one state becomes too powerful it threats the security of others, which respond to hegemonic power by engaging in counterhegemonic balancing.[92]

In a unipolar world, realism would predict that new great powers would emerge to challenge the hegemon.[93] Notwithstanding this expectation many analysts have argued that the United States will prove to be the exception to the rule. Three basic arguments are advanced to support the proposition that America will be a successful hegemon.

First, it is sometimes suggested that the distribution of capabilities in the international system today is unprecedented, and likely to remain so, because America's economic and technological lead over potential great-power rivals is so large as to be insurmountable.[94]

Second, building on the 'balance of threat' theory, it is claimed that the United States can follow policies that will allay others' concerns about America's overwhelming power.[95]

Overlapping the contention that the United States is a non-threatening hegemon, a third argument holds that America's 'soft power' – its ideals, political institutions, and culture – will attract other states into Washington's orbit while simultaneously reassuring them that the United States will exercise its power benevolently.[96] Certainly, among both policymakers and the community of foreign policy scholars, conventional wisdom holds that, just as it gratefully accepted Washington's hegemony during the Cold War, Europe in the post-Cold War era will not engage in counterhegemonic balancing against the United States because it does not view American power as threatening, and because, by the creation of a transatlantic 'security community', shared democratic values have legitimated US preponderance.[97] That thesis – both as history and as prediction – is problematic.

There is no question that the West Europeans willingly accepted Washington's leadership during the Cold War. America's post-1945 informal empire indeed was 'an empire by invitation'.[98] Voluntary subordination to the United States clearly was preferable to the alternative: forcible subordination to the Soviet Union. Nevertheless, although the United States, unlike the USSR, managed its European empire without recourse to heavy-handed coercion (although with plenty of less blatant pressure), *realpolitik* was always the crucial factor that shaped transatlantic relations. It is unsurprising, therefore, that West European perceptions of the United States were always far more ambiguous than US policymakers and foreign policy analysts have cared to admit.[99]

It is too easily forgotten that there always was among the European allies an underlying fear and distrust of US power. For example, in the immediate aftermath of World War II, the West Europeans (especially the British) hoped to establish themselves as a geopolitical 'third force' in world politics, because they had no more wish to be dominated by Washington than by Moscow. As British diplomat Gladwyn Jebb put it, it was important to prevent the geopolitical equilibrium from being undermined 'by a "bi-polar" system centering around what Mr [Arnold] Toynbee calls the two "semi-barbarian states on the cultural periphery"'.[100] Only when it became evident that the resources to implement that policy were lacking was a formal security alliance with the United States accepted as an alternative.

Even after NATO was established, American preeminence within the alliance was challenged by France under the leadership of Charles de Gaulle.[101] And beginning in the late 1960s, West Germany's *Ostpolitik* explicitly challenged Washington's desire to maintain the post-1945 status quo in Europe. For precisely that reason, *Ostpolitik* aroused the suspicions of US decision makers.[102] On the supranational level, even if it only occasionally acknowledged, from the early days of the European Common Market the desire to create a political and economic counterweight to the United States has always been a major impetus behind the creation of what today is the European Union.

Although realists would have predicted otherwise, the first post-Cold War decade did not witness a lessening of the Atlantic Alliance's bonds, nor – although there was no lack of verbal expressions of concern about America's unbalanced power – did Western Europe react to unipolarity by engaging in counter-hegemonic balancing against the United States. The Maastricht Treaty committed Europe to developing the capabilities to pursue an independent foreign and security policy, and the break-up of Yugoslavia seemingly offered the European Community (EC) its first post-Cold War opportunity to step out of Washington's shadow. Indeed, Jacques Poos for the EC proclaimed that with the Yugoslav crisis, 'the hour of Europe had arrived'. But the EC/EU's failure to develop a coherent, effective response to Yugoslavia's unraveling demonstrated that Europe's view of itself as an autonomous geopolitical actor was rhetorical rather than real.

The Kosovo war, however, may have been a turning point.[103] In the coming years it is likely to be seen as a crucial moment when Europe began to move concretely toward becoming an independent actor in international security affairs, and in the process deliberately set out to constitute itself as a geopolitical counterweight to US hegemony.

In the aftermath of the Kosovo conflict, the West Europeans have been much more vocal in expressing their fears of American hegemony. European concerns were articulated by French President Jacques Chirac and his Foreign Minister, Hubert Védrine. Arguing that US economic and military dominance is so formidable that the term 'superpower' is inadequate to convey the true extent of America's preeminence, Vedrine called the United States a 'hyperpower', and added: 'We cannot accept either a politically unipolar world, nor a culturally uniform world, nor the unilateralism of a single hyperpower. And that is why we are fighting for a multipolar, diversified, and multilateral world.'[104]

The US Senate's rejection of the Comprehensive Test Ban Treaty (CTBT) in late 1999, and the growing likelihood that Washington would abrogate the 1972 Anti-Ballistic Missile (ABM) Defense Treaty and deploy a national ballistic missile defense system (NBMD) fanned European (as well as Russian, Chinese, and Indian) concerns that the United States was acting unilaterally to maintain its global military dominance.[105]

Finally, the Kosovo war dramatized for the West Europeans the vast disparity between their military power and America's, especially the US superiority at the high-end of military technology. Alarmed by their military inferiority to the United States, and resentful of their continued dependence on Washington, the West Europeans were jolted by the Kosovo episode into a recognition that they needed to give substance to the concept of a common

European defense and security policy by developing their own advanced military capabilities (including satellite reconnaissance, precision guided munitions, and power projection).[106]

The American response to Europe's drive to develop autonomous military capabilities has been extremely ambivalent.[107] Despite public assurances from the EU that the proposed European Security and Defense Identity (ESDI) will complement NATO rather than compete with it, many American policymakers fear that ESDI, in fact, will come to be a rival of the alliance.[108] For Washington, ESDI can only have one legitimate purpose: creating a European 'pillar' of NATO that will enable the Europeans to share more of the burdens of the Continent's defense. As Secretary of State Madeleine Albright has said: 'We believe that [ESDI] is a very useful way to think about burden sharing.'[109] Thus, for the United States, ESDI must be based on 'the principle that these institutions should be the European pillar of a strong trans-Atlantic alliance and not separate and competing entities'.[110]

To ensure that ESDI does not undercut NATO, Washington has proclaimed the so-called 'Three D's': ESDI must not *diminish* NATO's role, must not *duplicate* NATO's capabilities, and must not *discriminate* against the United States.[111] Of course, if these 'Three D's' are implemented – especially the proscription on the EU duplicating military capabilities already possessed by NATO – Europe would be foreclosed from achieving strategic autonomy and would remain subordinate to the United States. And that really is the point of US policy. Washington seeks to uphold NATO's centrality in order to maintain its leadership role in European security affairs.[112]

Thus, as it did during the Cold War, the United States pays lip service to the idea of European unity while opposing the idea of an independent Europe. Hence, the United States insists that European integration, and ESDI, can occur only within the framework of transatlantic partnership. As Undersecretary of State Stuart Eizenstat has said: 'We will continue to celebrate the dream of a continent united through the European Union, but we must also hold before us another essential vision – that of a transatlantic partnership.'[113] American policymakers warn the EU that if it goes far down the road to real autonomy in defense and security – that is, if it seriously challenges US preponderance – the Atlantic Alliance could be shattered.[114]

NATO's days are numbered, and Kosovo was likely the last American war in Europe. The Soviet Union was the glue that simultaneously held the alliance together and legitimated US hegemony in Europe. Yet, even during the Cold War – especially from the mid-1960s on – NATO's cohesion was eroded significantly. US and West European political and strategic interests often conflicted sharply. Although allied against the Soviet Union, the United States and Western Europe were locked in a deepening, intense economic rivalry. And, as 'successor generations' came to power on both sides of the Atlantic, the sense of a common Euro-Atlantic identity – forged by the struggles of postwar recovery and the dangers of the early Cold War years – faded. With the Cold War's passing, these factors continue to gnaw away at the alliance's fabric.[115]

This time, however, there is no common external threat to hold these fissiparous forces at bay and keep the alliance together. Moreover, in the aftermath of the Kosovo conflict, Europe predictably is beginning to respond to United States hegemony by balancing against the United States. That the United States and Europe are destined to drift apart strategically and politically is no longer open to doubt. The only issue is how this distancing occurs. An amicable separation is better than a nasty divorce. For that to happen, however, the United States will need to give up its hegemonic pretensions, and accept Europe's emergence as an equal power center in international politics. Whether the US foreign policy elite is prepared to accept gracefully the transition from unipolarity to multipolarity is, however, an open question.

NOTES

1. John Mearsheimer, 'The Future of America's Continental Commitment', in Geir Lundestad (ed.) *No End to Alliance – The United States and Western Europe: Past, Present and Future* (NY: St Martin's 1998) pp.221–44.
2. Kenneth N. Waltz, *Theory of International Politics* (Reading, MA: Addison-Wesley 1979) pp.126, 209. As Waltz puts it (p.209), 'Alliances are made by states that have some but not all of their interests in common. The common interest is ordinarily a negative one: fear of other states.'
3. Christopher Layne, 'Superpower Disengagement', *Foreign Policy*, No.77 (Winter 1989–1990) pp.17–40; C. Layne, 'Atlanticism Without NATO', ibid. No.67 (Summer 1987) pp.22–45; C. Layne, 'Toward German Reunification?' *Journal of Contemporary Studies* 7/4 (Fall 1984) pp.7–37; C. Layne, 'Ending the Alliance', ibid. 6/3 (Summer 1983) pp.5–31; John J. Mearsheimer, 'Back to the Future: Instability in Europe After the Cold War', *International Security* 15/1 (Summer 1990) pp.5–56; Mearsheimer (note 1); Stephen Walt, 'The Ties That Fray: Why Europe and America are Drifting Apart', *National Interest*, No.54 (Winter 1998–99) pp.3–11; and Kenneth N. Waltz, 'The Emerging Structure of International Politics', *International Security* 18/2 (Fall 1993) pp.44–79.
4. Jeffrey Herf, *War by Any Other Means: Soviet Power, West German Resistance, and the Battle of the Euromissiles* (NY: Free Press 1991).
5. This argument was developed in Layne, 'Toward German Reunification?' (note 3).
6. On the interplay between NATO nuclear strategy and West Germany's diplomacy *vis-à-vis* Washington and Moscow in the 1980s, see Jeffery Boutwell, *The German Nuclear Dilemma* (London: Brassey's 1990). The chasm between America's and West Germany's respective strategic interests that was revealed by the Euro-missile debate is illustrated by Egon Bahr, 'Peace: A State of Emergency', in Rudolf Steinke and Michel Vale (eds.)

Germany Debates Defense: The NATO Alliance at the Crossroads (Armonk, NY, M.E. Sharpe 1983) pp.141–54; McGeorge Bundy, George F. Kennan, Robert S. McNamara, and Gerard Smith, 'Nuclear Weapons and the Atlantic Alliance', *Foreign Affairs* 60/4 (Spring 1982) pp.753–68; Karl Kaiser, Georg Leber, Alois Mertes, and Franz-Joseph Schulze, 'Nuclear Weapons and the Preservation of Peace: A German Response to No First Use', *Foreign Affairs* 60/5 (Summer 1982) pp.1157–70; and Ekkehart Krippendorff and Michael Lucas, '"One Day We Americans Will Have to Consider the Destruction of Europe"', in *Germany Debates Defense, supra,* pp.33–43.

7. See Mikhail Gorbachev, *Perestroika: New Thinking for Our Country and the World* (NY: Harper & Row 1987) pp.135–60, 190–209.

8. For the view that Gorbachev was 'for real' see Jerry Hough, *Russia and the West: Gorbachev and the Politics of Reform* (NY: Simon & Schuster 1988); and Jerry F. Hough, 'Gorbachev's Politics', *Foreign Affairs* 68/5 (Winter 1989–90) pp.26–41. For somewhat more cautious expressions of this view, see the chapters by Joseph S. Nye, Jr., William G. Hyland, and Seweryn Bialer in Seweryn Bialer and Michael Mandelbaum (eds.) *Gorbachev's Russia and American Foreign Policy* (Boulder, CO: Westview Press 1988). Typical of the view that Gorbachev's new thinking was simply a tactical ploy designed to buy time for the Soviet Union to rebuild its strength for renewed competition with the West is Robert C. MacFarlane, 'Effective Strategic Policy', *Foreign Affairs* 67/1 (Fall 1988) pp.33–48.

9. In his own words, Bush was 'probably less suspicious of Gorbachev than were others in my incoming team', especially his National Security Advisor, Brent Scowcroft, who believed 'that Gorbachev's goal was to restore dynamism to a socialist political and economic system and revitalize the Soviet Union domestically and internationally to compete with the West'. George Bush and Brent Scowcroft, *A World Transformed: The Collapse of The Soviet Empire, The Unification of Germany, Tiananmen Square, The Gulf War* (NY: Knopf 1998) pp.9, 13.

10. Hans Dietrich Genscher, 'Taking Gorbachev at His Word', German Information Center, New York, 6 Feb. 1987.

11. Bush and Snowcroft (note 9) pp.9–10.

12. Ibid. pp.37–56. Representative of the foreign policy community's intellectually sterile response to Gorbachev's initiatives is Graham T. Allison, 'Testing Gorbachev', *Foreign Affairs* 67/1 (Fall 1988) pp.18–32.

13. Bush and Scowcroft (note 9) p.43. The administration was deeply concerned that Gorbachev's policies of *perestroika*, and 'new thinking' would chip away at NATO's cohesion: 'The danger was growing that NATO would fragment in the face of Gorbachev's charm offensive and a diminishing Soviet military threat.' James A. Baker III, *The Politics of Diplomacy: Revolution, War & Peace, 1989–1992* (NY: Putnam's 1995) pp.43–4, 92.

14. Layne, 'Superpower Disengagement' (note 3); Christopher Layne, 'Continental Divide – Time to Disengage in Europe', *National Interest*, No.13 (Fall 1988) pp.13–27; and Ronald Steel, 'NATO's Last Mission', *Foreign Policy*, No.76 (Fall 1989) pp.83–97. Although these proposals were criticized in some quarters as 'isolationist', in the Bush administration's early months in office, Brent Scowcroft toyed with mutual disengagement as a policy response to Gorbachev. As he recounts, the mutual withdrawal of US and Soviet forces from Central Europe 'made military sense because NATO minus most of its US troops would was better off than the Warsaw Pact without Soviet troops. But primarily, such a move would reduce the smothering presence of Soviet forces in Central Europe – one of our goals.' Bush and Scowcroft, p.43. See also Philip Zelikow and Condoleezza Rice, *Germany Unified and Europe Transformed: A Study in Statecraft* (Cambridge, MA: Harvard UP 1995) p.27. Scowroft's proposal was opposed by the administration's leading Europeanist, Robert Blackwill of the NSC staff, and Assistant Secretary of State Rozanne Ridgway. Ibid.

15. Allison (note 12) pp.21–2.

16. Two key members of the Bush administration's foreign policy team state that by 1988 the US government defined the end of the Cold War in terms of attainment of three main objectives: '(1) Stabilize and reduce any danger from US–Soviet rivalry in the

development and deployment of nuclear forces. (2) Defuse and ameliorate any major areas of tension in the US-Soviet competition for influence or advantage in the Third World. (3) Persuade Moscow to move toward respect for the fundamental human rights of its citizens as a basis for full Soviet participation in the international community.' Zelikow and Rice (note 14), pp.18–19.

17. As applied to Europe, Gorbachev's 'new thinking' appears to have unfolded on an *ad hoc* basis. Gorbachev seems not to have had a step-by-step strategy either with respect to European security affairs or to the German Question. Although a few officials in Moscow seem to have appreciated the opportunities that the German reunification gambit held for Moscow, Gorbachev himself apparently did not realize the potentialities inherent in the playing the 'German card'. See Hannes Adomeit, *Imperial Overstretch: Germany in Soviet Policy From Stalin to Gorbachev* (Baden-Baden, Germany: Nomos 1998) pp.191–381; William C. Wohlforth, 'Realism and the End of the Cold War', in Michael E. Brown, Sean Lynn-Jones, and Steven E. Miller (eds.) *The Perils of Anarchy: Contemporary Realism and International Security* (Cambridge, MA: MIT Press 1995) pp.27–30.

18. See David P. Calleo, *The Bankrupting of America: How the Federal Budget is Impoverishing the Nation* (NY: Morrow 1992); and Calleo, *The Imperious Economy* (Cambridge, MA: and Harvard UP 1982).

19. Most of those who argued America's economic leadership was in jeopardy believed that Japan was emerging as the main challenger to US preeminence. For example, see Ronald Morse, 'Japan's Drive for Preeminence', *Foreign Policy*, No.69 (Winter 1987–88) pp.3–21. Samuel Huntington, however, viewed Western Europe as a superpower-in-embryo that could, if it fulfilled its political and economic potential, become 'the preeminent power of the 21st century'. Samuel P. Huntington, 'The U.S. – Decline or Renewal?' *Foreign Affairs* 67/1 (Winter 1988–89) pp.93.

20. See Richard Rosecrance, *The Rise of the Trading State* (NY: Basic Books 1986).

21. *Report of the Defense Burdensharing Panel, Armed Services Committee, US House of Representatives, 100th Cong., 2nd sess.* (Washington DC: US Government Printing Office 1988).

22. Paul Kennedy, *The Rise and Fall of the Great Powers: Economic Change and Military Conflict From 1500 to 2000* (NY: Random House 1987). Kennedy's thesis provoked a sharp debate between those who found his thesis compelling, and the self-styled 'anti-declinists' who took issue with him. Anti-declinists argued that the picture of an America in relative decline was substantially overdrawn. It was true, they admitted, that America's relative power position indeed had eroded from its artificial post World War II apogee. Nevertheless, this slippage notwithstanding, the United States had merely reverted to its 'normal' level of relative power, and was still preeminent economically and militarily. Moreover, they argued, the intense focus on on the relative decline of America's 'hard power' overlooked its formidable 'soft power'. See Henry Nau, *The Myth of America's Decline: Leading the World Economy into the 1990s* (NY: OUP 1990); and Joseph S. Nye Jr, *Bound to Lead: The Changing Nature of American Power* (NY: Basic Books 1990).

23. Kennedy's thesis was anticipated by Robert Gilpin, *War and Change in World Politics* (Cambridge: CUP 1981).

24. Representative of those who saw the United States engaged in an increasingly fierce economic competition with its West European and Japanese allies is Lester Thurow, *Head to Head: The Coming Economic Battle Among Japan, Europe, and America* (NY: Morrow 1992).

25. Walter Lippmann had defined the objective of national strategy as the 'bringing into balance, with a comfortable surplus of power in reserve, the nation's commitments and the nation's resources'. Walter Lippmann, *US Foreign Policy: Shield of the Republic* (Boston: Little, Brown 1944) p.9.

26. See James Chace, *Solvency: The Price of Survival* (NY: Random House 1981); David P. Calleo, *Beyond American Hegemony: The Future of the Western Alliance* (NY: Basic Books 1987); James Chace, 'A New Grand Strategy', *Foreign Policy*, No.70 (Spring 1998) pp.3–23; and William G. Hyland, 'Setting Global Priorities', *Foreign Policy*, No.73 (Winter 1988–89) pp.22–40. For arguments that the United States should terminate its

security commitments in Western Europe and East Asia, see Melvyn P. Krauss, *How NATO Weakens the West* (NY: Simon & Schuster 1986); and Earl C. Ravenal, *NATO: The Tides of Discontent* (Berkeley, CA: Inst. of Int. Studies 1987).

27. Representative of this sense of post-Cold War grand strategic possibilities are Robert E. Hunter, 'Starting at Zero: US Foreign Policy for the 1990s', *Washington Quarterly* 15/1 (Winter 1992) pp.27–42; William G. Hyland, 'The Case for Pragmatism', *Foreign Affairs: America and the World 1991–1992* 71/2 (1991–92) pp.38–52; Michael Mandelbaum, 'The Bush Foreign Policy', *Foreign Affairs* 'America and the World 1990–1991' 70/1 (1990–91) pp.4–22; Charles William Maynes, 'America Without the Cold War', *Foreign Policy*, No.78 (Spring 1990) pp.3–25; and James Schlesinger, 'The Quest for a Post-Cold War Foreign Policy', *Foreign Affairs* 'America and the World 1992–1993' 72/1 (1992–93) pp.17–28.

28. For example, see James Chace, *The Consequences of the Peace: The New Internationalism and American Foreign Policy* (NY: OUP 1992); David Abshire, 'Strategic Challenges: Contingencies, Force Structures, Deterrence', *Washington Quarterly* 15/2 (Spring 1992) pp.33–5; John Lewis Gaddis, 'Toward the Post-Cold War World', *Foreign Affairs* 70/2 (Spring 1991) pp.102–22;' Mandelbaum, 'The Bush Foreign Policy' (note 27) pp.12–13; Joseph S. Nye Jr, 'What New World Order?' *Foreign Affairs* 71/2 (Spring 1992) p.95; Elizabeth Pond, 'Germany in the New Europe', *Foreign Affairs* 71/2 (Spring 1992) pp.114–30; and Gregory F. Treverton, 'The New Europe', *Foreign Affairs* 'America and the World 1991–1992' 71/2 (1991–92) pp.94–112.

29. As Fareed Zakaria puts it: 'The strong are all the same… Over the course of history, states that have experienced significant growth in their material resources have relatively soon redefined and expanded their political interests abroad, measured by their increases in military spending, initiation of wars, acquisition of territory, posting of soldiers and diplomats, and participation in great power decision-making.' Fareed Zakaria, *From Wealth to Power: The Unusual Origins of America's World Role* (Princeton UP 1998) p.3.

30. Ibid. pp.18–20. An earlier statement of the link between capabilities and intentions is Robert Gilpin's observation that, 'As the power of a state increases, it seeks to extend its territorial control, its political influence, and/or its domination of the international economy'. Gilpin, *War and Change in World Politics* (note 23) p.106. A.F.K. Organski also suggested that it is rising great powers that seek to expand their influence in, and control over, the international system. A.F.K. Organski, *World Politics* (NY: Knopf 1968) p.97.

31. Ibid. pp.5, 184–5. As Zakaria says (note 29; pp.184–5), a state's 'definition of security, of the interests that require protection, usually expands in tandem with a nation's material resources'.

32. Eric J. Labs, 'Offensive Realism and Why States Expand Their Security Aims', *Security Studies* 6/4 (Summer 1997) p.15. Zakaria offers a slightly different formulation, contending that instead of attempting to maximize their relative power, states act to maximize their *influence* over the international system (Zakaria, note 29, p.19). The utility of this distinction is problematic, because whether one views a state as seeking to maximize its 'relative power' or its 'influence', the state's goal in either case is the same: an attempt to enhance its range of grand strategic options, to increase its control over the external security environment, and thereby to bolster its security. A similarly problematic semantic distinction is that between offensive realists and defensive realists over whether states maximize their relative power, or maximize their security. In fact, the distinction between 'power' and 'security' that is drawn by defensive realists is an illusory one. In an anarchic, self-help realm like international politics, a state's power is the very foundation of its security, a point nicely captured in John Herz's description of the 'security *and power* dilemma' at the heart of international politics. John Herz, *Political Realism and Political Idealism* (U. of Chicago Press 1951) p.24.

33. Zakaria (note 29) p.20. There is a conflict that runs throughout Zakaria's analysis of expansion because he makes two contradictory claims. On the one hand, after acknowledging that great powers have the *luxury* of defining their interests in ways that go beyond the mere attainment of minimal security (p.182), he argues that expansion occurs in response to the opportunities for successful expansion that are presented as the state's

relative power increases. The implication of Zakaria's argument is that a state's decision to expand is volitional. However, later Zakaria also argues (pp.29–30) that states expand for security reasons because the international system's constraints compel them to do so. According to this explanation, a state's decision to expand is reflexive.

34. John J. Mearsheimer, *Great Power Politics* (NY: Norton, forthcoming) Ch.2. I am grateful to John Mearsheimer for allowing me to read, and cite from, his manuscript.

35. Ashley J. Tellis, 'The Drive to Domination' (Ph.D. dissertation, Dept. of Political Science, U.of Chicago 1994) p.11. Tellis's subcategorization of hegemonic grand strategies is a potentially useful framework. Unfortunately, he neither elaborates on the differences between these subcategories nor does he define them. For my purposes, I would define these categories as follows. Elimination is self-explanatory. An example would be Rome's extinguishing of Carthage at the end of the Third Punic War. Elimination of rivals would seem to be a relatively rare path to hegemony. Subjugation encompasses a state's use of its military and economic capabilities to establish a relationship of dominance over its rivals. Often, but not always, subjugation is accomplished by defeating one's rivals in war. By establishing a clear power advantage over its rival(s), a hegemon is able to circumscribe the rival's autonomy, and reduce its material capabilities, thereby decreasing the likelihood that a defeated rival will resurface as a future threat. Subordination is the most interesting path to hegemony. Subordination is a subtle strategy that combines elements of both hard and soft power. The hegemon uses its hard power to define the power relationship between itself and others. The hegemon's hard power serves to circumscribe others' freedom of action and to dissuade, or prevent, them from developing their power capabilities to a point that would enable them to challenge the hegemon's preeminence. The hegemon uses its soft power to coopt others and to legitimize its dominance over them.

36. This is because: multipolar systems have more 'conflict dyads', which means that there are more chances for wars to erupt and spread; deterrence is difficult because power imbalances frequently occur in multipolar systems and, when they do, wars often occur because the powerful are tempted to aggress; and 'collective action' problems impede timely and successful balancing against aggressors, and encourage states to engage in buck-passing and 'free-riding' behavior. The most succinct critique of multipolarity, upon which this discussion is based, is Mearsheimer, 'Back to the Future' (note 30) pp.13–19. Also, see Waltz (note 2) pp.164–5. As Waltz points out, another reason balancing sometimes fails to occur effectively in multipolar systems is that it is not always clear (or it often is unclear) who threatens whom. On collective action problems generally, see Mancur Olson, *The Logic of Collective Action* (NY: Schocken Books 1968). On free riding, see Richard Zeckhauser and Mancur Olson, 'An Economic Theory of Alliances', *The Review of Economics and Statistics* 48/3 (Aug. 1966) pp.266–79. On buck passing, see Thomas J. Christensen and Jack Snyder, 'Chain Gangs and Passed Bucks: Predicting Alliance Patterns in Multipolarity', *International Organization* 44/1 (Spring 1990) pp.137–68.

37. Mearsheimer, *Great Power Politics* (note 34) Ch.2, p.9.

38. As Hans Morgenthau puts it: 'Since no nation can be sure that its calculation of the distribution of power at any particular moment is correct, it must at least make sure that its errors, whatever they may be, will not put the nation at a disadvantage in the contest for power. In other words, the nation must try to have at least a margin of safety that will allow it to make erroneous calculations and still maintain the balance of power. To that effect, all nations actively engaged in the struggle for power must actually aim not at a balance – that is, equality – of power, but at superiority of power in their own behalf'. Hans J. Morgenthau, revised by Kenneth W. Thompson, *Politics Among Nations: The Struggle for Power and Peace*, 6th ed. (NY: Knopf 1986) pp.227–8.

39. Ibid. p.377. The classic expositions of how differential economic growth rates affect the distribution of relative power in the international system are Gilpin (note 23) and Kennedy (note 22).

40. Morgenthrau (note 38) p.378.

41. Quoted in Robert B. Strassler (ed.) *The Landmark Thucydides* (NY: Free Press 1996) p.372.

42. See Walter F. Hahn, 'West Germany's *Ostpolitik*: The Grand Design of Egon Bahr', *Orbis*, 16/4 (Winter 1973) pp.859–80; and Karsten Voigt, 'The Function of Defence Alliances in the Future', address to the conference on 'NATO at 40', Cato Institute, Washington DC, 4 April 1989.

43. In American foreign policy circles, George F. Kennan was the leading advocate of this view. In 1948, while serving as director of the State Department's policy planning staff, Kennan had urged mutual superpower disengagement from Central Europe, coupled with German unification as an alternative to the creation of NATO, which he feared would solidify Europe's bipolar division for decades to come. See PPS 43, 'Considerations Affecting the Conclusion of a North Atlantic Security Pact', 23 Nov. 1948, in Thomas H. Etzold and John Lewis Gaddis (eds.) *Containment: Documents on American Policy and Strategy, 1945–1950* (NY: Columbia UP 1978) p.157. Out of office, Kennan revived this idea in 1958. George F. Kennan, 'A Chance to Withdraw Our Troops in Europe', *Harper's* 216/1293 (Feb. 1958) pp.34–41.

44. As Defense Secretary Richard Cheney said, 'America should continue to anchor its strategy to the still-valid doctrines of deterrence, flexible response, forward defense, [and] security alliances... Even the extraordinary events of 1989 do not mean that America should abandon this strategic foundation.' 'Statement of Secretary of Defense Richard B. Cheney', Senate Budget Committee 101st Cong., 2nd sess., 5 Feb. 1990, p.3. If the events of 1989 did not indicate that a review of US grand strategy was needed, it is difficult to imagine what would trigger the need for such a reassessment.

45. The American foreign policy community came to believe that US interests in Europe were best furthered by the 'Yalta' system of a divided Continent and a divided Germany. The flip side of this viewpoint was the belief that any change in the post-1945 European *status quo* would be inimical to the United States. The classic statement of this dominant American outlook is A. W. De Porte, *Europe Between the Superpowers: The Enduring Balance* (New Haven, CT: Yale UP 1979).

46. News Conference in Brussels, Belgium, 4 Dec. 1989, *Weekly Compilation of Presidential Documents*, 11 Dec. 1989 (25, No.49).

47. Zelikow and Rice (note 14) pp.169–70 (emphasis added).

48. Bush and Scowcroft (note 9) pp.230–31 (emphasis added).

49. For example, in early 1990, when Britain and France suggested that CSCE play a more important role in post-Cold War Europe's security architecture, the Bush administration believed that this could lead to NATO's being supplanted. As Scowcroft said, that was an 'unacceptable notion' because of 'the centrality of NATO to US strategy'. Ibid. p.249.

50. Ibid. p.188. President Bush himself, who, prior to Nov. 1989, seemed more willing than his senior advisors to entertain the possibility of German reunification, has nevertheless made clear that his support for that outcome was rather tepid. He recalls that he 'did not feel that strongly' about whether Washington should push German reunification, and that if 'the NSC or the State Department had avowed it was a bad idea, I certainly would have been receptive'. Ibid. pp.187–8.

51. As two mid-level Bush administration officials who were involved intimately in the German reunification process put it, the Bush administration was resolved that NATO's essential functions – especially the containment of German power – would remain unchanged even if the Cold War ended: 'Germany would continue to rely on NATO for protection... The Germans would thus forego pursuit of a purely national defense, including the development of their own nuclear weapons'. Zelikow and Rice (note 14) pp.169–70.

52. American concerns that Bonn would trade NATO membership in exchange for Moscow's consent to reunification were fanned both by German Chancellor Helmut Kohl's Dec. 1989 'Ten Point' plan for reunification, and by Foreign Minister Hans Dietrich Genscher's policy statements, notably his Jan. 1990 speech at Tautzig on 'German Unity in a European Framework'. As Scowcroft says, Washington was worried about Kohl's speech because the German Chancellor was silent about the security implications of German reunification, and Germany's future relationship to NATO: 'It was important that Germany remain firmly within the alliance, not just because it was important to anchor that nation to the West and

to assuage the fears of its neighbors, but also because it was crucial to NATO...A Germany outside NATO would "gut" the Alliance.' Bush and Scowcroft (note 9) pp.196–97.

In his Tautzig speech Genscher acknowledged that a unified Germany would remain in NATO, but he also called for a special arrangement to govern the relationship between the alliance and the territory of the former GDR. This worried US policymakers, as did intelligence reports suggesting that Genscher wanted to create a new pan-European security framework that would quickly supersede NATO. Zelikow and Rice (note 14) pp.174–5. In Dec. 1989, Washington had determined that Germany's full membership in NATO was the *sine qua non* of reunification. Ibid. pp.113, 133, 147.

When Kohl and Bush met at Camp David in late Feb. 1990, it was made clear to the Germans that the US support for reunification was predicated on Bonn's commitment that a reunified Germany would remain a full NATO member. Ibid. pp.172–3, 211. With respect to the role of the Two Plus Four talks in ensuring US interests, Baker observes that: 'Without such a process, the odds of the Germans and the Soviets going it alone and cutting a private deal disadvantageous to Western interests (as they had with the agreements of Brest-Litovsk in 1918, Rapallo in 1922, and the Molotov-Ribbentrop accord in 1939) would increase. I felt it important to have the major players at one table, where we could all see the cards that each of us was playing.' Baker (note 13) pp.198–9.

53. As Baker told Gorbachev in May 1990, 'unless we find a way to truly anchor Germany in European institutions we will sow the seeds for history to repeat itself. If Germany was not anchored to the existing security institution [NATO], then we would have a powerful new entity in Europe concerned about developing its [own] security measures.' Baker (note 13) p.273.

54. Bush and Scowcroft (note 9) p.205; and Zelikow and Rice (note 14) p.197. Gorbachev certainly came to understand that Washington was seeking to fashion a post-Cold War European settlement that would give the United States the upper hand. As he told Baker when they met in Moscow in May 1990, 'Sometimes I have the sense that you want an edge, you may seek an advantage [on Germany and NATO]... that's going to mean a very serious development in the strategic balance; it's going to mean a serious shift in the balance.' Baker (note 13) pp.248–9.

55. This became a point of friction between Washington and Genscher, who was prepared to be more accommodating to Moscow because he worried that US policy would undermine Gorbachev. However, 'Genscher may not have understood that the Americans had decided that the US objectives for Germany were more important than protecting Gorbachev.' Zelikow and Rice (note 14) p.252.

56. Ibid. p.197.

57. As Baker says, the Bush administration recognized the need to give Gorbachev and Foreign Minister Eduard Shevardnadze political 'cover' in the form of arguments they could make domestically to justify accepting Washington's terms. And, he says, 'That meant we had to work with our European partners to adapt NATO and CSCE to make them *appear* less threatening to the Soviet people.' Baker (note 13) pp.231–2 (emphasis added).

58. Bush and Scowcroft (note 9) pp.239, 273; and Zelikow and Rice (note 14) pp.18–182. No doubt, those arguments were self-serving. At the same time, however, it is also true that, for its own part, the United States did worry about the geopolitical implications of a reunified Germany, which posed a latent threat to US interests.

59. Gorbachev found it inconsistent for the United States to argue, on the one hand, that a democratic, unified Germany could be trusted to behave responsibly, but to maintain, on the other hand, that a reunified Germany could be a trouble-maker unless embedded in NATO. Bush and Scowcroft (note 9) pp.257, 272. Gorbachev also insisted that the American insistence on maintaining NATO was in conflict with the goal of ending the Cold War. Ibid. p.272.

60. Bush and Scowcroft (note 9) p.253. Also see Zelikow and Rice (note 14) p.215.

61. This is what Baker told Gorbachev when the two met in Moscow in May 1990. Bush and Scowcroft (note 9) p.273.

62. Zelikow and Rice (note 14) p.274. See text and references at note 55.

63. Baker (note 13) p.257.

86   *NATO Enters the 21st Century*

64. In early 1990, when the diplomatic process leading to German reunification was just beginning to gather momentum, Genscher assured Moscow that reunification would not mean NATO's eastward extension. As Genscher said, 'To think that the borders of NATO could be moved 300 kilometers eastward, via German unification, would be an illusion... No reasonable person could expect the Soviet Union to accept such an outcome.' Quoted in Zelikow and Rice (note 14) p.175. In Feb. 1990, Baker told Shevardnadze that if a reunified Germany remained in NATO, Moscow would receive firm guarantees 'that NATO's jurisdiction or forces would not move eastward'. Ibid. p.180; Bush and Scowcroft (note 9) p.239.

65. As President Clinton said: 'I know that some in Russia still look at NATO through a Cold War prism and, therefore, look at our proposals to expand it in a negative light. But I ask them to look again. We are building a new NATO, just as we support the Russian people in building a new Russia. By reducing rivalry and fear, by strengthening peace and cooperation, NATO will promote greater stability in Europe and Russia will be among the beneficiaries. Indeed, Russia has the best chance in history to help build that peaceful and undivided Europe, and to be an equal and respected and successful partner in that sort of future. The great opportunity the Russian people have is to define themselves in terms of the future, not the past; to forge a new relationship with NATO as enlargement moves forward.' President Bill Clinton, 'Remarks to the People of Detroit', 22 Oct. 1996, White House Press Office transcript, http://www.pub.whitehouse.gov/uri-res/I2R?urn:pdi://oma.eop.gov.us/1996/10/22/4.text.1

Arguing that NATO enlargement was not drawing new lines of division in Europe, a senior Pentagon official said: 'NATO is a defensive alliance created to ensure more security and stability for Europe as a whole, Russia included, whatever its formal or informal relations with the alliance. NATO is not an alliance against Russia. NATO's basic principles – collective defense, democracy, consensus and cooperative security – are no threat to the Russia of today or, we trust and hope, of the Russia of tomorrow.' Undersecretary of Defense for Policy Walter Slocombe, 'Partnership for Peace and NATO-Russian Relations', Speech to the Center for Strategic and International Studies, Washington DC), *Defense Issues* 10/28 (online), 2 March 1995. Also see Strobe Talbott, 'Why NATO Should Grow', *New York Review of Books* 42/13 (10 Aug. 1995) pp.27–30.

66. The most detailed account of Russia's reaction to NATO expansion is J.L. Black, *Russia Faces NATO Expansion: Bearing Gifts or Bearing Arms* (Lanham, MD: Rowman & Littlefield 2000). See also Susan Eisenhower, 'The Perils of Victory', in Ted Galen Carpenter and Barbara Conry (eds.) *NATO Enlargement: Illusions and Reality* (Washington DC: Cato Institute 1998) pp.103–19.

67. Ronald D. Asmus, 'Double Enlargement: Redefining the Atlantic Partnership After the Cold War', in David C. Gompert and F. Stephen Larrabee (eds.) *America and Europe: A Partnership for a New Era* (Cambridge: CUP 1997) pp.19–50.

68. For example, a senior Pentagon official made the case that post-Cold War NATO would need to focus on 'out of area threats', stating that 'real, immediate challenges to NATO allies have been mounting to the south. Flash points have emerged in the Mediterranean, in Southwest Asia, in the Balkans and in North Africa. The potential spread of instability across the Mediterranean would not only threaten friendly regimes of North Africa and the prospects for peace in the Middle East, it would also threaten Europe with new social and security problems.' Slocombe (note 65). The most robust vision of how NATO should serve to defend a geographically expansive notion of US strategic interests is Zbigniew Brzezinski, *The Grand Chessboard: American Primacy and its Geostrategic Imperatives* (NY: Basic Books 1997). Brzezinski calls for ultimately transforming NATO into a Trans-Eurasian Security System (TESS), that would encompass all of Europe, Central Asia and the Caucasus, and East Asia.

69. As Secretary of State Albright put it, 'instability that is dangerous and contagious is best stopped before it reaches NATO's borders'. Secretary of State Madeleine K. Albright, 'Press Conference at NATO Headquarters', Washington DC: US Department of State, Office of the Spokesman, 8 Dec. 1998.

70. President Bill Clinton, 'Remarks on Foreign Policy', San Francisco, 26 Feb. 1999, White House Press Office transcript, http://www.pub.whitehouse.gov/uri-res/I2R?urn:pdi:// oma.eop.gov.us/1999/3/1/3.text.1.

71. Melvyn P. Leffler, 'National Security', in Michael J. Hogan and Thomas G. Paterson (eds.) *Explaining the History of American Foreign Relations* (Cambridge: CUP 1991) p.204.

72. President Clinton, 'Remarks on Foreign Policy' (note 70).

73. Slocombe, 'Partnership for Peace and NATO-Russian Relations' (note 65).

74. President Bill Clinton, 'Remarks to the American Society of Newspaper Editors', Annapolis, MD, 1 April 1993, White House Press Office transcript, http://www.pub.white house.gov/uri-res/I2R?urn:pdi://oma.eop.gov.us/1993/4/1/10.text.1.

75. Deputy Secretary of State Strobe Talbott, 'Robert C. Frasure Memorial Lecture', Tallinn, Estonia, 24 Jan. 2000, State Dept. Website, http://www.state.gov/www/policy_remarks/ 2000/000124_talbott_ Tallinn.html.

76. Deputy Secretary of State Strobe Talbott, 'Remarks at a Conference on the Future of NATO', The Royal Institute of International Affairs, London, 7 Oct. 1999, http://www. state.gov/www.policy_remarks/1999/991007_talbott_London.html.

77. Ibid. Also see John Lancaster, 'Albright Signals Strong Backing for Milosevic Foes', *Washington Post*, 4 Nov. 1999, p.A27.

78. Marc Lacy, 'US Will Reconsider Ties if Haider Joins Coalition', *New York Times*, 2 Feb. 2000.

79. President Bill Clinton, 'Remarks to the People of Detroit' (note 65).

80. An early expression of US fears of 'renationalization' was the Pentagon's 1991 Summer Study, which argued that the main threat to America's post-Cold War preponderance was of 'Germany and/or Japan disconnecting from multilateral security and economic arrangements and pursuing an independent course'. Undersecretary of Defense (Policy), *1991 Summer Study*, Organized by the Director, Net Assessment, held at Newport, RI, 5–13 Aug. 1991, p.17.

81. For the argument that the American commitment to NATO is vital to preventing Europe from relapsing into security competitions, see Robert J. Art, 'Why Western Europe Needs the United States and NATO', *Political Science Quarterly* 111/1 (Spring 1996) pp.1–39. Also see Stephen Van Evera, 'Why Europe Matters, Why The Third World Doesn't', *Journal of Strategic Studies* 13/2 (June 1990) pp.1–51. Simply put, US policymakers believe that a unipolar world in which America is hegemonic is more peaceful than a multipolar system. The case against multipolarity is set forth in the *Regional Defense Strategy*, prepared by the Pentagon during the Bush administration: 'It is not in our interest....to return to earlier periods in which multiple military powers balanced one against another in what passed for security structures, while regional, or even global peace hung in the balance'. Dept. of Defense, *Regional Defense Strategy*, 1992, p.12.

82. If this 'reassurance' provided by the United States ever was doubted by America's allies, the entire fabric of European security would unravel. As a recent Pentagon strategy document puts it, a loss of confidence in US reassurance 'could cause allies and friends to adopt more divergent defense policies and postures, thereby weakening the web of alliances and coalitions on which we rely to protect our interests abroad'. *Report of the Quadrennial Defense Review* (May 1997) p.12. As a consequence, Europe 'could unravel into unrestrained military competition, conflict, and aggression'. *Regional Defense Strategy* (note 81) p.12. The 'virtuous circle' theory of US strategy has been outlined by Secretary of Defense Cohen. He argues that, 'Peace and stability are the very cornerstones of prosperity. When our diplomats and military forces combine to help create stability and security in a nation or region, that same stability and security attracts investment. Investment generates prosperity. And prosperity strengthens democracy, which creates more stability and more security.' Cohen went on to emphasize the connection between peace and stability, and the US military presence in Europe (and in East Asia): 'Our wisest and most-cost effective actions are those that encourage peace and discourage violence and instability – instability which destroys lives and markets. That means being forward deployed in Asia and Europe...and addressing instability before it turns into war.' Secretary of Defense William Cohen, 'Remarks at Microsoft Corporation', Redmond, WA, 18 Feb. 1999, DoD website,

http://www.defenselink.mil/speeches/1999/s19990218-secdef.html.

83. Since the Cold War's end, US grand strategy has aimed at perpetuating America's role as the only great power in a unipolar world. The most forthright statement of this grand strategic objective was the Bush administration's Draft Defense Planning Guidance for FY 1994–99, which stated, 'We must account sufficiently for the interests of the large industrial nations to discourage them from challenging our leadership or seeking to overturn the established political or economic order', and that 'we must maintain the mechanisms for deterring potential competitors from even aspiring to a larger regional or global role'. 'Excerpts from Pentagon's Plan: "Prevent the Emergence of a New Rival"', *New York Times*, 8 March 1992, p.14. The Bush administration disavowed that document when such leaks triggered a public relations backlash (especially with US allies in Europe and East Asia). However, the substance of the strategy has been reaffirmed in innumerable policy statements and documents during both the Bush and Clinton administrations.

84. For elaboration, see Christopher Layne and Benjamin Schwarz, 'American Hegemony – Without An Enemy', *Foreign Policy*, No.92 (Fall 1993) pp.5–23. Also see Benjamin Schwarz, '"Cold War" Continuities: US Economic and Security Strategy Towards Europe', *Journal of Strategic Studies* 17/4 (Dec. 1994) pp.82–104.

85. The term 'double containment' is from Wolfram F. Hanreider, *Germany, Europe, and America* (New Haven, CT: Yale UP 1989). Also see, idem, 'The German-American Alliance at Forty', *Aussenpolitik* (II/89) 40/2, 2nd Quarter 1989, pp.148–59.

86. See Joseph Joffe, 'Europe's American Pacifier', *Foreign Policy*, No.54 (Spring 1984) pp.64–82.

87. The link between America's security, its preponderance, and an American-led world order was articulated in NSC-68, which stated: (1) the purpose of American power was 'to foster a world environment in which the American system can survive and flourish' and (2) the strategy of preponderance was 'a policy which [the United States] would probably pursue even if there were no Soviet Union'. Text of NSC-68 in Thomas Etzold and John Lewis Gaddis (eds.) *Containment: Documents on American Policy and Strategy, 1945–1950* (NY: Columbia UP 1978) p.401.

88. As diplomatic historian John Lewis Gaddis states: 'Few historians would deny, today, that the United States did expect to dominate the international scene after World War II, and that it did so well before the Soviet Union emerged as a clear and present antagonist.' John Lewis Gaddis, 'The Tragedy of Cold War History', *Diplomatic History* 17/1 (Winter 1993) pp.3–4.

89. Quoted in Melvyn P. Leffler, *A Preponderance of Power: National Security, the Truman Administration, and the Cold War* (Stanford UP 1994) p.19.

90. See Russell D. Buhite and Wm. Christopher Hamel, 'War for Peace: The Question of American Preventive War against the Soviet Union, 1945–1955', *Diplomatic History* 14/3 (Summer 1990) pp.367–85.

91. Leffler (note 89) p.17.

92. See Waltz, *Theory of International Politics* (note 2) pp.126–7. As Hans Morgenthau observes, 'A nation that throws into the scale of international politics the maximum of material power it is capable of mustering will find itself confronted with the maximum effort of all its competitors to equal or surpass its power. It will find that it has no friends, but only vassals and enemies.' Morgenthau (note 38) p.183. It should be noted that offensive realists, as well as defensive realists, acknowledge that a would-be hegemon must surmount formidable barriers to attain its objective. Even Mearsheimer, the leading proponent of offensive realism, says: 'Hegemony is rarely achieved, however, because power tends to be somewhat evenly distributed among states, because threatened states have strong incentives to join together to thwart an aspiring hegemon, and because the costs of expansion usually outrun the benefits before domination is achieved, causing extension to become overextension.' John Mearsheimer, 'Back to the Future', *International Security* 15/1 (Summer 1990) p.13, n.15.

93. For elaboration of this argument, see Christopher Layne, 'The Unipolar Illusion: Why New Great Powers Will Rise', *International Security* 17/4 (Spring 1993) pp.5–55.

94. William C. Wohlforth, 'The Stability of a Unipolar World', *International Security* 24/1 (Summer 1999) pp.5–41.
95. For example, see Michael Mastanduno, 'Preserving the Unipolar Moment: Realist Theories and US Grand Strategy', *International Security* 21/4 (Spring 1997) pp.49–88. On balance-of-threat theory, see Stephen M. Walt, *The Origins of Alliances* (Ithaca: Cornell UP 1987).
96. On the role of soft power in US grand strategy, see Nye, *Bound to Lead* (note 22). In an important speech in the autumn of 1999, National Security Advisor Sandy Berger invoked the ideas of 'soft power' and 'balance of threat' theory to refute European claims that the United States was an overbearing hegemon. Berger acknowledged that the United States is seen in Europe, Russia and China as 'a hectoring hegemon' and a country that is 'unilateralist and too powerful'. Berger did not deny that the United States indeed is hegemonic, nor did he suggest that Washington is going to renounce its geopolitical preponderance. What he tried to do, however, was to allay others' fears of American power by arguing that the United States is a benign hegemon: 'We are accused of dominating others, of seeing the world in zero sum terms in which any other country's gain must be our loss. But that is an utterly mistaken view. It's not just because we are the first global power in history that is not an imperial power. It's because for 50 years, we have consciously tried to define and pursue our interests in a way that is consistent with the common good – rising prosperity, expanding freedom, collective security.' Samuel R. Berger, 'American Power: Hegemony, Isolationism or Engagement', speech at the Council on Foreign Relations, New York City, 21 Oct. 1999, on the White House website at http://www.whitehouse.gov/WH/EOP/NSC/html/speeches/19991021.html.
97. For example, see Karl Deutsch *et al.*, *Political Community and the North Atlantic Area* (Princeton UP 1968); Thomas Risse-Kappen, *Cooperation Among Democracies: The European Influence on U.S. Foreign Policy* (ibid. 1995); Mary N. Hampton, 'NATO at the Creation: US Foreign Policy, West Germany and the Wilsonian Impulse', *Security Studies* 4/3 (Spring 1995) p.653; and Robert G. Kaufman, 'A Two-Level Interaction: Structure, Stable Liberal Democracy, and US Grand Strategy', *Security Studies* 3/4 (Summer 1994) pp.681–5.
98. Geir Lundestad, *The American 'Empire' and Other Studies of US Foreign Policy in a Comparative Perspective* (NY: OUP 1990).
99. See for example D.C. Watt, 'Perceptions of the United States in Europe, 1945–1983', in Lawrence Freedman (ed.) *The Troubled Alliance: Atlantic Relations in the 1980s* (NY: St Martin's 1983) pp.28–43. As Watt notes, the West Europeans have perceived the United States both as a friend and as an adversary.
100. Quoted in Michael J. Hogan, *The Marshall Plan: America, Britain, and the Reconstruction of Western Europe, 1947–1952* (Cambridge: CUP 1987) p.113.
101. As Edward Kolodziej observes, 'In the closing years of Gaullist rule, the possible development of a unipolar system became one of the major concerns of the French government.' Edward A. Kolodziej, *French International Policy Under De Gaulle and Pompidou: The Politics of Grandeur* (Ithaca, NY: Cornell UP 1974) p.91.
102. On US distrust of the motives underlying Bonn's *Ostpolitik*, see Henry A. Kissinger, *White House Years* (Boston: Little, Brown 1979) pp.408–10.
103. As University of Munich political scientist Ulrich Beck put it, 'Kosovo could be our military euro, creating a political and defense identity for the European Union in the same way as the euro is the expression of economic and financial integration.' Quoted in Roger Cohen, 'In Uniting Over Kosovo, A New Sense of Identity', *New York Times*, 28 April 1999, p.A11.
104. Quoted in Craig R. Whitney, 'France Presses For a Power Independent of the US', *New York Times*, 7 Nov. 1999, p.A5.
105. German Foreign Minister Joschka Fischer hinted that Germany would respond to US NBMD deployment by developing its own nuclear forces. See William Drozdiak, 'Possible US Missile Shield Alarms Europe', *Washington Post*, 6 Nov. 1999, p.A1. Arguing that NBMD deployment would render Europe more vulnerable than the United States to nuclear attack and disrupt the strategic coupling of Europe and America, Fischer observed that Germany's commitment to forego nuclear weapons 'was always based on our trust that the United States would protect our interests, that the United States, as the leading nuclear

power, would guarantee some sort of order'. Fischer said NBMD deployment would undercut Germany's trust in the efficacy of American security guarantees.

106. See Craig R. Whitney, 'Hey, Allies, Follow Me. I've Got All the New Toys', *New York Times*, 30 May 1999 (online ed.); Roger Cohen, 'Dependent on US Now, Europe Vows Defense Push', *New York Times*, 12 May 1999 (online ed.); John-Thor Dahlburg, 'Battle for Kosovo Shows Europe Still Needs US', *Los Angeles Times*, 20 April 1999 (online ed.).

107. This ambivalence is deeply rooted. Henry Kissinger warned that while it might prove to be a price worth paying, the United States indeed would pay a price if Europe achieved political and economic unification. A unified Europe would be no longer subservient to Washington, and would pursue its own agenda in international politics. It was naive, Kissinger said, to suppose that 'Europe would unite in order to share *our* burdens or that it would be content with a subordinate role once it had the means to implement its own views. Europe's main incentive to undertake a larger cooperative role in the West's affairs would be to fulfil its own distinctive purposes.' Henry A. Kissinger, *Years of Upheaval* (Boston: Little, Brown 1982) p.131. Kissinger first made this point in a 1965 book on transatlantic relations, where he argued explicitly, that a united Europe would 'challenge American hegemony in Atlantic policy'. Henry A. Kissinger, *The Troubled Partnership: A Re-Appraisal of the Atlantic Alliance* (NY: McGraw-Hill 1965) p.40.

108. See Joseph Fitchett, 'EU Takes Steps to Create a Military Force, Without Treading on NATO', *International Herald Tribune,* 1 March 2000 (online ed.); James Kitfield, 'European Doughboys', *The National Journal*, 26 Feb. 2000, pp.610–14; Carol J. Williams, 'Conference Highlights Flaws of NATO's Kosovo Campaign', *Los Angeles Times*, 6 Feb. 2000 (online ed.).

109. Secretary of State Madeleine K. Albright, 'Press Conference at NATO Headquarters', US Department of State, Office of the Spokesman, 8 Dec. 1998.

110. Slocombe, 'Partnership for Peace and NATO-Russian Relations' (note 65). Talbott has made the same point, stating that US support for ESDI would depend on the answer to a the key question: 'will it help keep the alliance together…?' As Talbott said, the United States does 'not want to see an ESDI that comes into being first within NATO but then grows out of NATO and finally grows away from NATO, since that would lead to an EDSO [European Defense and Security Organization] that initially duplicates NATO but that could eventually compete with NATO'. Talbott, 'Remarks at a Conference on the Future of NATO' (note 76).

111. Albright, 'Press Conference at NATO Headquarters' (note 69).

112. NATO, Deputy National Security Advisor James Steinberg has declared, is the 'bedrock' of post-Cold War Europe's security, and 'underpins Europe's best hopes for a continent that is democratic, undivided and at peace'. He went on to note that while some in Europe perceive 'that US leadership is heavy handed', nevertheless the 'fact is, our leadership is essential in support of the larger cause of an integrated Europe'. James B. Steinberg, Deputy Assistant to the President for National Security Affairs, 'Remarks before European Institute', Mayflower Hotel, Washington DC, 15 Jan. 1998, at http://www.whitehouse.gov/WH/EOP/NSC/html/speeches/19980204-6020.html.

113. Stuart E. Eizenstat, Under Secretary of State for Economic, Business, and Agricultural Affairs, 'Address to the Secretary's Open Forum', 6 April 1999 (State Dept. website).

114. Strobe Talbott warns: 'If ESDI is misconceived, misunderstood, or mishandled, it could create the impression – which could eventually lead to the reality – that a new, European-only alliance is being born out of the old, trans-Atlantic one. If that were to happen, it would weaken, perhaps even break, those ties that I spoke of before – the ones that bind our security to yours'. Deputy Secretary of State Strobe Talbott, 'Address at the Royal United Services Institute, London, UK', 10 March 1999 (State Dept website).

115. The most recent iteration of these points is Stephen Walt, 'The Ties That Fray: Why Europe and America are Drifting Apart', *National Interest*, No.54 (Winter 1998–99) pp.3–11. Walt's analysis is compelling and builds on the work of such analysts as David Calleo, James Chace, Earl Ravenal, and Ronald Steel acutely identified the external and domestic factors that could ultimate cause the transatlantic alliance to fracture. By the mid-1980s, NATO's fraying was discernible, the result of: the contradictions imbedded in the alliance's

extended deterrence strategy; the recrudescence of the German question; the attenuation of the Soviet military threat to Western Europe; the coming to power of successor generations on both sides of the Atlantic; and the divergence of interests between the United States and an economically resurgent Europe. There was also a strong argument to be made that the time had come for the United States to capitalize on the incipient multipolarity suggested by Western Europe's post-World War II recovery, and to contemplate disengagement from the Continent's security affairs. For discussions of these issues, see Layne, 'Superpower Disengagement' (note 3); Layne, 'Continental Divide' (note 14); Layne, 'Atlanticism Without NATO' (note 3); Layne, 'Toward German Reunification' (note 3); Layne, 'Ending the Alliance' (note 3). Also see Ted Galen Carpenter, 'Competing Agendas: America, Europe, and a Troubled NATO Partnership', in idem (ed.) *NATO at 40: Confronting a Changing World* (Lexington, MA: Lexington Books 1990) pp.29–44; and Carpenter, *A Search for Enemies: America's Alliances after the Cold War* (Washington DC: Cato Institute 1992) pp.11–46.

Previously associated with strong support for NATO, Walt now concurs with my analysis of more than a decade ago that, because the alliance's disintegration is inevitable, the best course of action is for the United States and Western Europe to begin a process of gradual disengagement, rather than risk its precipitous rupture in a future transatlantic crisis. For his previous support of the US commitment to NATO, see Walt, 'The Case for Finite Containment: Analyzing US Grand Strategy', *International Security* 14/1 (Spring 1989) pp.5–50.

5

The New NATO and Relations with Russia

ALTON FRYE

One of Jean Monnet's great maxims framed an essential goal of statecraft: The first task in a negotiation is to get the people on one side of the table – and the problem on the other. That insight is an apt description of the challenge facing NATO and Russia after the end of the Cold War and the splintering of the Soviet Union into 15 independent states. After half a century of staring ominously at each other, NATO and Russia are still searching for ways to shape a common approach to the security of Europe. This analysis reviews difficulties that have arisen in that quest, assesses the relative importance of cooperation between NATO and Russia, and sets forth some ideas for lubricating major points of friction between the two.[1]

Since the time of Mikhail Gorbachev, the ambition for stability in Europe's common home has elicited admirable rhetoric on both sides of the former Iron Curtain. Beyond rhetoric, the closing decade of the twentieth century has seen real and dramatic achievements in bolstering European security – major reductions in the massive conventional forces that dominated the continental landscape, significant cuts in the vastly overblown strategic nuclear deployments that defined the balance of terror, and a remarkable shift toward direct political discourse at the highest levels of the major governments.[2]

Yet, as the Clinton and Yeltsin eras come to an end in America and Russia, along with far-reaching changes in European regimes, relations between NATO countries and Russia have degenerated, in the words of a leading US official, to a state of 'mutual strategic mistrust'.[3] Where not long ago both sides nourished hopes for a durable strategic partnership, they now approach each other with far more modest expectations and far more grudging acknowledgement that they cannot avoid doing some business together. The dynamics between NATO and Russia have turned decidedly perverse. Shifting them to a more benign and mutually advantageous direction will require a prodigious salvage job. It must begin with a clear-headed understanding of how the 1990s failed to fulfill the promise of a more wholesome relationship with which the decade began.

MOUNTING DISARRAY IN NATO-RUSSIA RELATIONS

The catalogue of irritations, resentments and conflicts of interest between Russia and NATO has grown long. Many of its elements are familiar, but recalling them gives one a fresh appreciation of the sour context they have created. They include disagreements specific to NATO as an institution and other irritants arising between Russia and individual countries, especially the United States, that bear heavily on the general environment of the alliance's relations with Moscow.

NATO's decision to enlarge its membership is, of course, the first factor in Russia's growing suspicion of Western intentions.[4] The open-ended character of the enlargement scheme virtually guaranteed that, while Russian objections might be tempered in the short-run by the fact of Moscow's declining strategic leverage and its hope for a special connection to NATO, expansion beyond the initial three invitees (Poland, Hungary and the Czech Republic) would meet mounting Russian opposition.[5] That decision stemmed from understandable desire to reassure peoples who had been subject to decades of Soviet oppression that they would find a secure harbor in the West. However, it also embodied a degree of triumphalism and moral hubris that could not but trouble those Russians who felt that they, too, had suffered from the Soviet experience and that they, too, deserved assurance that the new security order would consider their concerns.

Attempts to assuage Russia through the arrangements made in the so-called NATO-Russia Founding Act of 1997 and the NATO-Russia Permanent Joint Council were briefly, but only symbolically, successful. Those arrangements, though formal, were tenuous at best and predictably vulnerable to disturbance from several directions.

In important respects, the process of seeking accommodation with NATO appeared to many Russians as a form of appeasement imposed upon their government; that perception contributed to weakening the hand of some Russian leaders struggling to build a workable relationship with their former adversaries. It was not an asset for democratically inclined Russians to be seen at home as eager to strike bargains with the Americans and West Europeans, as former Foreign Minister Andrei Kozyrev learned. Yevgeny

Primakov managed to rise to the prime ministership only by dint of a careful balancing act to maintain his reputation as a skillful defender of Russian interests. Boris Yeltsin and other proud Russians, looking over their shoulders at the currents of embittered nationalism flowing through their body politic, were prone periodically to bombastic outbursts to demonstrate that they were standing up to a haughty West.

NATO observers, American more often than European, tended to proceed from the hard-nosed premise that Russia was too weak to mount effective resistance against alliance expansion or policy. While voicing concern for Russian sensibilities, there was little inclination to give much weight to them. The theme of Western policymakers for the Russian link to NATO was explicit: 'a voice not a veto'.

The strategic logic that propelled NATO enlargement had an understandable appeal to the US administration, for domestic political reasons as well as international ones.[6] It was hard to resist the claims of Central Europeans who, once the American president raised the prospect of their membership in NATO, yearned ever-more-vocally for acceptance into the alliance. That ambition reverberated through important ethnic communities in the United States, constituencies with significant weight in American elections. However plausible the security rationale for NATO enlargement, there was also a suspicion that the Clinton administration's motives were tinged with a self-interested desire to mobilize the voters in those constituencies.

From the beginning of debate on NATO expansion, Mikhail Gorbachev and other Russian leaders smelled betrayal. They claimed that such a move was a clear violation of assurances they had received as part of the agreement to accept German unification and continued German membership in NATO. It was difficult for them to accept the concept that NATO would be the cornerstone of Europe's new security order, not only because the alliance had long represented an 'enemy' explicitly poised to threaten the Soviet Union but also because they feared the creation of new dividing lines in the heart of the Continent.[7] How could the extension of a Cold War alliance into new territory fail to create such divisions? It was difficult to persuade Russian leaders that the vaunted stability offered by NATO's embrace of new members was good for Russian security. Those responsible for Russian security, particularly in the military establishment, saw an expanding NATO not as a vehicle for shoring up stability in Europe but for isolating Russia from Europe.

Proponents of NATO expansion regularly dismissed Russian antagonism to the idea as either a misunderstanding that could be alleviated or a reflection of recidivist imperialism that must be resisted. They argued that Russian opposition to expansion was merely an elite issue in Moscow and that opinion polls showed little popular attention to the matter. The characterization was probably accurate, but it downplayed the critical fact that it was the Russian elite with which Western governments would have to collaborate in shaping compatible political and strategic relationships.[8] There was a price to be paid for breeding such deep mistrust among Russian political leaders that it infected the broader effort to build practical working arrangements on a host of issues. Moreover, apprehension over NATO encroachments into former Warsaw Pact territory would not long remain exclusive to the Russian elite. By 1999 it had spread broadly throughout Russian society.

Three developments were critical to intensifying and diffusing fresh anti-NATO sentiment among the Russian populace: US bombing of Bosnian Serb forces in 1995, the revision of NATO's strategic concept to emphasize interests beyond the territory of NATO members, and NATO's 1999 intervention in Kosovo. After the failure over several years to tame the violence in Bosnia Herzegovina, NATO's assumption of the central responsibility for enforcing the Dayton accords followed brief, but notable, bombing operations against Bosnian Serbs. Careful negotiations brought Russia into constructive participation in the NATO deployment to maintain the peace there, but accompanying that good news was an undercurrent of resentment against the bombing strikes the United States had carried out against Orthodox coreligionists.

Moscow undoubtedly wished to demonstrate its capacity to share responsibility for an exercise in international peacekeeping in a zone of historic interest to Russia. One reason for the Russians' participation was certainly concern that, absent their presence, implementation of the Dayton accords would be prejudicial to the Serbs. Another was the need to keep a close watch on NATO's extension of its activities beyond the territory of its own members. On the ground and in the channels linking Russian forces to NATO headquarters, the results were impressive. Officers of both NATO and Russia found ways to make the arrangements work and began to gain the kind of mutual confidence on which deeper ties might be built.

That hopeful beginning of military cooperation came under a cloud with changes in NATO doctrine that pointed toward the possibility of widespread engagement in regions well outside the territory of the alliance's members.[9] The 1991 Persian Gulf War had already demonstrated that, even when NATO did not act as an alliance *per se*, its infrastructure would be essential to coalitions of the willing, subgroups of allies who chose to intervene in crises beyond the areas defined in the NATO treaty. Even with the versatile globe-spanning military forces of the United States, the ability to tap NATO resources was indispensable to repulsing Saddam Hussein and projecting a potent deterrent against others who might emulate him in unstable regions.

This value of NATO as the base for such coalitions of the willing was a major argument used by those who opposed expanding the alliance.[10] A compact alliance offered the advantages both of intensive experience in joint operations among a relatively manageable number of countries and of a tauter decision-making structure than would be possible with a larger organization. As an alternative to further enlargement, several analysts posed the model of NATO as a sturdy military organization on which to build flexible coalitions, among members and other states, to cope with the unknowable range of future contingencies. With the initial stage of enlargement advertised as merely a first step, prospects that NATO would follow such a model were unclear. To Russian skeptics, the evolution of NATO's doctrine carried with it a flavor of assertive interventionism that was incompatible not only with the concept of a defensive alliance, but also with international norms against interference in the domestic affairs of sovereign states.

The dynamics of the situation are worth noting. Calm in Europe left some NATO leaders fearing that the organization would deteriorate unless it reframed its *raison d'être*. One theme became that NATO 'must go out of area or out of business'. Both those who favored enlargement and those who favored limiting NATO to its present scale as a more effective base for coalitions envisaged circumstances in which, as in the Persian Gulf, the alliance needed to be ready to support operations at a distance from NATO territory. The internal debate on NATO's strategic concept put on display for Russia and others wary of the alliance's intentions a clear disposition among member governments to sustain the alliance by transforming the scope of its mission. Not surprisingly, NATO's benign self-description did not seem persuasive to all observers.

Thus, the multiple catastrophes that arose in the Balkans during 1999 were bound to compound frictions that were already arising in NATO-Russian relations. NATO's intervention in Kosovo confirmed to many Russians that the alliance could not be trusted to respect either its own defensive precepts or international norms. By evading the UN decision-making processes that would have brought Russian influence to bear, NATO's action obscured for many Russians the viciousness of Serbian President Slobodan Milošević's treatment of Kosovar Albanians. It also ended whatever indifference the Russian public at large may have felt toward NATO. Elites and non-elites alike now share the view of NATO and the United States as unfriendly, prepared to disregard Russian interests, and working to isolate their weakened state still further.

In this mood of soaring resentment it was remarkable that the Russian government undertook a central role in bringing the Kosovo conflict to a diplomatic conclusion. President Yeltsin's dispatch of former Prime Minister Viktor Chernomyrdin to serve as a key interlocutor with Milošević proved more than helpful. Having catered to Serbian sensibilities in many ways, the Russians were in the best position to make clear to the Serbian demagogue that he was completely isolated and could not rely on Moscow to intervene further in his behalf. No one can say what course the war would have followed without the multilateral diplomacy to which Chernomyrdin contributed. It is clear, however, that the ground campaign NATO had threatened might well have been necessary to force the Serbian army out of Kosovo – and it could have been a very bloody campaign indeed.

In Russia something else was clear. Russia's suspension of its formal cooperation with NATO (though not of its deployment to Bosnia as an adjunct to the NATO-led force there) had marked a severe setback, signaling a basic turn in Moscow's attitude toward the alliance. Seventy-eight days and thousands of NATO sorties later, the attitude was even grimmer. If there was a degree of pride that Russian diplomacy was instrumental to ending the NATO bombing, there was a more vivid moment of widespread elation when Russian troops moved preemptively to occupy Pristina airport.[11] Militarily, the maneuver may have involved only 200 men and meant little strategically, but the finger it poked in NATO's eye was a source of much satisfaction to Muscovites and their fellow countrymen. The tide of anti-NATO and anti-American sentiment surged strongly, even while Russian leaders were groping toward participation in the international occupation of Kosovo once that occupation gained UN blessing and authority.

It is hard to believe that such participation would have been possible if British Lieutenant General Sir Michael Jackson had not refused to carry out an early order by NATO Supreme Commander General Wesley Clark to move forces against the Russian troops that had raced to the Pristina airport. Without that episode of evident insubordination in the field, resolved only at the highest levels of the US and UK governments, even greater dangers to NATO-Russian relations would have been likely. Jackson's awareness of the risks in a situation both fluid and volatile helped salvage the dwindling possibilities for restoring the cooperation both sides had worked to achieve before the war.

One result of the Kosovo experience was less strange than it might have appeared. NATO's European members, properly disturbed by their continued inadequacies to cope with security crises in their neighborhood and perplexed by the disparity between their military capabilities and those of the United States, moved to bolster their ability to act independently in such cases. Among American observers, some feared that this initiative might undermine NATO, but the Europeans pledged to harmonize their efforts with the alliance structure and decision-making processes. Selection of NATO Secretary General Javier Solana to lead the European foreign and defense initiative was designed to reinforce that commitment.

In any event, enhancing European military capabilities would take years. It was an open question how this new departure in European security arrangements would relate to the need to revive a valid working relationship with Moscow. But it was no secret that in some quarters and to some degree the European members of NATO were determined that the alliance not remain quite so dominantly an American organization. They were struggling to balance the classic NATO function of keeping the Americans in Europe with the need for the Europeans to play a role in security policy commensurate with their economic and political standing.

In that struggle there were points of convergence between Western European views and those of Russia. France was not the only NATO ally that worried about aspects of US policy. Absent the threat of a monolithic Soviet empire, even among allies appreciative of American leadership there was latitude for, and an incipient inclination toward mixed emotions about, entrusting too much authority to the 'sole superpower' that sometimes seemed to believe the myth of the 'unipolar moment'. As Samuel Huntington and other astute analysts noted, the dynamics of world politics made any such moment, if it existed at all, highly perishable, as other states found it important to coalesce in ways designed to temper the proclivity of any dominant power, well, to dominate.[12]

With the security compulsions of the Cold War diminished, that counterbalancing phenomenon is encouraged by clashes of interest in nonsecurity realms. The American preoccupation with domestic issues that marked the Clinton era was matched by Europe's rising self-absorption in economic problems and in the further development of the European Union's common institutions. The net result was not to displace NATO as the principal transatlantic link, but to open some daylight for differences of view and emphasis among allies that had generally been suppressed during the decades of the Cold War standoff with the USSR.

One topic on which France and other European allies shared Russian worries about US policy was Washington's revival of steps toward active defense against ballistic missiles. Without the concurrence of its allies, but responsive to powerful political pressures in the United States, the Clinton administration committed itself to decide on deployment of an anti-ballistic missile (ABM) system by the end of its term. Congressional demands for such a deployment erupted to new heights after two major events in 1998: the publication of the so-called Rumsfeld Report and the launching of a long-range rocket by North Korea.

While it did not make a specific recommendation regarding missile defenses, the Rumsfeld Commission found evidence that proliferation of long-range missiles to several 'rogue' regimes could take place much sooner than previously expected.[13] Within a matter of weeks the North Korean launch punctuated that warning. Even though independent evaluation by former US Air Force Chief of Staff General Larry Welch and other experienced military professionals cautioned against a 'rush to failure' by premature deployment of inadequately tested technology, President Clinton committed the government to reach a decision after only a few tests of a complex hit-to-kill system – and in the midst of a presidential election campaign. If technical skeptics found the technology dubious, political skeptics thought the timing had as much to do with denying an issue to Republicans as with confidence that the decision to deploy was ripe.

Whatever the factors influencing the US movement toward fielding an ABM system, the alarm in Russia was highly vocal. Washington offered repeated assurances that the ABM plan would focus on limited threats that might emerge from such states as North Korea, Iran and Iraq, and that it would be configured to avoid threatening Moscow's still-massive strategic deterrent. The administration was striving to map a path that did not disrupt the possibility of continued reductions in US and Russian offensive nuclear forces, but dealt effectively with the worrisome implications of missiles and weapons of mass destruction in the hands of the Kim Jong-Ils and Saddam Husseins of the world. From the American strategic point of view, looming proliferation of such capabilities to those types of regimes posed grave dangers, both globally and regionally. From a Russian perspective, however, a modest deployment of active defenses against rogue state missiles was hard to distinguish from a foundation to build more substantial defenses that would erode Russia's deterrent – and pose serious impediments to the drastic reductions in missiles that a cash-starved Moscow was proposing for the two principal nuclear powers.

Apart from concerns about strategic stability, the revived interest in ABM provoked deep anxiety, not only in Russia, about the impact of such deployments on arms control. Even the limited deployment advertised by the United States, beginning with perhaps 100 interceptors based in Alaska but with the likelihood of a second tranche of 100 to follow, would be incompatible with the 1972 Anti-Ballistic Missile Treaty's ban on a national missile defense. The treaty provided for possible amendments, and the United States sought repeatedly to engage Russia in negotiations to make such amendments.

In its resistance to tinkering with the ABM Treaty, Russia found much sympathy among America's NATO allies. France, Germany and others worried that changing the treaty could ignite a new competition in nuclear arms and further damage the fragile structure of arms control that had contributed much to Europe's more auspicious security environment. The French had particular apprehensions that, if the ABM Treaty collapsed, the burden on its own *force de frappe* deterrent would increase. In a situation made less predictable by the possibility of both a competition in defenses and an abandonment of reductions in the major nuclear arsenals, it would become more difficult for France to exercise the restraint it (as well as Britain and China) contemplated in its own nuclear forces. The economic and political consequences of pressure to allocate additional resources to defense spending were daunting for a country wrestling with chronic high unemployment and other problems. These considerations helped explain the vigorous arguments against any hasty steps on ABM that President Jacques Chirac presented directly to President Clinton. The sense that the United States was leaping before it looked, that it was not fully taking account of allied interests, persuaded France and others to join Russia in advocating a UN endorsement of the need to maintain the ABM Treaty as a cornerstone of international stability.

The international reaction on the ABM issue was amplified by the dismay that greeted the US Senate's refusal to ratify the Comprehensive Nuclear Test Ban Treaty, for which the United States has labored since the Eisenhower administration. The Senate's action affronted not only President Clinton, but also Chirac, British Prime Minister Tony Blair and German Chancellor Gerhard Schröder, all of whom appealed to senators to avoid such a dire result. Unless that blow to the worldwide nonproliferation regime was reversed or somehow softened, it would compound the damage threatened by US proposals to weaken the ABM Treaty. Broadly speaking, NATO's European allies and Russia held a common view of US action on those issues as provocative and verging on irresponsible. That discontent did not mean the unraveling of the alliance, but neither did it augur well for deference to American leadership.

What one sees in this partial review of the interplay between Russia and NATO is a complex pattern of tensions and cross currents, interests that diverge and converge at various points, problems that simultaneously spawn friction and invite common approaches.[14] To some scholars and policymakers, it matters little whether Russia cooperates willingly with NATO and the United States; at any rate, Russian cooperation on security and political affairs is worth too little to pay a significant price to win. For the foreseeable future Russia is weak, the West is strong. Russia needs international investment, economic modernization and access to the world market – none of which it can attain without Western assistance or acquiescence. It cannot afford to compete in a revived strategic competition with the United States and therefore, even if the US ABM deployment proceeds, it has no alternative to the continued shrinkage of the nuclear arsenal it inherited from the Soviet era. Why pay Russia, the implicit argument goes, to do what its circumstances compel it to do anyway?[15]

The superficial appeal of that *realpolitik* calculation is undeniable. Russia's leaders face stark and intimidating choices, with little room for maneuver. As they operate in a political system with the trappings but not yet the full substance of democracy, and in an economic system whose transition is heavily freighted with debilitating corruption, self-interest should point those leaders toward an accommodating posture toward NATO. Yet it takes no deep reflection to know how often leaders are drawn to act against their interests – at least as perceived by others.

Russia's brutal intervention is Chechnya is a case in point. Even while acknowledging Russia's right to deal forcefully with terrorism within its own borders, the United States and European countries were appalled at what they saw as excessive and counterproductive force. Although it seemed offensive to those who characterized NATO's operations in Serbia as discriminating and precise, Russians portrayed their second military assault in Chechnya as in key respects analogous to the Kosovo war – long-range artillery and aerial bombardment of Chechen rebels designed to minimize Russian casualties. Lacking the precision-guided weapons employed by the United States in the Balkans, however, the Russian destruction of Grozny was far more costly to civilians caught in the maelstrom. Yet Moscow's action in Chechnya was a notable demonstration that the Russian government was prepared to disregard the general verdict of other states about how it should proceed in the region – and that the government could gain wide political applause among the Russian electorate for doing so.[16]

One should not ignore the evidence of rising nationalism and anti-Americanism that may reinforce the Russian government's willingness to defy Western preferences even at the price of acting against what others assert is its own interest. Without suggesting a comparison on the merits of the cases, one recalls many episodes of a state pursuing measures that others depicted as clearly contrary to its interests: America's closest allies argued that US intervention in Vietnam was against its interest; Israel has been admonished for years that its treatment of the Palestinians was against its interest, even while Arab states were told that attempts to isolate Israel were against their interest.

So what? one may argue. If Russia chooses to act against its interest in ways that obstruct relations with NATO, let it pay the price in lost economic opportunities and greater political isolation. That easy inclination disregards the leverage that Russia retains and the options it has to obstruct US and NATO objectives. Both in terms of promoting a stable Europe based on democratic institutions and market-oriented economies, and in terms of wider strategic considerations, there is need for a balanced engagement of Russia, not an indifference to the course it follows at home or abroad.[17] If that guiding insight is not always clear to Americans, it is very vivid in the minds of European statesmen. Few things would do more to alienate NATO Europe from the United States than an American policy that Europeans blamed for sacrificing the opportunity to forge cooperative relations with Russia.

An obvious lever for Russia's countervailing power is its permanent, veto-carrying membership in the UN Security Council. At a time when many American politicians are impatient with the United Nations, viewing it as a frequent obstacle to unilateral American action, there remains deep-seated sentiment in most parts of the world that major decisions on security need to be taken through UN procedures. One already sees in the *de facto* collaboration among France, China and Russia to urge changes in the sanctions imposed on Iraq the increased difficulty that the United States faces in building the necessary Security Council consensus to deal with matters vital to US security. For crises yet to come, the ability to act effectively through the Security Council will be extremely important.

There are many opportunities for a hostile or resentful Russia to impose costs on the United States. Recent contacts among Russia, China and India reveal a shared determination to find means to resist what they perceive as a too assertive American policy, as well as what they see as vaulting NATO ambition to operate beyond the territory defined in its treaty. Commercial and strategic interests play in these channels, as Russia's need to market its modern weaponry matches Chinese and Indian desires to upgrade their military capabilities. It will be said, correctly, that *rapprochement* among weak states is not a serious or immediate threat to NATO or to US security arrangements in other regions. That short-term fact should not obscure the long-term potential of those states, individually and collectively, to become strong enough to pose troublesome security dilemmas. One of the profound lessons of the Cold War is that exploiting short-term advantage can be very costly in lost opportunities to define more durable mutual advantage for the long haul.

Nor should complacency blind one to the capacity even of a weakened Russia and its associates to complicate already difficult situations in their neighborhoods. Moscow's incentives to do so are likely to grow when Georgia's distinguished leader, Eduard Shevardnadze, lauds the Kosovo intervention as a model for reversing the ethnic cleansing that has occurred in his vicinity. They are bound to be heightened still more when Azerbaijani authorities begin to speak of relocating a NATO air base from Turkey to their territory. Coupled with Western competition for privileged access to Central Asian oil and related maneuvers over pipeline routes, NATO's developing links with former Soviet republics in the Trans-Caucasus and Central Asia are seen as inflammatory schemes to encircle Mother Russia.[18]

The recent shocks to Russia's relations with the United States and NATO have already combined to produce adverse policy tremors in Moscow. Bluster it may have been, but Boris Yeltsin's agitated reminder that Russia is a state with many nuclear weapons conveyed the profound irritation of a nation that finds itself confronted with numerous red lines drawn by others while none of its own red lines is being respected. The calamitous decline of Russian military capability, accompanying the degeneration of the nation's economy, has triggered significant changes in strategic doctrine. With its conventional forces in disarray and under severe stress, Russia has altered its longstanding pledge not to be the first to use nuclear weapons in the event of conflict.[19]

Ironically, Russia has now embraced a version of NATO's longstanding threat to use nuclear weapons if it was faced with defeat at the conventional level. Throughout the Cold War, NATO felt it necessary to compensate for what it thought was inferiority to Soviet conventional capabilities by threatening to escalate any conflict to the nuclear level. Unlike NATO's doctrine of flexible response, however, because of the grievous state of Russian conventional forces, in reality Moscow's doctrine is likely to be one of inflexible response. The revival of a threat of early use of nuclear weapons, this time by Russia, is a grim reversal of the trend toward diminishing the nuclear element in the strategic balance.

This ominous development is not solely a function of Russia's sense of a forward-leaning NATO bent on placing Russia at a strategic disadvantage, but one can hardly dissociate it from the rising fears that infect Moscow's attitude toward the alliance. If NATO proceeds heedlessly to enlarge its ranks to include the Baltic republics or Ukraine, there is every reason to expect Russia to move some of its theater nuclear weapons forward into Kaliningrad and Belarus.

Indeed, of all the options available to Russia to retaliate, if it chooses, for objectionable actions by NATO and the United States, its capacity to disrupt the process of progressive nuclear restraint is the most worrisome. In the event of a breakdown in the START process, it would be foolish to expect that the Russians will retire obsolescent nuclear weapons at the rate currently predicted. Even at great cost and at the risk of accidents in the forces, one must assume that the Russians will somehow husband the large payload MIRVed missiles that are scheduled to be dismantled under the START agreements. As one element in the equation, US pursuit of a limited ABM capability to cope with a potential small threat from rogue states could well result in the perpetuation of the vast threat that already exists in the Russian nuclear force, both strategic and theater. That is a dubious tradeoff, to put it mildly.[20]

Moreover, the current apprehensions about Russian nuclear and missile exports to other countries are likely to seem mild by comparison with the flows of such technologies that could occur in an environment of disintegrating arms restraint. Without Russian cooperation, the task of curbing proliferation of weapons of mass destruction could well become unmanageable.[21] The assurances Russia now offers that it will exercise prudence in nuclear sales to Iran, for example, are likely to dissolve under conditions of heightened tensions with the West and the greater need for export revenues. Missile collaboration with North Korea, a country still dependent on strapping together rather ancient Soviet technology to increase the range of its rockets, could well generate a more substantial threat to stability in East Asia.

Under those circumstances, Russia and China, despite their history of mutual suspicion, could be drawn into pragmatic arrangements to counter the alleged hegemonism of NATO's leader. Those arrangements might well involve even greater transfers to China of modern Russian arms than have already been planned.

Were matters to take so dire a turn, it is not at all certain that the effect would be to bind the NATO allies more closely together in the face of a new menace. Indeed, if the perception develops that insensitive or inept American leadership was largely to blame for the deterioration in the international security climate, it could well corrode the alliance. Thus, it is crucial to arrest the negative trends in relations with Russia and steer the relationship back toward mutual accommodation. With new leadership coming to authority in Russia and the United States, the moment is at hand to adjust some policies and advance fresh initiatives that hold promise of setting relations on a sounder course.

CHANGING SOME OF THE QUESTIONS

The arrival of a virtually unknown Vladimir Putin at the pinnacle of Russian power is at once unsettling and auspicious. Judging from his first pronouncements as Acting President in December 1999, Putin brings to office an intelligent awareness that Russia's overwhelming needs are to put its social, political, and economic house in order. Toward that awesome challenge he displays a capacity for self-criticism that augurs well. Needless to say, a politician's rhetoric does not always foretell what he will do, but the expectations Putin established in his opening statements point toward a concentration on reform in Russia, not xenophobic fear-mongering about foreign enemies as the source of his country's troubles. The fact that Putin's rise owed much to popular approval of his leadership in devastating the Chechen rebel strongholds has to cause concern, but until it is disproven by other behavior the premise of Western policy must be that he is a pragmatic nationalist with whom reasonable bargains are possible.[22] Those bargains can hardly be based on the notion that Russia will simply yield to US and NATO preferences without achieving some of its own objectives.

Three major paths toward common ground with Russia commend themselves. The first concerns the pace and character of any future enlargement of NATO. While the Baltic republics, Romania and some other countries have had their expectations of early entry kindled by repeated stress on the open-ended nature of enlargement, second thoughts are apparent even among many NATO expansionists. That is true especially in Europe, but one notes that 43 senators, among them a number who voted to accept Poland, Hungary and the Czech Republic as allies, also supported ratification language calling for delay in further admissions. It is not plausible that the Clinton administration would abandon the now-habitual rhetoric depicting the enlargement process as open, of indefinite scale, and practically inevitable, but it is important to buy time to explore ways to re-orient any future expansion in the least provocative directions.[23] That argues for giving the alliance the full opportunity to integrate the first three countries from the former Soviet bloc.

It also argues for reconsidering whether it is conceivable that Russia itself can be seen as a credible candidate for NATO membership. Charles Kupchan has made a convincing case that, if the process is truly an open one, it is important to make clear to Moscow that it, too, can aspire to membership. President Clinton and Secretary of State Madeleine Albright have stated repeatedly that eventual Russian membership is not precluded, although that idea sends shivers down some European spines. The Russians have often seemed indifferent to such a prospect, or at least reluctant to reveal any interest in pursuing the possibility. What that reluctance disguises is not evident. A firm judgment that Russia's security interests would be better served otherwise? A fear of rejection? Or a conviction that the US remarks are mere tranquillizers to soften Russian objections to the entry of others?

Nevertheless, the sharp decline in Russia-NATO relations makes it worth revisiting this question sooner rather than later. Early indications are that the Putin administration sees the need to restore working contacts with NATO.[24] Putin himself has alluded to eventual Russian membership in the alliance as a possibility, and his government has returned to sessions of the NATO-Russia Permanent Joint Council. If the new Russian administration manages to move the country toward meaningful democratic reform, NATO should offer specific overtures to demonstrate that, if the alliance is to be the arch in the architecture of European security, Russia will have an opportunity inside it, rather than outside it.

The second path toward recalibrating NATO's approach to Russia involves the accelerated movement toward enlargement of the European Union (EU), including Estonia and perhaps other Baltic states as candidates during the next decade. As many NATO supporters have argued, including former Secretary of State James Baker, the main need of the countries aspiring to alliance membership is economic modernization, not investment in military capabilities to qualify for joining a defense organization. That makes a compelling case for giving priority to EU enlargement before considering any further enlargement of NATO. The EU enlargement process is perceived as much less threatening in Russia, yet membership in the Union would embed new entrants in the web of Western institutions. With

Europe's commitment to bolster its own security capabilities as a compatible adjunct to NATO, EU membership implies gradual inclusion in a developing zone of stability that need not involve formal NATO membership.

To put another point on the matter, the hundreds of thousands of Kosovars who were returned to their homeland were not covered by the NATO Treaty. Whether or not a consensus can be built to offer Russia membership in the alliance, cooperation with Moscow will be facilitated by making clear that the EU process will be the pacing factor in future decisions on NATO expansion.

A third path toward forging meaningful cooperation between NATO and Russia must address the impending collision of views on nuclear arms control. The ABM dispute is at the heart of that problem and a fresh approach to resolving it is both necessary and possible. Dealing with the threat of missiles in the hands of reckless or unreliable states may someday require a comprehensive approach, but for the cases now anticipated it should be technically feasible to factor the problem into regional components. Studies by Richard Garwin and Theodore Postol have shown that it would be possible to defeat long-range missiles launched from North Korea, Iraq and Iran by using ground-based boost-phase interceptors deployed close to those territories. Putin has now invited discussion of this option and it could be decisive in opening the way to cooperative action on this issue. Regionally-oriented missile defenses based in the theaters of special concern would not jeopardize Russia's deterrent, nor would they constitute the infrastructure for the kind of national missile defense Russia fears the United States will deploy.[25] The adjustments they would require in the ABM Treaty would be less wrenching than those required for terminal or mid-course interceptors based on US territory. And such a factored defense would offer both technical challenge and political opportunity for the United States and Russia to cooperate actively in fielding it.

There is a promising basis for such collaboration in the agreement reached in 1998 by Clinton and Yeltsin to provide continuous exchange of early warning information on missile and space launches throughout the world. Yeltsin then spoke of his excitement that the plan would 'set up on the territory of Russia a joint center' for this purpose. Implementation of the early warning agreement has faltered in the face of rising tensions between Washington and Moscow, but the concept could provide a starting point for a different concept of cooperative defense. In the specific case of North Korea, high-velocity interceptors based on nearby Russian territory or in adjacent waters could be more capable of suppressing long-range missiles than interceptors based in the continental United States. Such a deployment can also be configured to assure China that it would not jeopardize the PRC's deterrent or require Beijing to expand it in major degree. Toward that end, China should also be invited to cooperate in aspects of any US-Russian defenses against North Korea.

Postol's analysis has shown that similar options exist for interceptors based in the Caspian area or Turkey to defeat potential future missile threats from Iraq or Iran. The key to such a system is prompt launch detection, agile and fast interceptors, and proximate deployments able to exploit the vulnerability of large missiles during the few minutes of their boost phase when they cannot be hidden by decoys or other countermeasures.

A crucial distinction between this concept for factored missile defense and current plans is that it could provide Russia with security comparable to that sought for the United States. In a sense, the idea is a practical variation of Ronald Reagan's suggestion that defense against ballistic missiles should be shared with Russia. It offers substantially more negotiating room to define a common approach. Informal, preliminary discussions with Russian experts indicate that changing the question in this way holds much promise. The threat of missile proliferation, though problematic in its timing and potency, is not one to be ignored. The dictate of prudence is that it be addressed in a manner that does not compound or perpetuate other dangers, particularly those associated with the existing arsenals.

Nothing would better serve to dampen the impulses of states moving clandestinely toward weapons of mass destruction or missile capabilities than the emergence of active Russian-American cooperation to defeat those efforts. Such collaboration could lend vital impetus to the restoration of the desired engagement between Russia and the West. Several leading proponents of ABM deployment, notably Senators Chuck Hagel (Republican-Nebraska) and Gordon Smith (Republican-Oregon), have called for a delay in committing to a system, thereby allowing the next administration to consider the matter. That wise counsel would allow time to begin exploring with Russia the possibility of a joint approach to defenses along the lines sketched here.

As this essay has discussed, missile defense is but one of the elements bearing on Russia's relationship with NATO and the United States. It is, however, one on which an accelerated timetable for the deployment of a US system could prejudice other aspects of the relationship. In weighing how to proceed on all the main issues in the relationship – future enlargement of the alliance, the connection between EU and NATO expansion, further restraints on strategic nuclear forces, and the need to relate NATO actions

to UN procedures – the guideline could well be the one formulated five
years ago by Robert Blackwill in a Trilateral Commission report: 'There is
no problem on the continent that is not made more manageable through
Russian cooperation, and none that does not become more intractable if
Moscow defines its interest in ways that oppose Western interests.'[26] Unless
the United States and its NATO allies pay that insight more than lip service,
stability in Europe and beyond will remain precarious.

NOTES

1. *U.S.-Russian Relations at the Turn of the Century*, Report of Carnegie Endowment for
   International Peace Working Group on U.S.-Russian Relations, Washington DC, chairman
   Arnold Horelick; and *Russian-American Relations at the Turn of the Century*, Report of the
   Council on Foreign and Defense Policy (CFDP) Working Group on Russian-American
   Relations, Moscow, co-chairmen Sergei Karaganov and Yuli Vorontsov. Both reports were
   published by the Carnegie Endowment for International Peace in Feb. 2000.
2. Jonathan Dean, *Ending Europe's Wars: The Continuing Search for Peace and Security* (NY:
   Twentieth Century Fund Press 1994) pp.55–106.
3. Off-the-record meeting attended by author.
4. A prescient view of the dilemmas NATO expansion would present is Coral Bell, 'Why an
   Expanded NATO Must Include Russia', *Journal of Strategic Studies* 17/4 (Dec. 1994)
   pp.27–41, also in Ted Galen Carpenter (ed.) *The Future of NATO* (London and Portland, OR:
   Frank Cass 1995).
5. Dale R. Herspring, 'Expanding the Alliance: The Military Factor', in Susan Eisenhower (ed.)
   NATO at Fifty: Perspectives on the Future of the Atlantic Alliance (Washington DC: Center
   for Political and Strategic Studies 1999) pp.151–68.
6. James M. Goldgeier, *Not Whether But When: The U.S. Decision to Enlarge NATO*
   (Washington DC: Brookings 1999) especially pp.36–40. See also Susan Eisenhower, 'The
   Perils of Victory', in Ted Galen Carpenter and Barbara Conry (eds.) *NATO Enlargement:
   Illusions and Reality* (Washington DC: Cato Inst. 1998) pp.103–19; Jonathan Dean, 'NATO
   Enlargement: Coping with Act II', in ibid. pp.121–7; Stanley Kober, 'Russia's Search for
   Identity', in ibid. pp.129–41; and Anatol Lieven, 'The NATO-Russian Accord: An Illusory
   Solution', in ibid. pp.143–56.
7. Raymond L. Garthoff, 'NATO and Russia: Looking to the Future', in Eisenhower (note 5)
   pp.211–16.
8. Gernot Erler, 'Russia's Role in Europe and the Russian Security Concerns', in Eisenhower
   (note 5) pp.205–10.
9. Russia was not the only country concerned about the change in alliance doctrine. Regarding
   the widespread wariness to NATO's new posture, the US Information Agency published
   extensive reports of international reactions. See US Information Agency, 'NATO Summit
   Results: Promulgation of "A Dangerous New Doctrine"', 3 May 1999, edited by Katherine
   L. Starr, which assembles diverse commentary from several continents.
10. Howard Baker Jr, Alton Frye, Sam Nunn, and Brent Scowcroft, 'NATO: A Debate Recast',
    New York Times, 4 Feb. 1998; and Alton Frye, 'Precursor to NATO Enlargement',
    Washington Post, 4 March 1998.
11. Oksana Antonenko, 'Russia, NATO and European Security After Kosovo', *Survival* 42/4
    (Winter 1999–2000) pp.124–44.
12. Samuel P. Huntington, 'The Lonely Superpower', *Foreign Affairs* 78/2 (March–April 1999);
    and Robert F. Ellsworth and Dimitri K. Simes, 'Imposing Our "Values" By Force',
    Washington Post, 26 Dec. 1999. Agence France Presse, 'Russia Accuses US of Brainwashing
    the World', 17 Feb. 2000 quotes Gen. Ivashov speaking in Geneva: 'The US are
    brainwashing the world... Even Russian people are being brainwashed.' He raised the

prospect of 'a very dangerous cold war' with Russia, India and China united against a Western 'diktat policy'.

13. The Rumsfeld Commission, chaired by former Defense Secretary Donald Rumsfeld, submitted its report to Congress as *Report of the Commission to Assess the Ballistic Missile Threat to the United States*, 15 July 1998, Pursuant to Public Law 201, 104th Congress.

14. Andrew J. Pierre, NATO at Fifty: New Challenges, Future Uncertainties (US Institute of Peace Special Report, Washington DC, 22 March 1999); and Dimitri V. Olshansky, *The Disintegration of Russia – A View From Within* (Potomac Foundation, McLean, VA, Oct. 1999) pp.33–4.

15. Typical of such perspectives is the Center for Security Policy Decision Brief no. 00-D 6, 17 Jan. 2000, 'Beware the "Grand Compromise": Arms Control Deal Threatens Effective U.S. Missile Defenses, Nuclear Deterrence'. According to one passage, 'Economic realities seem likely to compel the Kremlin sharply to reduce its obsolescing nuclear arsenal, regardless of the bellicosity of its rhetoric or doctrine. We do not necessarily want to follow suit, though.'
    The Center's earlier Decision Brief no. 98-D150 of Aug. 1998 was already arguing that point as a basis for rejecting negotiated reductions in US strategic forces: 'The fact is, however, that the Russian Federation cannot maintain its current forces over the long-run, while the United States clearly can… The Russian Federation is now an economic basket case that cannot support its current strategic forces.'

16. Mark Kramer, 'Putin is Only Part of the Russian Picture', *Washington Post*, 23 Jan. 2000.

17. Dimitri K. Simes and Paul J. Saunders, 'A New Course for NATO: Toughness with Restraint', in Eisenhower (note 5) pp.39–44.

18. James Brusstar, 'Russia and Its Neighbors: Faltering Progress?' in *Strategic Assessment 1999: Priorities for a Turbulent World*, Institute for National Strategic Studies (Washington DC: National Defense Univ. 1999) pp.89–100.

19. Michael Wines, 'Moscow Issues New Policy Emphasizing Nuclear Arms', *New York Times*, 15 Jan. 2000.

20. Andrew Kuchins, 'US-Russian Discussions on Strategic Stability', Center for International Security and Cooperation, Stanford University, *CISAC Monitor* (Autumn 1999) pp.1–2.

21. Stephen Blank, 'Russia As Rogue Proliferator', *Orbis* 44/1 (Winter 2000) pp.91–108.

22. Harvey Sicherman, 'Yeltsin's Legacy and Putin's Plans', Foreign Policy Research Institute E-Note, 18 Jan. 2000.

23. Roland Dannreuther, 'Escaping the Enlargement Trap in NATO-Russian Relations', *Survival* 41/4 (Winter 1999–2000) pp.145–64.

24. Col. Gen. Leonid Ivashov, head of Russian Defense Ministry international military cooperation department: '… there is no alternative to Russia-NATO cooperation and Moscow is ready to restore relations with the alliance'. RFE/RL Newsline, 31 Jan. 2000. Michael Wines, 'Russia and NATO, Split Over Kosovo, Agree to Revew Relations', *New York Times*, 17 Feb. 2000, reported Putin's decision gradually to restore formal relations with the alliance, but comments by Foreign Minister Ivanov and Russian defense ministry sources made clear that Moscow would maintain a stiff attitude in dealing with NATO.

25. Theodor A. Postol, 'A Russian-US Boost-Phase Defense to Defend Russia and the US from Postulated Rogue-State ICBMs', Briefing at the Carnegie Endowment for International Peace, 12 Oct. 1999.

26. Robert D. Blackwill, Rodric Braithwaite, and Akihiko Tanaka, *Engaging Russia* (NY: Trilateral Commission 1995) p.24.

6

NATO's 'Fundamental Divergence' over Proliferation[1]

KORI SCHAKE

Even as Western leaders and NATO advocates breathe a sigh of relief that the alliance held together during the 1999 bombing of Serbia, a new crisis is brewing in NATO with more important implications for the alliance's core missions. The problem is how to address the proliferation of weapons of mass destruction and their delivery vehicles. The failure of non-proliferation regimes is the central issue in US defense debates, and consensus is growing in favor of building military defenses against ballistic missiles. America's European allies are openly opposed to this assertive, military-oriented approach. They believe the United States is overstating the threat of weapons of mass destruction (WMD) proliferation. They also fear 'decoupling', with a protected United States destabilizing the beneficial strategic status quo that has allowed the European states to focus their attention on the challenges of creating an Economic and Monetary Union in the European Union (EU) and managing smaller-scale problems in the Balkans.

European leaders have been resisting efforts to make proliferation a major focus of NATO defense efforts since at least 1994, when the United States pushed proliferation onto the NATO agenda. The divergence between European and American attitudes became apparent in October 1999 with the inability of the Clinton administration to persuade the Senate to consent to ratification of the Comprehensive Test Ban Treaty; horrified European reactions extended so far as to suggest that the United States had become a rogue state.[2] America's European allies want the United States to be bound by an approach to security problems that stresses the consensus rule of international norms and the primacy of deterrence and arms control to manage proliferation. A different consensus is growing in the United States, however

– one that believes this approach is negligent, given the magnitude of the threat to America's homeland and military forces posed by proliferation.[3]

The difference in views is more than simply another NATO crisis to be weathered through extensive consultation and papered over in careful language that preserves alternative interpretations. Countering proliferation will dominate the US policy debate in the months leading up to the expected 2000 decision on whether to proceed with deploying a national missile defense. The decision will likely be delayed until a new presidential administration takes office in January 2001, but it is almost certain to be in favor of deploying national missile defenses.[4] It is difficult to imagine a president of either political party choosing not to spend $15 billion over ten years (out of a defense budget of $270 billion per year) to try to defend America's territory.

However, the United States cannot construct a national missile defense without the active participation of several NATO allies on whose territory are stationed essential radars.[5] At a minimum, Canada, Denmark, and the United Kingdom hold vetoes over America's ability to create a national missile defense system and will need to concur with the US policy. The conflict cannot be avoided, and it is conceivable that America's allies will actually prohibit use of their territories for the purpose of collecting radar data for use in tracking and destroying ballistic missiles attacking the United States.

The transatlantic relationship would collapse if America's allies prevented us from defending our national interests and our territory. It would amount to a refusal by the NATO allies to honor the alliance's Article 5 commitment to consider an attack on one member as an attack on all. Perhaps even more important, it would poison the good will and political commonality that make credible the treaty's terms.

How can this destruction of the alliance be avoided? Several steps need to be taken.

First, gain Russian acceptance of US policy, which would make European claims about instability more difficult to sustain.

Second, include in a missile defense arrangement any ally who participates in the functioning of the system and its supporting intelligence collection.

Third, offer to assist European allies in developing their own national missile defenses and share theater missile defenses to diminish European concerns about 'decoupling' a less vulnerable United States from a Europe that would be more threatened by the larger nuclear forces likely to be developed by Russia, China and other potentially hostile states.[6]

Fourth, seriously and consistently make countering proliferation – and allied resourcing and compliance with counterproliferation plans – a priority in NATO.

Fifth, support the development of strategic intelligence collection and assessment capabilities by European allies and institutionally by the European Union (EU).

Sixth, create a US-EU mechanism for sharing information on proliferation threats in the EU's 'justice and home affairs' channels. This will give an incentive to address proliferation to European governments for whom the ever closer union of the EU is a higher priority than are defense issues. A policy along these lines could successfully bridge the gap between the United States and its European allies on proliferation.[7]

AMERICAN THREAT PERCEPTIONS

While concern about ballistic missile and WMD proliferation has been a substantial factor in US threat assessments since the Strategic Defense Initiative in the 1980s, the 1998 Rumsfeld Commission Report on Ballistic Missile Threats to the United States greatly heightened concern about proliferation in US defense circles. The bipartisan Rumsfeld Commission reached four major conclusions:

- 'Concerted efforts by a number of overtly or potentially hostile nations to acquire ballistic missiles with biological or nuclear payloads pose a growing threat to the United States, its deployed forces, and its friends and allies;'
- North Korea, Iran and Iraq could inflict major damage on the United States within five to ten years of a decision to acquire the capability;[8]
- US intelligence community is incapable of determining when proliferant states might have made the decision to acquire WMD and long-range delivery systems;
- North Korea could reach major US cities in Alaska and Hawaii with its current inventory of Taepo Dong missiles – and could modify existing platforms to reach most areas of the United States.[9]

These findings were generally supported by the 1999 National Intelligence Estimate on ballistic missile threats and the United States Commission on National Security in the Twenty-First Century.[10] Other responsible US analysts conclude that two dozen countries are actively pursuing nuclear, biological and chemical weapons programs, and more than a dozen of those have operational ballistic missile programs. According to Robert Joseph and John Reichert of the Center for Counterproliferation Research, 'given the growing availability of dual-use technology and alternative suppliers, a determined proliferator of even modest resources is likely to succeed'.[11]

The erratic North Korean regime's August 1998 test of a three-stage Taepo Dong missile variant that flew over the Sea of Japan (attempting to put a satellite into orbit), construction of hardened underground facilities, and record of proliferating WMD technologies to additional states have made the political and national security consequences of proliferation shockingly real to the United States and many of its Asian allies.[12] The North Korean test reminded Americans not only of the growing vulnerability of US territory, but also of the cost of leaving American territory unprotected while maintaining an interventionist policy in support of US and allied interests.[13]

Expert evaluations of the rate and magnitude of WMD proliferation, coupled with North Korean missile tests, have galvanized concern inside the US government. Secretary of Defense William Cohen rates proliferation of advanced weapons technologies with military or terrorist uses second only to large-scale, cross-border aggression in his evaluation of threats to the United States.[14] The Department of Defense has been sufficiently concerned with countering proliferation that the 1997 Quadrennial Defense Review allocated an additional $1 billion in this area over the next five-year budget cycle.[15]

US COUNTERPROLIFERATION POLICY

Washington's approach to countering the threat of WMD proliferation continues long-standing US use of a variety of diplomatic means to persuade countries not to acquire WMD and threats to use its military power in response to any attack on US territory, forces, or allies. However, US policymakers have concluded that these traditional approaches are insufficient. More assertive measures are necessary because non-proliferation regimes appear to be breaking down in regions of critical interest to the United States. Evidence of that unsettling development includes:

- India and Pakistan have tested nuclear weapons;
- the status of North Korea's programs remains a concern as does Pyongyang's transfer of technology to other regimes hostile to the United States;

- both Russia and China continue to make commercial sales of nuclear power generators and missiles to Iran.

Revelations about Iraqi and North Korean nuclear programs since 1991 have badly eroded confidence that international agreements and inspection regimes can detect and monitor proliferation. The behavior of Iraq and North Korea has also impaired confidence that states hostile to the United States are likely to abide by agreements even if they can be persuaded to become signatories. These developments have reduced reliance on arms control agreements and international nonproliferation regimes in US security policy.[16]

US policy to counter proliferation currently has four major elements:

- deterring the use of WMD by threatening retaliation;
- shoring up, where possible, non-proliferation regimes;
- improving passive defenses to protect troops and respond to attacks; and
- developing active defenses to prevent effective use of WMD.[17]

Indications are that this basic approach would be supported by administrations of either political orientation. For example, defense and foreign policy experts associated with Republican presidential nominee George W. Bush, such as Condoleezza Rice and Robert Zoellick, consider proliferation a central US concern and would have it figure significantly in policies toward Russia and China.[18]

The element of US policy certain to cause greatest concern to allies is the development of active defenses, particularly ballistic missile defenses. In January 1999, the Clinton administration allocated $6.6 billion to build a network of radars and interceptors for a first phase national missile defense, and committed itself to decide in 2000 whether to deploy a national missile defense. Because the system is predominantly concerned with ballistic missiles emanating from North Korea, Iran or Iraq rather than Russia or China, the main location for the 100 interceptors is slated for Alaska. A more comprehensive deployment of an additional 100 missiles at a second location, along with advanced radars and space-based sensors is envisioned subsequently.[19] The system would be deployed between 2005 and 2010, at an estimated cost of $10.5 billion.[20]

THE RUSSIA PROBLEM

Such a system would not be compliant with the current constraints of the 1972 US-Soviet (now Russian) Anti-Ballistic Missile Treaty. Originally, the

ABM Treaty limited the United States and Russia to two missile defense sites each with 100 interceptors. Overseas radars – specifically, radars in the US early warning system located in Thule, Greenland, and Fylingdales, UK – were permitted to remain but were 'grandfathered' so they could not be replaced. The treaty was amended in 1974 to reduce the number of sites to one for each party; the Soviet Union deployed its ABM system around Moscow, the United States around missile sites in North Dakota.

The ABM Treaty would require three modifications for a system like that envisioned for the United States in the near-term.

First, there would need to be a protocol allowing the United States to move its single national missile defense (NMD) site to Alaska.[21]

Second, the United States would need latitude to upgrade and expand its network of overseas radars. Radars at Thule and Fylingdales would need both software and hardware improvements to provide sufficient data, and a radar would need to be constructed somewhere in Asia to provide coverage from the Pacific direction.

The most difficult modification to the ABM Treaty is related to Article I, which states that neither the United States nor Russia may create the basis for a territorial defense. A national missile defense would seem to contradict Article I. The United States has always maintained that Article I could not be violated unless other provisions of the treaty were also violated; and the fact that Russia will continue to have the ability to overwhelm the envisioned US ballistic missile defense system may provide a sufficient basis to convince Russia that a limited US system does not constitute a 'territorial defense' in the terms of the treaty.

Negotiations are underway to gain Russian acceptance of modifications to the treaty; to encourage Russian cooperation, the administration is offering a START III treaty with reductions of strategic nuclear warheads down to 2,000 each for the United States and Russia.[22]

The Russian government was, not surprisingly, hostile to any amendment to the ABM Treaty – especially since initial consultations occurred simultaneous to Russia's disagreement with the West over Kosovo. During those exchanges, Russian negotiator Gregory Berdennikov said: 'We see no variants which would allow the United States to set up a national ABM system and still preserve the ABM Treaty and strategic stability in the world.'[23] Whether former Russian President Boris Yeltsin's claims of an 'anti-NATO' alliance with China materialize, Russia and China do appear to be cooperating on the ABM issue, in military programs, in the United Nations Security Council, on the issues of Taiwan and Iraq, and on other issues contrary to US interests.[24]

As early as August 1999, then Prime Minister Sergei Stepashin said that Moscow recognized that the US desire for missile defenses resulted from proliferation to 'complex, difficult regimes' rather than from US concerns about Russia.[25] Despite President Putin's June 2000 rejection of the Clinton administration's proposals, it remains likely that Russia will eventually agree to changes in the ABM Treaty. Russia will need to continue reducing its own nuclear arsenal because of funding and safety concerns. Thus it would seem manifestly in Russia's interest to maintain some treaty-based constraints on US offensive and defensive systems. Moreover, given the extent of Russian strategic nuclear forces – and the insurance policy of a very large inventory of tactical nuclear weapons (which number in the tens of thousands) – an attack could still overwhelm the envisioned limited US ballistic missile defenses. US officials also appear to be negotiating on the basis that either Russia allows the United States the flexibility to deploy a limited defense or the United States will withdraw from the Treaty.[26] If amendments to the ABM Treaty were coupled with additional reductions in strategic nuclear forces and a public commitment to the value of mutual vulnerability between Russia and the United States, it seems likely that Russia will accede.[27]

EUROPEAN CONCERNS

Ironically, the Russians may be more easily persuaded than the NATO allies to support the deployment of ballistic missile defenses. The transatlantic problem of countering proliferation is that the United States and Europe view the problem and its solution in very different terms – indeed, in terms that are mutually exclusive.

By and large, European political leaders view their countries' security as assured. The four wars of Yugoslav secession were unquestionably a horrific reminder that 'war is possible in Europe', and an affront to European values, but they were not wars that threatened the territory of NATO countries. Their sense of security is reflected in the Europhoria that has blossomed after the Cold War: remember Luxembourg Foreign Minister Jacques Poos stating that the European Union would handle the collapse of Yugoslavia because 'this is the hour of Europe, not of the United States', or German Foreign Minister Hans-Dietrich Genscher's desire for Europe to move from 'power politics to a politics of responsibility in Europe'.[28]

It is reflected in their indulgence of institutional competition for advantage between NATO and the European-controlled security venues of the European Union and the Western European Union.

It is reflected in the continuing downward pressure on defense budgets in European capitals. Despite NATO's Defense Capabilities Initiative, most European members of NATO reduced their defense spending by around four per cent in 1999, and Germany recently announced a seven per cent reduction in its defense budget, with further reductions expected.[29]

In contrast to US perceptions of a dangerous world, America's European allies tend to view the strategic situation as relatively stable and beneficial to their interests, with significant warning times to address any threat that may evolve.

Different transatlantic perceptions of the proliferation threat do not account for all of the difficulty on the missile defense issue, however. Many European defense experts acknowledge the proliferation threat. Joachim Krause of the German Society for Foreign Affairs assessed in 1995 that proliferation was serious enough to warrant NATO action because of threats to NATO territory, military forces operating outside the NATO area, shifts in regional power balances, regional instabilities, erosion of international norms, danger of accidents, and new dimensions of terrorism.[30] French President Jacques Chirac, British Prime Minister Tony Blair, and German Chancellor Gerhard Schroeder stated in October 1999 that 'our greatest concern is proliferation of weapons of mass destruction, and chiefly nuclear proliferation. We have to face the stark truth that nuclear proliferation remains the major threat to world safety.'[31]

Even as they agree in assessing the threat of proliferation, however, the overwhelming majority of European defense experts and political leaders fundamentally disagree with the assertive and defense-focused US approach to managing the problem. Europeans are concerned that the US approach is destabilizing to the status quo that is so beneficial to their security. Secretary of Defense Cohen has explained European concern with US policy by saying, 'the fact is our European allies see this [the ABM Treaty] as one of the few remaining strategic stabilizing factors that we have'.[32]

European analysts are more likely than their American counterparts to raise concerns about missile defenses spurring arms races.[33] Their views in the current debate over ballistic missile defenses are also colored by the predominant European belief that the Reagan administration's Strategic Defense Initiative was a reckless endangerment of Washington's European allies. America's NATO partners remain much more wedded to arms control as the major means to address proliferation and are more concerned about Russian responses.[34]

NATO AND PROLIFERATION

Under considerable US pressure, NATO formally recognized proliferation as a threat in 1994, and proceeded to develop an Alliance Policy Framework and two senior-level groups to monitor the political and defense aspects of countering proliferation.[35] The Senior Politico-Military Group on Proliferation addresses the traditional diplomatic and deterrent components of counter-proliferation policy (SDGP).

NATO's Senior Defense Group on Proliferation focuses on the military capabilities necessary to effectively manage proliferation. The SDGP concluded in 1996 that 'greatest emphasis should be placed on core, integrative capabilities that would make the most substantial contributions ...strategic and operational intelligence; automated and deployable command, control and communications; wide area ground surveillance; stand-off/point biological and chemical agent detection, identification and warning; extended air defences, including tactical ballistic missile defence for deployed forces; individual protective equipment for deployed forces'.[36]

These capabilities were then translated into force goals through the NATO defense planning process in 1997.[37] Force goals are specific requirements, proposed by NATO military commanders and agreed to by nations, which accumulate into the five-year NATO defense plan and by which member states' national fulfillment of their respective alliance defense commitments is measured every year.

However, NATO was never seized with the threat of proliferation and has not remained focused on countering proliferation. Even though NATO's 1999 Strategic Concept states that 'the Alliance's defence posture against the risks and potential threats of the proliferation of NBC (nuclear, biological and chemical) weapons and their means of delivery must continue to be improved, including through work on missile defences', US diplomats concede that it is probably weaker than the 1996 NATO endorsement of counterproliferation.[38]

In fact, very little has actually been achieved in NATO on the proliferation issue. The alliance's proliferation force goals have not been met. The NATO Military Committee assesses that NATO's capability to counter proliferation is likely to remain low. The problems associated with creating a NATO Weapons of Mass Destruction Centre are illustrative. The Centre was approved at the 1999 NATO summit to 'improve coordination of all WMD-related activities at NATO headquarters, as well as strengthen non-proliferation related political consultations and defence efforts to improve the preparedness of the Alliance'.[39] However, the WMD Centre is not only not yet established, its functions have not even been agreed upon.

EUROPEAN DEFENSE INITIATIVES

To the extent that Washington's European allies are concerned with defense issues, the Balkans and building a European security and defense identity crowd out all other prospects. The European allies are focused on developing a small core of forces capable of deploying outside their home territory for peace and support operations. That European militaries were structured to fight on home territory with the support of civilian infrastructure was long known, and the problems associated with 'main defense forces' were amply demonstrated during European involvement in Bosnia.[40] However, the shocking degree of Europe's dependence on the US military to conduct high-intensity warfare that employs high-technology weaponry to increase effectiveness and reduce casualties has motivated a new interest – at least for the moment – in building better European forces.

NATO Secretary General George Robertson asks why Europe maintains such large forces when only two per cent of European forces could deploy to Kosovo, and those only with difficulty and substantial assistance from the United States.[41] Recent meetings of European leaders dedicated to defense have focused on giving the European Union an autonomous capacity for decisionmaking.[42] Military capabilities identified for improvement are intelligence, lift, command and control, and making the Eurocorps into a reaction force – the kinds of improvements that would replicate the conventional capability to intervene in the Balkans under conditions consistent with past conflicts.[43] The scathing criticism of Europe's failure to understand the nature of its challenges at the end of the Cold War by Oxford University's Timothy Garton Ash could well merit repeating if Europe focuses on building peacekeeping forces instead of imagining and addressing emerging security threats such as proliferation.[44]

America's European allies have dedicated themselves to the goal of being able by 2003 to deploy a corps (50,000–60,000 troops) within Europe, given 60 days of preparation.[45] The missions assigned to the force will be limited to the so-called Petersburg tasks: humanitarian assistance, peacekeeping, and peace enforcement – but not combat.[46] Given that the European NATO members are a collection of states with a gross domestic product greater than that of the United States, and with already very capable military forces consisting of over two million troops, this is a very modest ambition. In addition, these forces are for the non-Article 5 mission of projecting stability rather than for the direct defense of NATO territory, which countering proliferation addresses.

US DEPENDENCE ON ALLIED SUPPORT

On most issues, the United States and its European allies could agree to disagree or create another of the creative NATO 'dual-track' decisions that could be interpreted in mutually exclusive terms by different NATO states. However, missile defenses will require active participation by at least three other NATO members. Even if the United States were willing to brook open conflict over policy on proliferation with its NATO allies, it cannot build a national missile defense without the consent of its allies.[47]

Radar sites essential to a national missile defense for the United States are located in Denmark and the United Kingdom. And the United States is strategically bound to Canada through the joint command structure of the North American Air Defense Command (NORAD). For this reason, the United States has already conceded that it will only make decisions on a national missile defense system after full consultations within NATO.[48]

ACTIONS THAT NEED TO BE TAKEN

What then must we do? The United States is beginning to create the groundwork for a common policy by sharing information with allies through NATO, and by adopting an incremental approach to ABM Treaty adaptations in response to European concerns.[49] However, much more must be done to avoid a serious crisis in the transatlantic relationship. Specifically, the following six policy initiatives would probably be adequate to move proliferation into the category of manageable and perennial NATO crises.[50]

Gain Russian Acceptance. As the matter of first priority, the United States needs to get Russia at least to countenance changes to the ABM treaty. If Russia, as the major country affected by alterations to the ABM Treaty and a formerly powerful state now faltering in its efforts to secure its interests, could accept the US approach, European allies would have a difficult time vetoing Washington's actions.

A package of initiatives that included reassurances for Russia, reductions in strategic nuclear systems, and a face-saving way to alter the ABM Treaty would likely suffice. As Brookings Institution scholar Michael O'Hanlon has persuasively argued, it will be essential to reassure Russia that the United States has abandoned any pursuit of nuclear superiority. The means needed to give Russia that assurance include: unilaterally reducing US strategic force levels, reducing alert levels of US nuclear forces, assisting Russia in rebuilding its early-warning network, and collaborating where possible on national missile defenses.[51] Given the importance to US security of countering proliferation and the importance Europeans accord to Russian concerns, other incentives may also be worth considering, if necessary to gain Russia's acceptance.

Protect Participating States. Allies that provide key nodes for any missile defense system are understandably concerned about becoming targets, since the most effective way to attack the system would be to destroy radars that provide targeting information. Those allies (Canada, Denmark, and the United Kingdom) should have their concerns addressed as a priority in US efforts to build a consensus for a missile defense system. Given that they will be sharing the risk of deploying a missile defense, they deserve to share the benefit.

Any ally that participates in the functioning of the system and its supporting intelligence collection should be included in its protection. Even if those allies will not contribute to the financial costs of developing and deploying a missile defense, they should ultimately be offered its protection, since they hold a veto over US deployment of a national missile defense.

Assist Development by Other Allies. Allies that do not provide facilities critical to the functioning of a US national missile defense should not be allowed to become free riders on American efforts, though. There is no compelling reason for the United States to underwrite European states equally at risk from proliferation unless their cooperation is necessary to build and operate a US missile defense system. Washington should not countenance European claims that the United States is creating zones of greater and lesser security within the alliance. Zones of differing security have always existed in NATO; Germany as a front-line state during the Cold War was always more vulnerable than Canada. And it remains within the power of states concerned about becoming more vulnerable to take action to reduce their vulnerability. They can choose to develop their own national missile defenses or buy into the US system. The United States should assist allied states in that effort but not absolve them of responsibility for paying the costs of their own security.

Several NATO nations are already involved in theater ballistic missile defense programs intended to protect alliance troops during operations. European allies have already crossed an important threshold in choosing to protect their troops; what is needed now is a political choice to extend to their populations and territories the protection being offered their military forces.

Make Proliferation a NATO Priority. The United States is not without blame in NATO's failure to make more progress in assertively addressing the threat of proliferation. In his Annual Report to Congress, Secretary Cohen identified two key Department of Defense counterproliferation challenges: institutionalizing counterproliferation as an organizing principle in all US defense activities, and 'internationaliz[ing] those same efforts to ensure US allies and potential coalition partners train, equip, and prepare their forces to operate with US forces under NBC [Nuclear, Biological and Chemical] conditions'.[52]

Yet harnessing NATO's strength to counter proliferation has received only sporadic attention by US leaders. Despite pressing for creation of the NATO WMD Centre, the United States has not followed up with policy implementation. By contrast, within the same amount of time in 1994, the United States had the equally controversial Partnership for Peace well underway conducting field exercises.

The United States has allowed the shortcomings in European conventional military forces to become the sole focus of European defense efforts. Secretary Cohen has frequently upbraided European allies to increase their defense spending and restructure their forces. However, preparing to counter proliferation has not figured in any of these appeals; they are all focused on producing more cost-efficient forces for operations like Kosovo.[53]

Deputy Secretary of State Strobe Talbott reinforced this tunnel-vision with his castigation of Europe's performance in Kosovo in which he stated that 'never again should the US have to fly the lion's share of risky missions in a NATO operation and foot by far the biggest bill'.[54] This is certainly true, but it justifies Europe's sole focus on the last war. Admiral James Ellis, NATO AFSOUTH Commander, raised as a primary concern in his review of NATO operations in Kosovo how the alliance would have reacted to Serbia's attacking NATO allies with ballistic missiles.[55]

By allowing Europe to perfect its ability to conduct the Petersburg tasks within Europe using a force of 50,000–60,000 troops, the United States is not helping Europe to come to terms with the equally important challenges of countering proliferation. The rate at which ballistic missiles and weapons of mass destruction are proliferating, and the attraction of asymmetric strategies to adversaries of the West, suggest that the next NATO operation could well have to address both conventional military operations and the use of WMD by NATO's adversary. Certainly NATO operational planning will have to include these prospects.

The United States approved NATO's 2000–2004 defense program, with its predominant focus on the Kosovo-related conventional warfare priorities of the Defense Capabilities Initiative. While the internal NATO report is critical of the lack of allied progress, public NATO documents contain no mention of the failure to meet proliferation force goals. To the extent that the report of NATO defense ministers discusses counterproliferation at all, it is solely in terms of support for arms control.[56] The NATO report contains no mention of the failure to meet proliferation force goals. To the extent that it discusses countering proliferation at all, it is solely in terms of support for arms control. Washington needs to send a much clearer and stronger signal to its European allies about the value of countering proliferation.

Develop Better European Intelligence Systems. Part of the gap in perceptions about proliferation results from the smaller scale and lack of coordination among European intelligence programs. Europeans simply do not see what the United States does because they lack the intelligence assets to provide such information. The wide chasm in intelligence capabilities between the United States and its European allies has resulted in a lack of trust in US intelligence assessments by the European governments. Europeans do not believe US threat assessments, whether about proliferation or other issues, such as evidence of Sudanese complicity in attacks on US embassies in the summer of 1998.

Better intelligence assets would allow Washington's NATO allies to replicate and validate the factual basis of US assessments. While disagreements over interpretation would certainly occur (they routinely occur within and among US intelligence agencies), in the aggregate better European intelligence is likely to produce more agreement between the United States and Europe on the nature of threats to Western security.

In addition to improving national intelligence collection and assessment capabilities, the United States should also support greater intelligence cooperation in the EU. With the exceptions of modest multilateral satellite programs and the EU's Policy Planning and Early Warning Unit, intelligence collection and assessment by the European countries remain jealously guarded in national channels.[57] It is difficult to mask the sensitive sources and methods by which intelligence is gathered; this problem has restricted intelligence sharing within NATO. However, states that have placed themselves under the mutual authority of a collective Council of Ministers to the degree that EU members have already done in order to create a common currency and economic union, or end border restrictions among themselves, should be able find ways to share intelligence information.

EU intelligence collection and assessment will duplicate capabilities already existing in NATO – violating the Clinton administration's 'three D's' policy: opposition to duplication, discrimination and decoupling in efforts to build a European security and defense identity. That is a risk worth accepting, however, because the current distribution of power within NATO on intelligence issues is not conducive to cooperative policies or beneficial to either European or American interests. The United States should be bold enough to want strong allies, even at the risk of duplicating valued and valuable assets, rather than retaining allies because of their weakness.

A European Union Role in Countering Proliferation. European supporters of more robust European defense efforts argue that centering efforts in the EU rather than NATO will capitalize on momentum gained in the economic and monetary union. They suggest that EU defense spending convergence criteria or standards of performance (which have long been part of the NATO defense planning process but have not produced much action) may build more support for improving defenses and allow peer pressure of the kind that effectively kept EU states within government spending limits specified in the Maastricht treaty.[58] If that argument holds, the United States should also engage the EU in efforts to manage proliferation. The EU has a functioning mechanism that could be used to gather and assess information on proliferation threats and coordinate operations by intelligence services and law enforcement officials.

The 1985 Schengen Agreement among several EU members established a basis for cooperation among police, customs, immigration and judicial authorities that 'will drive a new wave of European integration'.[59] The Agreement commits signatories to:

- remove internal borders;
- tighten external frontiers;
- develop common policies on asylum, immigration, and visas;
- exchange information on migration; and
- cooperate in police affairs.

The Schengen Agreement started a process of common policies and common action that is likely to result in a 'European judicial space'.[60] By 1997 the Schengen information system contained 14 million records, and national authorities in the Schengen countries posted 5.5 million alerts in 1997 alone.[61]

A second EU invention, Europol, has been authorized to act in 'preventing and combating terrorism, unlawful drug trafficking and other serious forms of international crime where there are factual indications that an organized structure is involved.'[62] While Europol currently consists of only 200 staff with a $30 million annual budget, it holds great promise as a basis for conducting and coordinating investigations and operations. It may be that US interests are better served by working with the EU on a bilateral basis to counter proliferation rather than working through NATO, and the prospect should be carefully explored.

These six policy prescriptions would put the US and European approaches to proliferation on a cooperative, sustainable, and productive track. It is urgently important to both the United States and Europe that we create a transatlantic basis for managing the threat of proliferation. The United States cannot proceed in assertively countering proliferation unless it convinces European states whose participation is essential for an effective national missile defense to support the American approach. At the same time, Europeans can ill afford to have the United States cease to value the transatlantic security community on which Europe's security relies. Fortunately, the means for creating a common approach seem to lie within reach, if the United States moves quickly to build a sound approach to countering proliferation that maximizes the likelihood of allied support.

NOTES

1. French President Jacques Chirac, British Prime Minister Tony Blair and German Chancellor Gerhard Schroeder warned on the eve of the Congressional vote on the Comprehensive Test Ban Treaty that 'rejection would also expose a fundamental divergence within NATO'. See Chirac, Blair and Schroeder, 'A Treaty We All Need', *New York Times*, 8 Oct. 1999.
2. For an example of this characterization, see the cover and lead article in *The Economist*, 16 Oct. 1999.
3. For the most detailed and sensible assessment of missile defenses, which on balance supports deploying defenses, see Michael O'Hanlon, 'Star Wars Strikes Back', *Foreign Affairs* 78/6 (Nov.–Dec. 1999) pp.68–82.
4. While some have suggested that the unsuccessful 19 Jan. 2000 missile intercept could postpone the decision on whether to proceed with a decision, Secretary Cohen has asserted that the president will still decide in the summer, and the Department of Defense is programming money in the FY 01 budget for NMD. Bill Gertz, 'Cohen Touts Missile Test's "Near Miss"', *Washington Times*, 29 Jan. 2000.
5. The United States could, however, construct an autarchic national missile defense if it either redirected design of the interceptor missiles to reduce radar information requirements or relied on space-based sensors. Neither change is envisioned in the US national missile defense plans.
6. The CIA considers larger forces, penetration aids and countermeasures to be likely responses to US development of missile defenses. National Intelligence Council, *Foreign Missile Developments and the Ballistic Missile Threat to the United States Through 2015*, Sept. 1999, p.5.
7. The recommendations are focused on alleviating specifically European concerns about ballistic missile defenses. The concerns of Canada are similar in many respects but could well be more vexing to redress, given the unresolved differences in opinion between Canada and the United States over such issues as banning landmines.
8. Specifically, North Korea and Iran were judged to be within five years, and Iraq within ten years.
9. Rumsfeld Commission on Ballistic Missile threats [see p.110, note 13] pp.5–6, 11, 20–21.
10. National Intelligence Council, *Foreign Missile Developments* (note 6) p.5; The United States Commission on National Security / 21st Century, *New World Coming: American Security in the 21st Century* (Washington DC: 15 Sept. 1999) p.3.
11. Robert G. Joseph and John F. Reichart, *Deterrence and Defense in a Nuclear, Biological and Chemical Environment* (Washington DC: Inst. for National Strategic Studies 1996) p.4.

12. Steven Lee Myers, 'Missile Test by North Korea: Dark Omen for Washington', *New York Times*, 1 Sept. 1998.
13. Steven Mufson, 'Korean Missiles Push US Defense Plans', *Washington Post*, 5 Sept. 1999, p.6.
14. William S. Cohen, *Annual Report to the President and the Congress, 1999* (Washington DC: Government Printing Office 1999) p.2.
15. Ibid. p.19
16. For an excellent evaluation of the US failure to ratify the Comprehensive Test Ban Treaty, see Steve Cambone, 'An Inherent Lesson in Arms Control', *Washington Quarterly*, 23/2 (Spring 2000) pp.207–18.
17. Secretary of Defense William Cohen outlined this approach on Meet the Press, 23 Nov. 1997 (transcript p.9); Strobe Talbot basically outlined this approach in 'The State of the Alliance: An American Perspective', speech delivered at the 15 Dec. 1999 meeting of the North Atlantic Council, p.4. See the State Department website www.state.gov/www/policy_remarks/1999/991215_talbott_nac.html
18. Condoleezza Rice, 'Promoting the National Interest', *Foreign Affairs* 79/1 (Jan.–Feb. 2000) pp.46–7, 56, 59.
19. Bradley Graham, 'US To Go Slowly on Treaty', *Washington Post,* 8 Sept. 1999, p.13.
20. Bill Gertz, 'Cohen Sees Russia, US Allies as Hurdles to a Missile Defense', *Washington Times,* 5 Oct. 1999, p.1.
21. Alaska is the only site in the United States that provides adequate coverage of geographic areas of concern.
22. Secretary of Defense William Cohen, cited by Bryan Bender in 'Interview', *Jane's Defence Weekly*, 22 Sept. 1999.
23. Grigory Berdennikov, quoted in David Hoffman, 'Moscow Proposes Extensive Arms Cuts', *Washington Post*, 20 Oct. 1999, p.29.
24. Former Russian President Boris Yeltsin, cited in Ben Aris and David Rennie, 'Yeltsin Presses for Anti-NATO Alliance with the Chinese', *Daily Telegraph* (London), 26 Aug. 1999, p.1. See also Henry Chu and Richard C. Paddock, 'Russia Looks to China as an Ally Amid West's Ire', *Los Angeles Times*, 8 Dec. 1999, p.1.
25. Former Russian Prime Minister Sergei Stepashin, quoted in Alice Lagnado and Ian Brodie, 'Russia Angry Over Revived 'Star Wars' Plan', *The Times*, 18 Aug. 1999.
26. Commentators frequently discuss US abrogation of the ABM Treaty. This is inaccurate, or at least not necessarily accurate. The ABM Treaty contains a clause allowing either signatory to withdraw from the Treaty with six months notice. The United States could announce its intent and withdraw without violating the terms of the treaty. 'Treaty Between the United States of America and the Union of Soviet Socialist Republics on the Limitation of Anti-Ballistic Missile Systems', Article XV.2, printed in *Arms Control and Disarmament Agreements* (Washington DC: US Arms Control and Disarmament Agency 1982) p.142.
27. See the comments of Secretary of Defense William Cohen, in Bryan Bender 'Interview', *Jane's Defence Weekly*, 22 Sept. 1999.
28. Jacques Poos, quoted in Charles Grant, *Strength in Numbers: Europe's Foreign and Defence Policy* (London: Centre for European Reform 1997) p.7. Hans-Dietrich Genscher, 7 March 1989 speech to the Conference on Security and Cooperation in Europe, quoted in idem, *Rebuilding a House Divided* (NY: Broadway Books 1998) p.243.
29. Turkey and Greece are exceptions to this general NATO trend. Swedish International Peace Research Institute, *SIPRI Yearbook, 1999* (London: OUP 1999) pp.298–9. On German defense reductions, see 'The Week in Germany', 3 Dec. 1999 (German Information Center; reached at info@germany-info.org).
30. Joachim Krause, 'Proliferation Risks and their Strategic Relevance: What Role for NATO?' *Survival* 37/2 (Summer 1995) p.136.
31. Chirac, Blair and Schroeder (note 1).
32. Secretary of Defense William Cohen, quoted in Gertz, 'Cohen Sees Russia' (note 20).
33. Terry Taylor, IISS, quoted in 'Rogue States Raise Fears as Nuclear Arms Spread', *The Times*, 18 Aug. 1999.
34. Author's off-the-record discussions with European security experts in the second half of 1999.
35. *NATO at a Glance* (Brussels: NATO Information Service 1996) p.58.

36. Ibid. pp.60–1; see also Press Communiqué, M-NAC-2(95)118, Ministerial Meeting of the North Atlantic Council held at NATO Headquarters, Brussels, 5 Dec. 1995.
37. The United States viewed this 'off cycle' set of force goals as evidence of growing European support for countering proliferation and a major policy victory at the time.
38. *The Alliance's Strategic Concept* (Press Release NAC-S(99)65) para. 56.
39. Final Communiqué, Meeting of the North Atlantic Council in Defence Ministers Session held in Brussels, 2 Dec. 1999 (Press Release M-NAC-D(99)156) para. 20.
40. Main defense forces are the NATO categorization for units not required to be ready on short timetables, or deployable or sustainable away from their support bases.
41. Elizabeth Becker, 'After Kosovo, European Allies Discuss Modernizing Forces', *New York Times*, 22 Sept. 1999.
42. Anglo-French Summit Joint Declaration by the British and French Governments on European Defence, London, 25 Nov. 1999.
43. 74th Franco-German Summit Consultations: Statements by the Franco-German Defence and Security Council, Paris, 30 Nov. 1999.
44. Timothy Garten Ash, 'Ten Years in Europe', *Prospect* 1/43 (July 1999) pp.22–7.
45. Presidency Conclusions, Helsinki European Council, 10–11 Dec. 1999 (SN 300/00) p.6.
46. The Petersburg Tasks were identified at a 1992 meeting of the Western European Union Council of Ministers. Western European Union Council of Ministers, WEU Audit of Assets and Capabilities for European Crisis Management Operations, Luxembourg, 23 Nov. 1999.
47. Bradley Graham, 'US To Go Slowly on Treaty', *Washington Post*, 8 Sept. 1999, p.13.
48. Lord Robertson, quoted at NATO Foreign Ministers Meeting, cited on NATO home page, 4 Jan. 2000, http://www.nato.int/docu/speech/1999/s991215e.htm
49. Graham (note 47). Secretary Cohen briefed US concerns and policy at the Dec. 1999 NATO Defense Ministerial.
50. NATO expert Stanley Sloan has long argued that 'NATO in crisis' is the most consistent refrain since 1949.
51. O'Hanlon (note 3) p.81. Collaboration with Russia on NMB should proceed cautiously, however, given Russia's record of proliferating technologies. The United States would certainly not want to have Russia providing information on a US defensive system to the states against which it is designed to defend.
52. Cohen (note 14) p.19.
53. Secretary of Defense William Cohen, 'Europe Must Spend More on Defense', *Washington Post*, 6 Dec. 1999, p.27; see also Cohen comments in Tom Bowman, 'NATO Compiles Hits, Misses of Kosovo Campaign', *Baltimore Sun*, 14 Sept. 1999.
54. Undersecretary of State Strobe Talbott, quoted in David R. Sands, 'Talbott Scolds Europeans on Their Role in NATO', *Washington Times*, 8 Oct. 1999.
55. Briefing by Admiral James Ellis, NATO AFSOUTH Commander, cited in 'For US Commander in Kosovo, Luck Played Role in Wartime Success', *Inside the Pentagon*, 9 Sept. 1999, p.1.
56. Final Communiqué, Meeting of the North Atlantic Council on Defence Ministers Session held in Brussels, 2 Dec. 1999, NATO Press Release M-NAC-D(99)156, paras. 19–20; and Final Communiqué, Ministerial Meeting of the Defense Planning Committee and the Nuclear Planning Group, Brussels: 2 Dec. 1999, NATO Press Release M-DPC/NPG-2(99)157, para. 8.
57. Alessandro Politi, *Towards a European Intelligence Policy*, Chaillot Paper 34 (Paris: WEU Inst. for Security Studies, Dec.1998) p.1.
58. François Heisbourg, Centre for European Reform, *CER Bulletin*, June/July 1999, p.19; and Charles Grant, 'European Defence Post-Kosovo', Centre for European Reform Working Paper, June 1999.
59. Ben Hall, *Policing Europe: EU Justice and Home Affairs Cooperation* (London: Centre for European Reform 1999) p.1.
60. Ibid. p.29.
61. Ibid. p.30.
62. Ibid. p.31.

7

The Corruption of NATO: The Alliance Moves East

AMOS PERLMUTTER

NATO has survived longer than any other military-political alliance in the history of Europe. It was designed with clear political and military strategic objectives:

1. The deterrence of the Soviet Union; and
2. The resolution of the German problem.

The future of Germany was the central issue for European security throughout the Cold War. Divided Germany symbolized a divided Europe. The German question remained fresh in the minds of Europeans, especially the Russians, and was of great concern in view of the barbaric war that Nazi Germany conducted between 1939 and 1945. Yet the division of Europe between East and West did not lead to a stable peace.[1]

To guarantee that the emergent West German state would not pose a threat to Europe, the NATO alliance had to integrate Germany, politically and militarily, with the rest of Western Europe. In addition to protecting the security of Europe from German revanchism, the new alliance brought the United States into partnership with a West European alliance, which was absent during the years between the two world wars. An American nuclear monopoly was to shield Europe from an aggressive, Stalinist USSR and provide insurance against an unexpected German revanchism. Thus, American intervention and the creation of NATO, linking America and Western Europe, led to the stabilization of America's central strategic front – Europe.

The first Secretary General of the alliance, Lord Ismay, has been quoted as declaring that NATO means the Americans in, the Russians out, and the Germans down. According to that standard, NATO has achieved its purposes. Throughout the Cold War, it was essentially a military, collective security alliance system – an anti-Soviet political coalition of democratic, industrial welfare states. NATO marked the end of the historical European nation-state system that went back to the days of the Treaty of Westphalia (1648). It also brought an end to the traditional nineteenth-century concept of the balance of power. NATO symbolized a West European post-nationalist alliance..

The NATO alliance is different from previous military alliances in several ways. It no longer represents the military power of separate alliance members, but rather a forceful collective alliance. It no longer represents separate and narrow nationalist interests and aspirations of its members, but rather limits national sovereignty. At the end of the Cold War it was an open borders, grand democratic, West European alliance.

This multination federation in 40 successful years contributed to the collapse of the Soviet Union without firing a shot. That occurred despite the fact that there were ethnic challenges within individual member states of the alliance: for example, Irish in Great Britain, Walloons in Belgium, and Basques in Spain. The alliance did not surrender to ethnic minority protest movements, and it helped preserve the national sovereignty of the members of the political, military confederation.

One exception to NATO as an association of West European industrial, democratic states was the entry of Greece and Turkey into the alliance in 1952. Those two states were not part of the geography or the political development of Western Europe. In fact, Greece is in southeastern Europe and Turkey is divided between Europe and Asia – with most of its territory on the latter continent. The two states were invited into NATO mainly as partners against the Soviet Union, which was meddling in Greece after 1945. Hardly post-nationalist entities, they were passionately nationalist and less than full democracies, and Turkey had (and has) serious problems with its Kurdish minority, while Greece had significant problems with its Turkish minority. Nevertheless, neither Turkey nor Greece inherits all the dysfunctional properties that are characteristic of the post-1989 'new NATO'.

In the late 1980s, before the Soviet Union collapsed, a distinctly European security identity began to emerge. It took the form of an effort to relaunch the Western European Union (WEU) to provide an autonomous European capability. That effort culminated in the adoption of the Maastricht Treaty (1991). The drive reflected a growing European concern that, with the end of the Cold War, the United States would reduce its military forces in Europe. European leaders saw a need for a European

Defense Identity (EDI). This effort to establish a Eurocentric security system was driven by France, but it was not very successful and EDI was never more than an acronym.

The 1991 Gulf War awakened Europeans to their lack of military preparedness and the inferior nature of their weaponry compared to that of the United States. It became quite clear to the Europeans that they especially lacked capability in either strategic lift or electronic intelligence. The graphic nature of that gap in capabilities brought an end to the debate that had begun about the relevance of NATO. NATO emerged once again in the view of West European leaders as the institution that could best deal with European security.

Forty years of NATO success brought a peaceful end to the Cold War. Unquestionably, NATO's vigilance contributed considerably to halting Stalin's aggressions and blocking Soviet aspirations concerning Western Europe. As in any military organization, debates over purposes and actions continued throughout NATO's history. The political mission of NATO remained constant: to deter Soviet aggression in Europe; but how best to fulfill that mission, and with which military-type structure, were debated throughout the alliance's evolution. Revolutionary strategic concepts were introduced, such as the role of nuclear weapons. Such changes in turn required consideration about who would be in charge of the trigger, the idea of European participation in NATO's nuclear decisions, and above all, the credibility of the American nuclear umbrella. Issues of weapon modernization and troop deployment continuously challenged NATO. The French opted out of NATO's military component in 1966. That defection and the need to move NATO headquarters from Paris to Brussels were serious challenges. Yet NATO weathered all such difficulties.

At the end of the Cold War, the need for a debate about NATO's mission was obvious. Should the alliance come to an end now that the Soviet Empire had collapsed? Should it instead remain a small and cohesive military alliance of Western Europe and the United States? Or should it expand, incorporating the new nations of Eastern Europe? These were most serious issues, especially in view of the fact that over a dozen new nations were knocking on the doors of NATO, seeking integration. The role of the Soviet Union (and soon Russia as the principal successor state) was another significant issue. Should it be part of NATO, an associate, or kept completely outside NATO? All of these issues arose during the watch of President George Bush and his advisors. The position of the Bush administration concerning NATO is both interesting and revealing.

The administration's position was set forth concisely in the president's address to the 1990 Rome NATO Summit:

> The alliance is not an American enterprise nor a vehicle of American power. We never sought preponderance, and we certainly do not seek to keep it. Nor do we claim a monopoly on ideas for the alliance. If we did, none of us would be sitting here today, for the idea of the Washington treaty [establishing NATO] was Europe's.
>
> The United States has been, is, and will remain an unhesitating proponent of the aim and process of European integration. This strong American support extends to the prospect of a political union – as well as the goal of a defense identity.
>
> Even the attainment of European union, however, will not diminish the need for NATO... We support the development of the WEU because it can complement the alliance and strengthen the European role in it...But we do not see the WEU as a European alternative to the alliance.[2]

There were several reasons for the president's foray into a new strategy for NATO, but two were especially important. First, he was concerned that the end of the Cold War might bring an end to NATO's mission. Second, the President wanted to make sure that a united Germany would be part of NATO. On the latter issue, he succeeded in engaging a reluctant Chancellor Helmut Kohl of West Germany, who initially did not believe that he could secure from Soviet president Mikhail Gorbachev a united Germany in NATO – which had been a taboo for over a half-century of Soviet rulers. President Bush and his advisors thought otherwise and finally persuaded Kohl to join them in pressing Gorbachev to accept a united Germany within NATO.

Two years later, Secretary of State James Baker, during his visit to Moscow, listed his initiatives to transform the NATO alliance substantially and not threaten Russia. The Bush-Baker administration had decided to move NATO into the new era of East-West relations. According to former Bush administration official Robert Hutchings, the United States and its Western allies made eight assurances regarding legitimate concerns in Moscow arising from German unification:

- agreement to limit the size of the German armed forces;
- a commitment to negotiate on short-range nuclear weapons;
- reaffirmation of Germany's non-nuclear status;
- revisions of NATO strategy to make it less threatening;

- a transitional period for Soviet forces in Germany;
- German renunciation of any future territorial claims;
- strengthening the Conference on Security and Cooperation in Europe (CSCE) and the Soviet role therein; and
- extensive German economic assistance to Moscow.[3]

The London summit of August 1992 was a landmark for the transition of NATO. A new political mission was established: to combine with former adversaries; to change the character of conventional defense in favor of a mobile, multinational force; and, finally, to establish a new nuclear strategy, reducing the reliance on nuclear weapons and modifying the 'flexible response' regime that had governed NATO strategy since 1967.

The central dominating issue during the final years of the Bush administration, and lingering into the first Clinton administration, was NATO's post-Cold War vision. One possibility was that it would remain an *Atlanticist vision,* as advocated by the United States and Britain, requiring a permanent US military-political presence in Europe while accommodating an increasing assertiveness in the European community now that the rivalry with the Soviet Union and Eastern Europe no longer existed.

Another vision, known as the *European vision,* was championed by France and especially the EC bureaucracy known as 'Brussels'. That vision looked toward a more cohesive European community, widening political and economic relations between its members, and an objective of incorporating and accepting new members. The Brussels bureaucracy advocated a gradually diminishing role for the North Atlantic Alliance during the transition period from the old NATO to a 'new NATO'.

A third version was advocated by the pan-Europeans, advocates of a stronger CSCE. This group was the most dedicated to European integration. At the opposite end of the spectrum, a fourth vision, known as the *'Europe of States',* was openly embraced by British Prime Minister Margaret Thatcher – unbeknownst to other Western leaders, according to Hutchings. Hers was a neo-Gaullist conception of Europe, which was restricted to Great Britain and never found a home in the Continent, except when Charles de Gaulle reigned in France.[4]

None of these visions was explicitly adopted, and the 'new NATO' remained in limbo. What was clear is that an interregnum period of transition was taking place. The Bush administration, rather than calling for a specific NATO vision, preferred what Hutchings called a more ambitious goal – a 'New World Order' in which NATO would play a leading role. The Americans sought a more pragmatic transitory solution for an opening to the

East under a new concept of Partnership for Peace (PFP). It was never entirely clear what PFP meant, except that it was an effort to reassure the Central and East European states, now liberated, that they would not be abandoned or isolated.

To advocate the immediate integration of East and Central Europe into NATO, however, was a monumental political and diplomatic task for which the Bush administration was not prepared. Moving from the historical NATO to a 'new NATO' needed a great effort to persuade American domestic opinion, especially in Congress, of the need to change NATO's mission. The Bush administration, busy and deeply engaged in the Persian Gulf crisis, exhausted all of its political capital on that issue, leaving the future of NATO on the sidelines.

Nevertheless, governments have to show they are attending to the nation's security needs and, therefore, NATO could not be left in limbo. The Bush administration therefore embraced the Partnership for Peace concept, sponsored by Senator Sam Nunn (Democrat, Georgia), then chairman of the Armed Services Committee. It was an idea halfway between integration and isolation of the newly freed, Western-oriented nations of Central and Eastern Europe.

NATO'S ATTENTION MOVES EAST

The events that would follow the collapse of the Soviet Union in 1991 overwhelmed Western visions, aspirations, and plans for European security. The success of NATO's 'winning' against the Soviet Union without firing a shot was so stunning that it paralyzed statesmen in the United States and the European Union (EU). The breakdown of the empire from within was not predicted by even the most visionary American or European statesmen. Unprepared for the Soviet collapse, and shackled by the tasks of NATO strategy, it would become inevitable that the Partnership for Peace phase would pass rapidly into a new phase: NATO extension.

Neither the Rome summit nor the Maastricht Treaty settled the fundamental questions regarding the future of the West European nations. The Eurocentric vision conflicted with the Atlanticist vision on how to support of the newly independent states of the former Soviet empire. The debate was over such ambitious ideas as creating an all-European security council.[5] These were efforts to integrate the East into pan-European structures, short of extending NATO. In the CSCE, an all-inclusive body of 35 members during the last years of the Cold War, the addition of a few East European states would not produce as serious a political impact as integrating the East European countries into an overtly military organization: NATO. But making the CSCE the primary organization for European integration raised other issues. If CSCE was a political alliance, then what was NATO? Should it remain an alliance, or should it become something different from what its framers created?

The PFP did not resolve or satisfy the anxieties of the East Europeans, who sought to influence Congress and American public opinion, bombarding them with the need for NATO extension. NATO membership became almost a magic talisman to the East Europeans – symbolizing their acceptance into the West, represented by its democratic, liberal societies. No other form of integration would be acceptable. The East Europeans demonstrated willpower, determination, and unusual political savvy, drawing the West European governments and the administrations of Bush and Clinton into their orbit on the issue of expanding NATO. In the minds of the East Europeans, liberation meant inclusion in NATO. PFP would never satisfy either as a transitory solution or one that could become permanent; without expanded NATO membership, there would be a wall between NATO and Eastern Europe. But expansion of NATO eastward inevitably entangled the alliance in the many volatile disputes that still exist in Central and Eastern Europe.

Ethnic minority conflict has been a way of life since World War I in East-Central Europe and the Balkans. Civil wars have been endemic. The withdrawal of the USSR from its empire, and the subsequent collapse of the Soviet Union itself, unleashed the forces of raw nationalism. Political disorder and newly independent minorities disrupted interstate relations. The case of Slovakia seceding from Czechoslovakia in 1992–93, although bloodless, was the beginning of what would become more ominous divisions in Eastern Europe. The Armenian–Azeri struggle over Nagorno-Karabakh is ongoing, as are the wars in Georgia, Dagestan, and Chechnya. And there are many other flashpoints. There are significant minorities of Hungarians in Romania who have suffered economic and cultural discrimination under the Romanian regime. There are ethnic Turks in Bulgaria and Germans in Poland. There are 25 million Russians in the Baltic states, Ukraine, Moldova, and Kazakhstan.

The breakdown of Yugoslavia represents the most serious threat by ethnic groups to the stability of Eastern Europe. NATO extension strengthened the power of Hungary and encouraged the Hungarians in Romania to seek the protection of NATO's newest member. That could mean – as in the case of Yugoslavia – NATO involvement in another ethnic conflict in Eastern Europe. At the very least, the situation throughout much of Eastern Europe is unpredictable. NATO extension has facilitated the mobilization of ethnic groups and their capacity for political action, thereby contributing to instability in the area.

Western officials pressing for the next NATO extension round intend to incorporate the Baltic states.[6] Expansion into the Baltics guarantees a direct challenge to Russia – and post-Chechnya Russia will not likely tolerate another US-led intervention in East European affairs.

In addition to ethnic conflict, there is the legacy of the Communist apparat. Authoritarian elements from the Communist era still control the administrative bureaucracy, including the military, the intelligence agencies, and the educational system in most Central and Eastern European countries. All three of NATO's newest members, even the much praised Czech Republic, have alarmingly weak civil societies and less than robust democratic political cultures. The situation is even worse in the candidates for membership in the next round. Admitting fragile, unfinished democracies to NATO may undermine the prospects for long-term freedom and stability. NATO might also have to face the embarrassment (or worse) of dealing with a member that had regressed into authoritarianism.[7] Illiberalism still dominates much of this part of Europe. The rule of law is still not guaranteed and, with the exception of Russia, all former republics of the dissolved Soviet Union are run by former Communist apparatchiks (except, of course, for the three Baltic republics). This has become a familiar story in Central and East European countries that have emerged from communism. The former apparatchiks have retained their political and economic power and acquired considerable clout in the post-Communist era.

The short-run consequences of NATO extension have already included damage to the conduct of American foreign policy. Since the NATO intervention in Kosovo, US-Russian relations, already wounded by the first round of expansion, have gone even further downhill. As Ted Galen Carpenter warned in a *Washington Times* op-ed nearly four years ago, 'expanding the alliance to Russia's borders threatens to poison Moscow's relations with the West and lead to dangerous confrontations. Extending security commitments to nations in Russia's geopolitical "back yard" virtually invites a challenge.'[8]

NATO extension and NATO intervention in Kosovo have led to the creation of a new Russian-Chinese anti-American entente. The Russians have a $1-billion bilateral military sales agreement with China, according to *Washington Post* correspondent John Pomfret, and 2,000 Russian technicians are employed in Chinese research institutes. Pomfret writes,

'China and Russia are moving toward a closer security relationship largely in response to what they see as growing American hegemony around the world. This concern was spurred by US global military and economic dominance, NATO expansion into Eastern Europe, and what Beijing and Moscow view as US use of the United Nations as a foreign policy tool.'[9]

As a result of NATO's intervention in Kosovo, Russia's security doctrine has also changed. Defense correspondent Mark Kramer writes, 'There is no question that the document [October 1999 doctrine] marks a major departure from the previous Concept on National Security, which had been in effect since December 1997. Instead of referring to a "partnership" with the West, the new doctrine condemns alleged American efforts to dominate other countries…' Kramer concludes that the significance of Kosovo, NATO expansion, strategic arms control, and Chechnya is "evident" in the October document, which is confrontational. 'More important than the document itself, which may well remain a largely bureaucratic piece of paperwork is an understanding of the factors that precipitated its drafting. We should not allow our focus on leadership politics and personalities to detract from a sound understanding of the forces driving Russia's new security policy.'[10]

One cannot exaggerate the diplomatic surprise caused by the collapse of the Soviet Union and its empire. No short-or-long run US or NATO plan was even in sketch form for a nonviolent end of the Warsaw Pact. The policy shelf was full of options to deter a Soviet attack on Western Europe and ideas on how to make sure that NATO's integrity would be preserved under different orientations of key European states and regimes. NATO's response during the political crisis caused by Moscow's deployment of cruise missiles in the 1980s, reflecting the unrelenting Soviet effort to weaken the alliance and make it politically irrelevant, was typical of the kinds of challenges alliance leaders anticipated. The rapid, chaotic collapse of the Soviet Union was never considered in US or allied strategy.

US-Russian policy was deeply linked with US-European policy. Europe was America's strategic front: the conventions of nuclear force, the equal partnership, the flexible response doctrines, all were directed to total deterrence of the Soviet Union. There were no NATO plans for strategic operations *with* the Soviet Union. The left-wing German Social Democrats and various Polish Communist moderates tried and failed to establish a non-NATO, non-nuclear, secure Europe to be based on a pragmatic understanding between NATO and the Soviet Union. But any effort to accommodate the Soviet Union, even détente, did not change the structures and purposes of NATO. If détente meant coming to terms with Russians, it did not mean the dissolution of NATO. What kept NATO consolidated was precisely the American attitude that it represented the European-American common strategic structure; that one could not exist without the other; and any contact with Russia could unglue the alliance.

Beginning in 1989, and certainly after 1991, the United States had to rearrange its Russian policy. To formulate a new policy toward Russia, now that the Cold War had ended, demanded that NATO planners had to think of the following: how to reassure and bring Eastern Europe closer to the EU and NATO, but also how to bring Russia, as a new non-Communist European state, into security relationships. PFP was designed to be the solution, and the creation of the North Atlantic Cooperation Council (NACC) was directed to bring about the integration of Eastern Europe into NATO.

> The objective was to bring the new democracies of Central and Eastern Europe, particularly the Visegrad group [Poland, Hungary, the Czech Republic, and Slovakia], closer to the alliance, while also providing a forum for more regular interaction with the Soviet Union. Instead of irregular visits and exchanges, we had in mind an entirely new institution that would bring NATO allies and former Warsaw Pact adversaries together in a forum for political consultation and defense cooperation. Trying to square the circle between Soviet sensibilities and Central and Eastern European nervousness, we devised a formula that would treat all former Warsaw Pact members equally as a formal matter but would in practice be highly differentiated in favor of the new democracies.[11]

The features of the NATO-Russia Founding Act of 1997 were already evident by January 1995. Russia reluctantly accepted NATO's expansion and put conditions similar to those of Gorbachev concerning the unification of Germany: (1) there should be no nuclear weapons in the new Eastern European member states of the new NATO, and (2) there should be no NATO troops stationed in those states. According to an in-depth study of the process of NATO expansion by James M. Goldgeier, 'President Clinton was playing a difficult balancing game in 1995: assuring the ethnic communities that NATO enlargement was moving forward and that Russia had no veto, but also assuring Yeltsin that he was moving slowly and transparently.'[12]

NATO AND PARTNERSHIP FOR PEACE

The Partnership for Peace concept was formally approved in Brussels in January 1994, offering the East Europeans tangible security benefits. PFP states could participate in NATO peacekeeping exercises in UN or Organization for Security and Cooperation in Europe (OSCE, the re-named CSCE)-sponsored humanitarian operations. Institutionally, the PFP officers were given offices in NATO headquarters so that they could take part in planning and coordination under European command. They were also consulting with NATO over planning, military procurement, and civilian-military relations.[13]

The significance of PFP requirements for participating states were left deliberately vague, even if forces from such countries were to be combined with NATO forces for joint exercises and (possibly) for some missions. No firm security guarantees were offered to PFP states. The requirements did, however, accomplish two major goals: strengthening military assets within the OSCE states and creating functional programs to meet specific needs instead of simply providing a forum for consultation. Senator Nunn stated that:

> The NATO summit will build upon the NACC by formally endorsing 'Partnership for Peace' (PFP), a US-sponsored initiative calling for NATO military cooperation with any interested non-NATO European state. While the PFP does not entail the immediate extension of alliance security guarantees beyond the territory of NATO's current 16 members, it does envisage such cooperative military activities as disaster relief and peacekeeping operations, training exercises and planning aimed at raising non-NATO military establishments to NATO standards. The PFP also obligates NATO members to consult with NACC members who feel threatened by an external adversary, and implies NATO membership down the road for those countries meeting as yet undefined political and military criteria.[14]

Senator Nunn at the time was hoping that the PFP concept would buy both NATO and prospective members time to think more about the future of the alliance. After all, these were nations that had had contact with NATO only as adversaries. The senator was wise in wanting to allow more time for any form of NATO extension. Nunn emphasized that, for one thing, the orientation of Russia must be made more certain, having in mind not to provoke Russia. He was hoping that the idea of PFP could serve as a warning to 'aspiring imperialists in Russia' that 'the choice of a cooperative or confrontational relationship with the United States and NATO would depend on Russia's direction'.[15] PFP was, therefore, an effort to define NATO's purposes in the post-Cold War era without necessarily offending Russia.

Also, 'the PFP could place Russian and the Ukraine on the same prospective [partnership] list as Poland, Hungary, and the Czech Republic'.[16] But, of course, Nunn's proposed approach did not prevail. The administration, put under tremendous pressure from domestic lobbies – mainly the Polish-American lobby that has traditionally voted Democrat – eclipsed the wise PFP concept. The Poles, especially with help from the American-Polish lobby, wanted an immediate entry into NATO because, from their perspective, time was not in favor of NATO extension. The PFP did not guarantee, to the Poles especially, an equal partnership with NATO. The Poles also rushed the administration so that they could be ahead of the Russians, if and when the latter would join PFP. They did not want to play a second role to the Russians.

The leap from PFP to NATO enlargement was the work of diligent Clintonian bureaucrats at the National Security Council (NSC), Department of State, and Department of Defense. Those bureaucrats maneuvered to push the president out of his ambiguous stance concerning NATO enlargement. According to Goldgeier, 'The development of the Partnership for Peace as the focus of America's NATO policy in the fall of 1993 was the result of typical bureaucratic politics.'[17] The real breakthrough came when the 'enforcer' arrived in the person of Richard Holbrooke. Holbrooke, in his post as Assistant Secretary of State, became the hub of the administration's push for NATO enlargement. He understood clearly the role of politics and the political calendar in connection with NATO extension, and the critical role that would be played by Congress once the President had made up his mind. In various speeches of administration leaders, especially those of Vice President Al Gore, one can identify Holbrooke's language.[18]

It was Holbrooke who would establish the rationale for expansion. For Holbrooke, the 1995 Dayton Accords ending the civil war in Bosnia were a benchmark. The function of American leadership was now to settle dangerous disputes in the Balkans and elsewhere in the formerly Communist part of Europe. As James Goldgeier observes, 'After Dayton, American foreign policy seemed more assertive, more muscular. This may have been as much perception as reality, but the perception mattered.'[19] Typical of Holbrooke's attitude was his later defense of the Kosovo intervention. 'We see progress and problems. But at least we are in a free Kosovo, and with NATO to provide security, it allows the creation of a pluralistic democracy.'[20]

A key ally of Holbrooke was General Wesley Clark, head of strategic plans and policy for the Joint Chiefs of Staff and later NATO's Supreme Commander. 'While politics played a secondary role in the 1993–94 administration deliberations that led to the NATO enlargement policy',

Goldgeier relates, 'they played a major role in determining how and when the United States and NATO would proceed.'[21] The President's and the Democratic Party's support for NATO extension was largely political: first, to demonstrate presidential leadership in foreign affairs, and second for electoral reasons – an appeal to 'the Polish vote' (i.e. East European constituencies active in the Democratic Party).

All of this maneuvering was played out at a time when Republicans had captured the House of Representatives and new House Speaker Newt Gingrich announced the 'Contract With America'. The President, reeling from that political setback, had no choice but to assert himself. NATO extension soon became a prominent way for him to do that.

NATO EXTENSION

With the end of the Cold War, competing national interests and institutional developments were set to alter the landscape of European security. The 50th anniversary of NATO was coming in mid-1999 and the decision about whether to extend remained. The other option, to keep NATO as it was, without extending it to Eastern Europe, quickly faded. The point of view that retaining the existing version of the alliance made sense from both an economic and a military standpoint no longer prevailed since the politics of the Clinton administration had moved toward an irreversible decision to extend NATO. Unfortunately, the policy debate took place simultaneously with the political zeal to extend NATO. What that produced was a rushed effort to expand NATO, which proceeded relentlessly.

The PFP was eclipsed before it really had a chance to demonstrate its potential. NATO extension became an effort to emphasize the continued centrality of NATO as the foundation of Europe's security architecture. NATO, the oldest, most mature, and arguably most effective of all European institutions, has proven again that a gigantic political-military structure does not dissolve by fiat and that, despite its political victory in the Cold War, NATO will not end through dissolution. Indeed, its proponents consider the alliance the only effective European security system. There was no reason in the view of NATO partisans to freeze the organization. The hope was that the new security dynamic, and the West's political advantage within the European state system, could provide NATO with strategic concepts for the future, this time including both parts of Europe.

That is what Western leaders hoped for by extending NATO to meet the security needs of all of Europe. The military boundaries of NATO were torn asunder. It now entered an arena without a clear and definite enemy (or even rival), and the conversion of its military to better pursuance of peacemaking ventures began to distance NATO from its erstwhile mission.

There were impassioned arguments pro and con among foreign policy experts in the United States and Europe. William G. Hyland, former member of the NSC and former editor of *Foreign Affairs*, offered a concise criticism of the campaign to expand NATO's membership:

> The leaders of NATO are creating a trans-Atlantic monstrosity worthy of Mary Shelley. The Atlantic alliance is being buried. In its place, NATO, led by the Clinton administration, is stitching together a Frankenstinian horror: a military alliance with no clear enemy, a military alliance with rapidly diminishing capabilities but expanding geographical commitments, a military alliance that can no longer credibly defend its members, a military alliance that will degenerate into little more than a political club of first and second-class members plus a list of applicants that may never be allowed to join.[22]

There is no question that the decision to expand NATO and the first step of inviting Poland, the Czech Republic, and Hungary is, as Cato Institute foreign policy experts Ted Galen Carpenter and Barbara Conry write in their book, a 'fateful undertaking'.[23]

What are the rationales for and against NATO extension? The rationale for NATO extension was presented in the Pentagon's 'Report to Congress on the Establishment of the NATO: Rationale, Benefits, Costs, and Implications.'[24] The report is an overwhelmingly political argument supporting the Clintonian concept of US foreign policy in the twenty-first century, especially concerning Europe. In fact, the administration's concept of foreign policy is and continues to be neo-Wilsonian. The logic underlying NATO extension is that the Cold War was fought for democracy, not merely to curb the expansionist ambitions of a great power. The Eastern European countries have been liberated from Communist authoritarianism, and we should support them in joining the Western democratic system that had prevailed throughout the Cold War in Western Europe.

The other argument used by the administration and its supporters was that Central and Eastern Europe were a source of instability between the two world wars. The belt of weak and unstable nations between the Soviet Union and Germany made the post-World War I nations vulnerable to domination by either the totalitarian Soviet Union or Hitler's Germany. Proponents of NATO expansion argued, without sufficient explanation, that the instability in the areas between Russia and Germany was the major cause of World War II.

The strategy of NATO enlargement missed the point that the more important goal was a 'much larger, post-Cold War strategy to help create a peaceful, undivided, democratic Europe'.[25] Even the administration and its supporters in the press and the foreign policy community concede that the strengthening of European economic and political institutions (EU, OSCE, the Council of Europe, and the West European Union), will all help create 'a peaceful, undivided, and democratic Europe'. The question, therefore, is why emphasize NATO extension? We already have working West European security structures. Why convert and change NATO's mission – a most successful military alliance and coalition – into a politically oriented and dominated structure? As soon as one introduces political objectives and a new mission (i.e. extending NATO) the historical NATO is inevitably corrupted.

In what sense does the NATO extension corrupt the historical NATO? The Yugoslav wars are the first case in point. NATO's intervention in Kosovo pressured Hungary, Poland and the Czech Republic to take an anti-Serb military and political posture. Yet the majority of Hungarians and Czechs did not support the Kosovo war. Extending NATO into Eastern Europe imposes new and divisive responsibilities on the East Europeans.

The most significant change is the West's relationship with Russia and Belarus. With Nazi Germany long ago defeated, the new Germany democratic and non-expansive, and the Soviet Union defunct, Russia has no imperial desires in Europe. Even if they had expansionist ambitions, the Russians have no military wherewithal to expand through Eastern Europe. The Stalinist effort to dominate Eastern Europe was a reflex going back to the nineteenth century balance of power concept, to be fulfilled under Stalin by social revolutionary means. In other words, Stalin's plan to secure the Soviet Union was to dominate Eastern Europe.

That is over now. True, there is no love lost between Russia and Poland, but that does not mean that historical rivalries should be ignited for no legitimate political or military reason. A major argument against NATO expansion is posed by the question: against whom do we organize and extend? Who is the enemy? Western proponents of expansion insist there is no enemy, and the target is certainly not explicit. But for Russia, NATO extension means a beleaguering, Western European-American presence. The Czech, Polish, and Hungarian extension was meant to be the first circle, the next circle into the Baltic area will certainly represent a direct threat to Russia.

NATO extension is an affront to Russia. Even a democratic Russia has national interests, which may include a sphere of influence beyond its western borders. Moreover, the emergence of a nondemocratic or revanchist

Russia is still a possibility. The majority of Russians supported the second war in Chechnya, and nationalist sentiment is on the rise. An enlarged NATO must view Russia as its potential adversary for military planning purposes and that is certain to further alarm the Russians. Another argument against NATO extension is cost.[26] The administration's cost estimates, something like $30 billion in the next ten years, are disputed by a Congressional Budget Office report that puts the cost at around $125 billion.[27] The argument that the purpose of NATO extension is the democratization of Eastern Europe is hardly persuasive. I have offered elsewhere different alternatives to NATO expansion, beginning with an enlarged European Union, a stronger OSCE, and a 'Middle Europa' security structure.[28] The argument that, without an expanded NATO, we are going to witness another Yalta is erroneous in view of the difference in the international structure today compared with 1945, above all the collapse of the Soviet Union. At present there are no conditions even approximating the situation at the time of the Yalta agreement.[29]

An especially persuasive reason why post-Cold War NATO does not require extension is the argument delivered by William Hyland. The results of post-1989 are: '(a) the reunification of Germany, (b) the limitation of strategic armaments and conventional armaments in Western Europe and (c) the significant revision of Western-NATO military settlement'.[30] Hyland argues, 'the expansion of NATO threatens to upset that settlement'. Foreign policy scholar Alan Tonelson concludes that NATO expansion is clearly 'the wrong tool for fixing the main problems threatening the stability of either half of Europe'.[31] In other words, any expansion of what was an essentially military alliance, even if it claims to be a moderate, liberal foundation for the extension of democracy in Eastern Europe, cannot and should not be accepted by the implicit rival (Russia) as a benign political organization.

NATO ENTERING THE TWENTY-FIRST CENTURY: NEW SECURITY THREATS

There were several challenges to European security at the end of the Cold War. The emergence of multinational, multiethnic states and a variety of conflicting nationalist aspirations and ideologies presented a threat to the internal and external security of Europe. The new entities have pursued traditional national claims and deeds, sometimes violently. While the West European states and NATO represented the early phase of trans-European internationalism, the East European states, many of whom became independent only after World War I, reemerged from Communism on the basis of nationalism, ethnicity, and particularism. Minority problems were replete in Czechoslovakia, Hungary, Romania, Bulgaria, and especially Yugoslavia – not to mention the more recent emergence of Baltic, Ukrainian, and Belarusian nationalists. NATO leaders were also concerned about Russian nationalism, which was not simple paranoia but based on the history of Russia. Another factor was the stability of Russia itself and the Commonwealth of Independent States (CIS), where ethno-religious nationalism was widespread.

One of the new challenges to European security was the revolution in missile technology. Here, the gap between the US military and the militaries of other NATO members was widening as the US skyrocketed in technological developments. The probable nature of future wars also had to be reconsidered. Future international wars will no longer be conducted against a monolithic Soviet Union and the Warsaw Pact military organization. The present multiplicity of nationalism and ethnicity, and the absence of central control of majorities, exposes a serious structural flaw in Europe's security architecture.

Another issue was the rise and proliferation of Weapons of Mass Destruction (WMD). Biological and chemical warfare is cheap, primitive, does not need a large amount of resources in production, can be mounted on conventional and strategic weaponry, and can nonetheless destroy large parts of the targeted population. Although there is a heavy debate over the seriousness and effectiveness of WMD (such weapons may be easily manufactured, but perhaps not so easily deployed), this is an issue that will not go away and continues to plague national security planners.

Still another security issue is connected with proliferation. With the rise of pariah states possessing or developing nuclear capability, the issue of proliferation, especially for the United States, is critical. The major concern is the control of nuclear stockpiles and is symbolized by the nuclear infrastructure of the former Soviet Union. The weaknesses or impotence of the International Atomic Energy Agency and other UN structures connected with disarmament exacerbate the situation. The issue became most critical in the transfer of nuclear expertise and technology, especially from Russia, to the rogue states of Iran, Iraq, and North Korea, whose radical regimes pose the most dangerous threat to the United States and Europe. Nuclear proliferation will become a much more serious matter and will have to be addressed under the umbrella of NATO, the only institution that could be delegated for this task.

THE CORRUPTION OF NATO

The case of the war in Kosovo, as conducted by the United States and NATO under a new 'humanitarian doctrine', raises serious questions about the future of NATO. This doctrine has its origins with Richard Holbrooke's 1995 Dayton Agreements, ending the war in Bosnia. It was then applied to the situation in Kosovo. What was the Dayton link to the new NATO? Dayton established the new doctrine of humanitarian intervention, with a studied disregard of sovereignty, traditional international law, and UN principles. The United States and NATO imposed themselves as belligerents, while the UN is based upon a nation-state system in which national sovereignty is sacrosanct.

The new NATO doctrine is usually duplicitous. One nationality is preferred to the other and NATO, as prosecutor and judge, then decides who is the offender and should be judged accordingly. A target of NATO from the beginning of the Yugoslav secessionist wars was Serbia. Serbian atrocities, not Croatian, came to the attention of NATO, even though both sides committed them. The Clinton administration sought to preserve with the Dayton Agreements an unworkable, multi-national state called Bosnia, divided into a Croat-Muslim federation and a Serb republic. The political integrity of this so-called nation-state is completely at the mercy of NATO and UN occupiers working as self-styled civilian reform administrators.

The same 'humanitarian' doctrine has been applied to Kosovo, which stands even less chance than Bosnia does of becoming a viable multinational entity. In the various Yugoslav civil wars the United States and NATO supported Bosnian Muslims, Croatians, and Albanians, but never Serbians. In fact, NATO became a partner with Kosovar Albanians and specifically with the anti-democratic terrorist group, the Kosovo Liberation Army (KLA), to pursue the war in Kosovo.[32]

The Dayton doctrine was clearly anti-Serbian. This doctrine of 'humanitarianism' is reminiscent of Woodrow Wilson's concept of national self-determination and the American penchant for supporting so-called progressive, democratic, and moral-political causes. The fact is that with the exception of Czechoslovakia, all nation-states of the former Austro-Hungarian and Ottoman empires have established radical nationalist or fascist regimes during most of their history as independent countries. Multinational states survived in Eastern Europe, and especially Yugoslavia (a mini Austro-Hungarian empire), *only* under monarchical, fascist, Stalinist, or Titoist authoritarian regimes. After the death of Tito, Yugoslavia was torn apart. Instead of letting the natural processes take place for post-Titoist settlements, even if they were brutal, NATO's new humanitarian doctrine has been imposed on both Bosnia and Kosovo. These are the latest examples of the corruption of multinationalism pursued by NATO in the name of a forlorn Utopian idea that Bosnia and Serbia's province, Kosovo, will become democratic. Even Woodrow Wilson would not have gone that far in his optimism.

This humanitarian, military intervention doctrine has thus far been applied to areas that are irrelevant or insignificant to American national interests. The Yugoslav successor states are strategically important for the European Union, but they are of no strategic value to the United States. The Clinton administration could bomb Yugoslavia without worrying that such action could have negative repercussions for America's security. The differences between the interests of the United States and the European members of NATO will likely grow wider as such missions became the primary focus of the alliance.

The case of East Timor, obviously not of strategic concern to the Europeans, demonstrates the duplicity and hypocrisy of the humanitarian intervention doctrine. Indonesia is strategically important for the United States. Bombing Jakarta as part of a humanitarian crusade could deny the United States a significant ally in its rivalry with China. It could also alienate Japan, India, Taiwan, Singapore and other important Asian powers. There is no love lost for the Indonesian regime among the Southeast Asian states and regimes, but bombing Jakarta in the name of humanitarian goals in East Timor would have been an American strategic disaster. That is why the administration confined its intervention to support for the Australian-led peacekeeping force with intelligence, medicine, and other assistance short of American troop engagement.

What have we learned from the Kosovo War? The humanitarian intervention doctrine has reached its limit and with it the future of NATO. The corruption of NATO's strategic purposes will be a heavy burden for the alliance as we enter the twenty-first century. British Prime Minister Tony Blair is wrong when he says that humanitarian action in Kosovo is the beginning of a new era for NATO. I would submit that it is the beginning of the end.

NATO's war in Kosovo deeply split the alliance, especially on the issue of military burden sharing. The inferiority of European military equipment in the war was contrasted with American technological superiority. The United States was deploying sophisticated intelligence gathering, battlefield information systems, and precision guided munitions, which made clear to the Europeans the historic gap in weapon technology and usage between the United States and Europe at the end of the century.

This gap alerted the European NATO members to the need for establishing a new force structure in Europe. As reported by Craig Whitney, Javier Solana, the former NATO Secretary General, now the first EU coordinator of foreign security policy, has reassured Americans that 'Duplication is the last thing we should do.'[33] But Solana's statement is not in conformity with the facts. 'European Union leaders decided in Cologne in June 1999 to take concrete steps by the end of 2000 to build a capacity for "autonomous action, backed up by credible military forces" in future regional crisis like those in Kosovo and Bosnia, even if the biggest NATO ally, the United States, decided to stay out.' In fact, Whitney reports that the French have a plan for a European General staff and a council of 15 European ambassadors, 'which some diplomats thought was intended to keep Mr Solana from making European defense policy more deferential to NATO than the French would like'. The French 'action plan', an idea that President Jacques Chirac proposed at the end of July 1999 to other EU members, 'proposes both civilian and military standing committees for a new European system. This plan also called for "a European military staff progressively organized to assume the triple functions of oversight, analysis, and planning".'[34]

According to Whitney, 'American ears pricked up at this news. "We're somewhat skeptical when we hear about a need for a separate European command structure", one US official stated.' In fact, Whitney quotes François Heisbourg, former advisor to the French Defense Ministry, as emphasizing, 'It is unacceptable for Europeans to be spending 60 per cent as much as Americans spend on defense but getting in return only a small fraction of the defense capabilities the Americans get for their money.'[35] This is tantamount to European double-talk. As much as the French would like to distance themselves from the United States, they find themselves caught again and again by American financial and military superiority. The aim of the 'new NATO' policy to make all allied armies rapidly deployable to crisis areas on the periphery of Europe, such as Bosnia and Kosovo, is chimerical. I would tend to agree with Whitney's analysis that it is far from clear that the Europeans are prepared to spend the enormous sums necessary to carry it out. The fact is that Germany, the largest European military force in NATO, is going to reduce its already modest military budget by 50 per cent by 2003. The French have also been engaged in defense budget cutting and one does not expect to count on the smaller European NATO countries to build an American-sized, sophisticated military technology.

Nevertheless, European leaders met in Paris on 25 November 1999, 'aiming to create within three years a rapid intervention force that could field 50,000 soldiers and 300 to 500 aircraft for up to a year in a future conflict like the one in Kosovo earlier this year'.[36] This goal was supported by both Chirac and Blair. It is a reaction to the intense criticism in the US Congress and among the American public of NATO's humanitarian war in Kosovo. But a leading German paper (*Frankfurter Allgemeine Zeitung*) inquired if the Europeans are 'really ready to spend the billions of dollars it would take for them to catch up with the United States and acquire the technology, communications and intelligence systems, along with the rapid deployment aircraft and helicopters they found they lacked in Kosovo'.[37] Such critics also wonder how this 'nimble military wing' would be tied to NATO.

The campaign for an EU force as an alternative to NATO is vacuous. There are no resources and no will for already squeezed welfare states to increase their defense appropriations. The debate will go on within the circles of NATO: as Christopher Patten, the EU's new Commissioner for External Affairs, notes, 'I don't think the debate will be resolved anywhere but within NATO.'[38] The short-run consequence of the humanitarian war in Kosovo is that fissures are widening within the alliance – fissures that had already begun during the 78-day air war campaign against Yugoslav president Slobodan Milosevic. NATO's costly expansion eastward, as well as the technological and psychological gap between the United States and Europe, will further weaken the alliance.

The future of NATO is linked to an eastern strategy in two areas. One is NATO extension eastward, and the other is an extension of this extension: the new humanitarian intervention doctrine of NATO. NATO faces a second round of expansion in the future when the Baltic republics and the Balkan states of Romania and Bulgaria will be considered for membership. In Kosovo, that European humanitarian and Socialist evangelical Tony Blair and the neo-Wilsonian Clinton administration imposed the new strategic doctrine of NATO. This version of NATO is an unpromising, unworkable mini-United Nations. In effect, NATO is becoming either a paper collective security system or a humanitarian mission operation. It seems that NATO will go in the direction of the former, since the latter is a dead end street.

The Kosovo War will be remembered in history as the beginning of the end of the historical NATO. From the start, the Greeks, French, and Italians did not support the American commanders. NATO Supreme Commander General Wesley Clark and the commander of US Air Forces in Europe, Lieutenant General Michael Short, advocated an immediate air strike against Belgrade's strategic and economic infrastructure. As recounted in a BBC documentary, the two generals appeared to be frustrated by the political micro-management of the air campaign by the Europeans. The principal target of the generals' wrath was French President Jacques Chirac and his Foreign Minister, Hubert Védrine, who rejected the wise and necessary strategic advice of the American generals. Reading between the lines, it was quite clear that the generals were furious at the European political intervention.[39]

According to editorialist Peter Ridell, writing in *The Times*, 'Serious strains have developed within the Western Alliance since the Kosovo war last spring, which have exacerbated the post-Cold War divergence of security interests between America and Europe.'[40] Another *Times* editorialist, Michael Gove, writes, 'The Western effort to police Kosovo is a tragic failure on every level.' Védrine's jibes at the American 'hyperpower' indicate the division between the United States and France over NATO is deepening. Ridell paraphrases US Secretary of Defense William Cohen, 'warning that Europe may be creating a new bureaucracy but not any more deployable troops, especially given planned cuts in spending. The underlying worry is that NATO and the American commitment to the defence of Europe will be weakened.'[41]

Prime Minister Blair declared that the purpose of the war in Kosovo was to get 'Serb troops out, our troops in, the refugees back home'.[42] This was one of the Prime Minister's greatest spins, surpassing his friend Bill Clinton in the mastery of Orwellian double-speak. As we know very well by now, Serb troops await the Albanians just beyond the eastern corner of Kosovo, NATO troops were and are unable to stabilize and pacify the area, and the great majority of non-Albanian refugees, now numbering more than 200,000, are afraid to return home. As Gove writes, 'The bitterest irony of this juvenile Gaullism is that where European forces are supposed to be acting in concert, in Kosovo itself, they are paralysed by ethnic strife.'[43]

THE CONSEQUENCES OF NATO'S HUMANITARIAN INTERVENTIONS

In general, one can argue that all of the ethnic national groups that the United States and its NATO allies supported during and after the Cold War have turned out to be the opposite of what they were supposed to be: the creators of stable democracies. We have supported forces in Afghanistan, Bosnia, Somalia, and Kosovo in the hope that our clients would not only become democratic, but would also establish regimes that would bring an end to violence and repression. Instead, these revolutionaries have established regimes that are corrupt, anti-democratic, and autocratic. The regimes in charge in Bosnia and Kosovo now aim to destroy the ethnic group that formerly dominated them. The Albanian Kosovars, especially the KLA, have not hidden their aspirations or renounced their violent ways to establish mastery of their acquired territories.

So if, in the range of factors that are considered, the foundation for humanitarian action, and thus military intervention, does not consider the 'day after' and a careful analysis of the type of regime that will be established once the revolutionaries have taken over, the humanitarian purposes become corrupted, as do the officials who sponsored them.

The latest example is the experience of the NATO governors in Kosovo. Since we do not expect the impotent UN to establish a working regime in Kosovo (or any other 'failed state') the bulk of responsibility will be assumed by the United States and NATO. The fundamental corruption of NATO is that the alliance has become an imperial arbiter in the Balkans – and someday perhaps elsewhere. It is not exactly the Austro-Hungarian Empire, but some of the elements of domination are similar between NATO imperialism and Austrian rule..

The Austrian-Hungarian monarchy was a failed arbiter of the conflicts of ethno-religious rivalries. We must recall that the army of Austria-Hungary ultimately failed to quell ethnic uprisings within the boundaries of the empire. The conditions for NATO are even less favorable. To impose its military supervision and peacekeeping will involve NATO, as it already does, in armed peacemaking. In view of the nature and structure of the American political system and the Constitution, especially the separation of powers and the nature of American public opinion, this kind of imperial role will never be supported by Congress and the American people. Kosovo is the Philippines and Cuba of the twenty-first century. The era of American imperial rule under William McKinley and Theodore Roosevelt is over; it cannot be recreated as humanitarian intervention under NATO's auspices.

This leaves NATO still in limbo. Humanitarian purposes may be noble, but when they confront and contradict strategic national interests they are no longer useful. The national interest dictates the subordination of humanitarian intervention in most cases. In cases such as Kosovo and Bosnia, NATO has found itself in a cul-de-sac following its humanitarian bombing if it does not find other arenas to fulfill new roles and strategic needs. The alliance may survive, like the Army Corps of Engineers, as part of the defense budgets of the United States and member European countries. The form will remain but the substance will not. As in *Alice in Wonderland*, the smile may linger after the Cheshire cat is gone. Institutions left alone will always find a purpose or ideology so that they can continue to exist.

They will manufacture purposes, if necessary, so the bureaucracy will survive and maintain resources essential to survival.

NATO may be blended into some type of European institutional arrangement if the Europeans can put their act together, downsize their welfare states, and come close to acquiring the military capabilities the Americans displayed in Kosovo. I doubt that such an outcome is possible, though, given the lack of military and economic readiness. The military budgets of the 'new NATO' will not meet its purposes, except to allow the organization to linger on. NATO still has not emerged as the institution best suited to deal with the new security threats to Europe, such as those mentioned above: new nationalism, proliferation, the threat of WMD, and the possible threat of a militaristic Russia. Nor is it likely to do so.

NOTES

1. Marc Trachtenberg, *A Constructed Peace: The Making of the European Settlement, 1945–1963* (Princeton UP 1999).
2. Quoted in Robert Hutchings, *American Diplomacy and the End of the Cold War: An Insider's Account of U.S. Policy in Europe, 1989–1992* (Baltimore: Johns Hopkins UP 1997) p.290.
3. Ibid. p.129.
4. For a discussion of these ideas, see ibid. pp.145–53.
5. Ibid. p.284.
6. Ronald Asmus, one of the authors of the *RAND Report on NATO Extension*, who moved from the RAND Corporation to join Deputy Secretary of State Strobe Talbott's enlargement team, said 'small is beautiful', and suggested why not the Balts? After all, they were further along in reforms than Romania. Quoted in James M. Goldgeier, *Not Whether But When: The U.S. Decision to Enlarge NATO*, (Washington DC: Brookings 1999) pp.117–18.
7. Thomas M. Magstadt, 'Flawed Democracies: The Dubious Political Credentials of NATO's Proposed New Members', *Cato Institute Policy Analysis*, 6 March 1998.
8. Ted Galen Carpenter, 'NATO Expansion Risks', *Washington Times*, 19 Jan. 1997.
9. John Pomfret, *Washington Post*, 10 Feb. 2000; Ted Galen Carpenter, 'Damage to Relations with Russia and China' in Ted Galen Carpenter (ed.) *NATO's Empty Victory: A Postmortem on the Balkan War* (Washington DC: Cato Institute 2000) pp.77–91.
10. Mark Kramer, 'Putin is Only Part of the Russian Picture', *Washington Post*, 23 Jan. 2000.
11. Hutchings (note 2) p.290.
12. Goldgeier (note 6) p.91.
13. Nick Williams, 'PFP: Permanent Fixture or Declining Asset?' *Survival* 38/1 (Spring 1996) pp.20–2.
14. Sam Nunn, 'NATO and the Successors of the Soviet Empire', *Washington Post*, 26 Dec. 1993.
15. Ibid.
16. Ibid.
17. Goldgeier (note 6) p.24.
18. Ibid. pp.98–103.
19. Ibid. p.98.
20. Quoted in Steven Erlanger, 'U.N. Envoy Pushes for Kosovo Democracy', *New York Times*, 30 Aug. 1999.
21. Goldgeier (note 6) p.77.
22. William G. Hyland, 'NATO's Incredibly Shrinking Defense', in Ted Galen Carpenter and

Barbara Conry (eds.) *NATO Enlargement: Illusions and Reality* (Washington DC: Cato Institute 1998) pp.31–40.
23. Introduction, *NATO Enlargement* (note 22) p.1.
24. United States Department of Defense, 'Report to Congress on the Enlargement of NATO: Rationale, Benefits, Costs, and Implications', 24 Feb. 1997.
25. Amos Perlmutter, 'Political Alternatives to NATO Expansion', in *NATO Enlargement* (note 22) p.223.
26. Amos Perlmutter and Ted Galen Carpenter, 'NATO's Expensive Trip East', *Foreign Affairs* 77/1 (Jan.–Feb. 1998) pp.2–6.
27. Ivan Eland, 'The Cost of Expanding the NATO Alliance', Congressional Budget Office Papers, March 1996, p.26.
28. Perlmutter, 'Political Alternatives' (note 25) pp.236–42.
29. See the carefully argued chapter by Ronald Steel, 'Beyond NATO', in *NATO Enlargement* (note 22) pp.243–51.
30. Highland (note 22) p.33.
31. Alan Tonelson, 'NATO Expansion: the Triumph of Policy Incoherence', in *NATO Enlargement* (note 22) p.50.
32. Chris Hedges, 'Kosovo's Next Masters?' *Foreign Affairs* 78/3 (May–June 1999) pp.24–42.
33. Craig Whitney, 'U.S. Raises Objections to New Force in Europe', *New York Times*, 11 Oct. 1999.
34. Ibid.
35. Ibid.
36. Quoted in Craig R. Whitney, 'A Rapid Strike Force (for Europe Only) is Taking Shape', *New York Times*, 26 Nov. 1999.
37. Ibid.
38. Ibid.
39. 'Moral Combat: NATO at War', BBC 2, 12 March 2000.
40. Peter Ridell, 'America Will Have to Wake Up to its Allies', *The Times* (London) 13 March 2000.
41. Michael Gove, 'Only Now Can We See How We Lost in Kosovo', *The Times* (London) 14 March 2000.
42. Quoted in 'Moral Combat' (note 39).
43. Gove (note 41).

8

NATO 1949 and NATO 2000: From Collective Defense toward Collective Security

RICHARD RUPP

The decision to transform the NATO alliance and expand the organization's membership may well have been the most important US foreign policy initiative of the 1990s, if not the past 50 years. Cognizant or not of the ramifications, the Clinton administration has dramatically altered an alliance configured in 1949 to promote and defend selective US vital interests. NATO 2000 identifies no specific state as a threat. Rather, NATO is committed to engaging future and unspecified conflicts in many diverse countries. With little debate and with great difficulty in identifying US interests, the Clinton administration is gradually converting NATO from a collective defense organization (CDO), which permitted the United States to determine its interests, into a collective security organization (CSO) that allows little flexibility on the part of the nation's policymakers. When the history of US foreign policy in the 1990s is written, the decision to transform and expand NATO will be seen as a critical error.

NATO's transformation has been executed without fully appreciating and grasping the US national interests at stake. Dissecting interests, both in the abstract and in light of current events, will illuminate the dangers in converting NATO from the collective defense organization that emerged in 1949 and stood throughout the Cold War into a collective security organization that now seems NATO's fate. As new members join the alliance and NATO is called upon to engage an ever-growing array of crises and conflicts, the organization's credibility and effectiveness will be stretched – conceivably to breaking point. NATO still has a vital role to play in promoting US interests. But to serve those interests, it is a slightly modified NATO of 1949 that is required, not the radically altered organization of 2000.

NATIONAL INTERESTS

It is often noted that the Cold War containment strategy gave US foreign policy remarkable focus and purpose. While the implementation of containment was frequently flawed and led to waste in treasure and lives, the perceived threat of the Soviet Union created an environment in which American elites largely shared a common perception of the national interest. Nevertheless, identifying national interests, even when a state confronts a powerful enemy, is a complicated task. Identifying national interests when no state poses such a threat is an even greater challenge, and one that has been confronting the United States for nearly ten years.

A nation has a variety of interests, both foreign and domestic. Debating and deciding which interests are of greater import are at the heart of politics. Virtually all people would agree that a nation's survival tops its lists of interests, but deciding how best to secure even that goal is a complicated and difficult task. In the realm of foreign policy, Donald Nuechterlein, a former US State and Defense Department analyst, argues there are two key categories in which to consider interests: vital and major. According to Nuechterlein: 'An interest is vital when the highest policymakers in a sovereign state conclude that the issue at stake is so fundamental to the political, economic, and social well-being of their country that it could not be compromised – even if this conclusion results in the use of economic and military sanctions.'[1]

Compared to its major interests, a nation-state has relatively few vital interests. Certainly, the most paramount task a government confronts is assuring the survival and physical security of the nation, and responding to states, groups, or individuals posing serious threats. For example, the Japanese attack on Pearl Harbor, and the possibility that Great Britain would fall to the Nazis, were threats to US vital interests. At Pearl Harbor, the threat was stark. As to Great Britain, defeat by the Nazis would have constituted a threat to the survival of the United States because, with the resources of the British Empire in German hands, America would have confronted an extraordinarily powerful enemy state.

Beyond armed conflict, states have vital interests in maintaining their fundamental economic well-being. Most international economic issues a nation addresses – currency devaluations, import quotas, debt management – impact the nation's major interests. However, some economic interests are so crucial that they do affect a nation's vital interests. Saddam Hussein's invasion of Kuwait in 1990 posed such a threat to the United States. Although it was not as directly dependent as its allies in Japan and Western Europe on Middle East oil, the prospect of Iraq setting oil prices and regulating the flow of vast amounts of oil challenged the fundamental stability of the international political economy, and consequently threatened US vital, not just major, interests.

Of course, not all interests a nation possesses are vital. Indeed, it was the inability of US policymakers to distinguish threats to vital interests from those to nonvital interests that took America astray in Vietnam, Nicaragua, and other regions during the Cold War. On a daily basis, a nation's policymakers are much more likely to be engaged in monitoring and advancing major rather than vital interests. Nuechterlein defines a major interest as:

> One that a country considers to be important but not crucial to its well being. Major interests involve issues and trends, whether they are economic, political, or ideological, that can be negotiated with an adversary. Such issues may cause serious concern and even harm to…interests abroad, but policymakers usually come to the conclusion that negotiation and compromise, rather than confrontation, are desirable.[2]

Major interests are myriad. A partial list of US major interests would include: financial assistance to Ukraine, confronting drug trafficking, peacekeeping deployments in East Timor, the Arab-Israeli peace process and the general promotion of human rights and democratization. While all of these issues occupy the attention and resources of the American government, none of them threatens the physical security of the United States or its fundamental economic standard of living.

COLLECTIVE DEFENSE AND COLLECTIVE SECURITY

To promote and defend its vital and major interests, a nation devises strategies and tactics. In the realm of national security, states have frequently turned to collective security and collective defense as means of ensuring their military-security interests.

Perhaps the most frustrating aspect of the NATO expansion debate for this author has been the necessity to revisit the viability of collective security organizations. A valuable and important analytical concept, collective security has been subject to powerful and compelling theoretical and empirical criticism.[3] Yet, despite this evidence, NATO heads of state spent the 1990s transforming the organization into an alliance that Woodrow Wilson would have praised and supported.

The term collective security is widely used in the lexicon of policymakers, journalists, and the general public. For specialists in international relations, collective security is also a central concept. Yet the term remains ambiguous to many. The notion of collective security can be traced back at least one thousand years, and has been a recurring feature in international politics since the Concert of Europe. In 1815, following the Napoleonic Wars, the major European powers were eager to devise an international institution that would regulate their relations and ideally reduce the likelihood of armed conflict. The result of their efforts was the Concert of Europe. For many, the Concert was Europe's first step at building a collective security organization.

Although competing usages exist, all modern versions of collective security draw from the thinking and words of Woodrow Wilson. Renouncing power politics, Wilson argued that human beings possessed the capacity and reason to alter the manner in which international relations had historically functioned. Wilson championed the establishment of an international organization – a league of nations – that would be based on a near universal membership of states, encompassing both the great and small nations of the world. He assumed that all member states would be desirous of peace, and would commit themselves to repel and punish aggressor states regardless of specific circumstances.

Wilson rejected the contention that states inevitably function in a self-help system in which they necessarily place their own national interests above all other concerns. He assumed that because states have 'clear interests in protecting an international order that they see as beneficial to their individual security, they will contribute to the coalition even if they have no vital interests at stake in the actual theater of aggression'.[4] Wilson presumed that his collective security's 'all-against-one' formulation would serve as a deterrent to aggressor states because a potential violator of the international order would be subject to a massive and coordinated global response. Given that no state would possess the necessary resources to resist the combined military forces of the collective security organization, peace would become the norm in international politics.

Collective defense is far less ambitious than collective security. Whereas collective security seeks large-scale memberships, and seeks to unite diverse states against threats to peace, collective defense binds a limited number of states sharing the view that a particular state, or states, threatens the vital interests of each of them. Rejecting the idealist aspirations of Woodrow Wilson, advocates of collective defense, or military alliances, view states as parochial self-interested actors. Such nations do not join forces to confront unidentified future threats to a vague conceptualization of international peace and security. Rather, collective defense provides a home for states that identify a specific threat common to them all and agree to mount a mutual defense effort against that threat.

Collective defense has a long history in international relations. Many attempts have succeeded and many have failed, but they all share certain traits. Robert Art, Professor of International Relations at Brandeis University maintains that collective defense organizations:

> qualify their commitments either by retaining national control over the decision to use force, or by clearly specifying the exact circumstances under which military aid shall be rendered, or by doing both. What an alliance gives up in certainty of response, however, should be more than compensated for by the strength and intensity of the interest its member states have in preventing a specific aggressor from attacking them. By narrowing its scope (the range of aggressions it seeks to prevent), an alliance thereby strengthens its deterrent power.[5]

Cato Institute scholars Ted Galen Carpenter and Barbara Conry have argued that the Clinton administration's NATO reforms are 'a confusing hybrid that ignores the fundamental differences between a collective security organization and a traditional military alliance'.[6] To appreciate the magnitude of the administration's confusion and its policy implications, NATO's original collective defense mission must be reviewed.

NATO'S ORIGINS

By the time Nazi armies crossed into the Polish frontier in September 1939, the League of Nations and the concept of collective security had been thoroughly discredited. Throughout World War II, several military alliances were formed. Although not precisely collective defense as defined above, the wartime 'Grand Alliance' between the United States, Great Britain, and the Soviet Union approximated collective defense. Each state identified Nazi Germany as a threat to its survival and the three nations agreed to coordinate and combine their resources to destroy the Nazi regime. Few people during the war envisioned that this cooperation – or more accurately, a marriage of convenience – between the West and the Soviet Union would so quickly evaporate following the close of hostilities.

In the period after the defeat of Germany and Japan, an array of events would occur that would cement hostile relations between East and West. The events are well known and include: the establishment of a Soviet puppet regime in Poland, Moscow's pressure on Iran and Turkey, Stalin's February 1946 address on the likelihood of war, Churchill's reply in Fulton, Missouri (the 'Iron Curtain' speech) a month later, the Truman Doctrine, the Marshall Plan, the division of Germany, and the Communist coup in Czechoslovakia. By March 1948, in a cable to Washington, General Lucius Clay, the US military governor of Germany, concluded that events might culminate in war with the Soviet Union.

Coupled to General Clay's telegram was his assessment of the West's military position on the ground in Western Europe. Millions of American troops had made their way back across the Atlantic by 1948, and only 200,000 remained on duty in Europe.[7] Indeed, plans were afoot to continue demobilization, reducing the force to approximately 95,000 troops, most of whom would be committed to occupation duties, not maintaining a robust deterrence capability. Although US intelligence reports exaggerated the size of Soviet forces in Eastern Europe and the western Soviet Union following the war, Soviet forces did considerably outnumber those of the Western countries.

The imbalance of forces can be captured best in a pithy cable Field Marshal Viscount Montgomery sent to his superiors in September 1948. Montgomery had been dispatched to France to preside over the Western European Union's Commander-in-Chief Committee. Upon surveying the military situation, Montgomery queried, 'My present instructions are to hold the line at the Rhine. Presently available allied forces might enable me to hold the tip of the Brittany peninsula for three days. Please instruct further.'[8]

Lacking Montgomery's irreverence, the US Joint Chiefs of Staff (JCS) surveyed the same situation, and presented their conclusions in a document with the title 'Halfmoon'. The JCS asserted that if the Soviets chose to attack, the Red Army could quickly overwhelm Western forces in Europe, the Middle East, and the Far East. With regard to Europe, 'Halfmoon' 'predicted that in a matter of weeks, all of Western Europe likely would be lost and total US evacuation would be necessary.'[9] 'Halfmoon' and other JCS assessments anticipated the worst-case scenario. Over the years, critics of such forecasts have condemned the extreme pessimism and conclusions. For example, in his 1962 study on NATO, Robert E. Osgood, a prominent scholar of American foreign policy, concluded, 'There is no indication that Stalin wished to pursue his designs upon Western Europe by engaging Western forces in direct combat.'[10] While the debate will never be settled, it remains clear that most policymakers shared Secretary of State George C. Marshall's view that, 'European Communism threatens US vital interests and national security.'[11] More specifically, the widely held view in Washington in the late 1940s maintained that

> if the Soviets overran Western Europe and harnessed the vast resources of that region to their own war machine, they could confront America as an equal in terms of military-industrial potential. If it were not for nuclear weapons, this great Soviet-dominated bloc might well be unconquerable, and indeed might in the long run be more than a match for the United States.[12]

The architects of the NATO alliance lived through the years spanning World War I, the interwar period, and World War II. Sobered by the events of that calamitous period, those men recognized the folly behind collective security. In designing the NATO Charter, US diplomats and their Canadian and European counterparts recognized that the glue holding any alliance together came in the form of a shared and specific threat. On 4 April 1949, representatives of 12 nations met in Washington, and created the North Atlantic Treaty Organization.

In signing the NATO Charter, the North American and West European governments committed themselves to function in accordance with the concept of collective defense. The signatories did not forfeit the right to control the destinies of their foreign policies, nor did they radically alter the manner in which they defined and protected their national interests. Rather, the member states all agreed that, with regard to one aspect of their foreign policies, their interests coincided, and they agreed to establish a joint mechanism for advancing a shared goal. While the Soviet Union was not mentioned in the Charter, there was no doubt that Article 5, the key passage, spoke directly to the Soviet threat. As Article 5 read in 1949, and as it reads unchanged today:

> The Parties agree that an armed attack against one or more of them in Europe or North America shall be considered an attack against them all and consequently they agree that, if such an armed attack occurs, each of them, in exercise of the right of individual or collective self-defense recognized by Article 51 of the Charter of the United Nations will assist the Party or Parties so attacked by taking forthwith, individually and in concert with other Parties, such action as it deems necessary, including the use of armed force, to restore and maintain the security of the North Atlantic area.

In 1949, there was little doubt that the governments of the West believed that war with the USSR was possible, if not probable. Today, more than 50 years after the treaty's signing, the USSR no longer exists, and while Russia remains a concern to NATO, the current guardians of the alliance have made clear that the primary threat to NATO comes not from a specific nation, but from the unstable nature of the post-Cold War era. Through reforms adopted since 1991, including the Strategic Concept, Partnership for Peace (PFP) and the actual extension of membership, NATO is being modified so that it can confront threats, not from specified governments, but from an array of developments including nationalism, refugee flows and economic upheavals. To confront these new threats, NATO is being gradually transformed from a collective defense organization into a collective security organization.

NATO'S TRANSFORMATION

In many ways, the past ten years have witnessed more tumultuous change for the NATO alliance than did the decades of the Cold War. As the Soviet Union collapsed between 1989 and 1991, NATO took tentative steps to prepare for the impending post-Soviet period. NATO leaders met in London in July 1990 and instructed their governments to undertake a fundamental review of the organization's future purpose and goals. In November 1991, the organization's 16 members agreed upon a new Strategic Concept. Although the Soviet Union was little more than a question for historians to ponder by that time, the NATO heads of state recommitted themselves to collective defense. In light of the fact that the Soviet Union at the time had only one month's breath left, one wonders how serious the commitment to collective defense was. However, in a departure from NATO's traditional mission, the new Strategic Concept also identified conflicts and issues that would occupy the alliance's attention in the future. Declaring that 'the monolithic, massive and potentially immediate threat which was the principle concern of the Alliance in its first forty years has disappeared',[13] the NATO heads of state went on to assert their particular concern with the:

> adverse consequences of instabilities that may arise from the serious economic, social, and political difficulties, including ethnic rivalries and territorial disputes, which are faced by many countries in Central and Eastern Europe. The tensions which may result, as long as they remain limited, should not directly threaten the security and territorial integrity of members of the Alliance. This could, however, lead to

crises inimical to European security and even to armed conflicts, which could involve outside powers or spill over into NATO countries, and have a direct effect on the security of the alliance.[14]

A vague statement to many, the Strategic Concept's reference to instabilities in Central and Eastern Europe was not lost on leaders in Prague, Warsaw, and the rest of the region. NATO's declaration that domestic turmoil in these states could threaten NATO itself was seen as an opening for national leaders, including Poland's Lech Walesa and Czechoslovakia's Vaclav Havel, to press the organization for more tangible commitments, which would be, after all, in NATO's own interest. Membership in all of the West's international organizations quickly became the central foreign policy goal of the new Central and East European governments, but NATO membership was the priority. Only NATO could provide the internal and external security that each new government sought.

Beyond the general statements found in the Strategic Concept and the public statements by NATO leaders, the alliance took concrete steps toward reform by creating new formal associations with the governments of Central and Eastern Europe, as well as the governments of republics that comprised the former Soviet Union. In December 1991, NATO established the North Atlantic Cooperation Council (NACC) which was designed to provide a formal but limited link between the 16-member alliance and the new governments to the east. In signing the NACC protocols, participants acknowledged that instability was a primary concern to Europe's future, and that NATO should play a decisive role in addressing and ameliorating that instability.

The NACC called on members to meet at regular intervals to discuss a broad array of issues – ranging from traditional human rights concerns to economic transitions. As to military ties and cooperation, the NACC declared, 'the focus of our consultations and cooperation will be on security and related issues, such as defense planning, conceptual approaches to arms control, democratic concepts of civil-military relations, civil-military coordination and air traffic management and the conversion of defense production to civilian purposes'.[15]

As NATO continued its search for a new identity in 1992, the alliance agreed to develop linkages with both the Conference on Security and Cooperation in Europe (CSCE) and the United Nations. With war raging in the successor states of the former Yugoslavia, NATO agreed in June 1992 'to support, on a case-by-case basis in accordance with our own procedures, peacekeeping activities under the responsibility of the CSCE, including by making available Alliance resources and expertise'.[16] Six months later,

NATO agreed to cooperate with the United Nations regarding international peacekeeping operations.

With those policy initiatives, NATO began the process of moving 'out-of-area'. To facilitate peacekeeping and peacemaking in out-of-area operations, NATO created the Combined Joint Task Forces (CJTF) in late 1993. Although the CJTF have had limited use since their founding, this US-led initiative continued the process of linking permanent NATO member-states to the concerns of non-NATO states and aspiring NATO states.

As time passed, the NACC proved unable to satisfy the needs and demands of its new members. With the NACC, the CJTF, the CSCE, and even the European Union perceived as virtual way stations to membership in NATO, stronger pressure was placed on NATO governments to increase the alliance's formal membership. During 1993, the question of NATO expansion found itself debated within the Clinton administration. With voices on both sides of the debate, the US government initially chose a middle road. Like most policy initiatives, Partnership for Peace (PFP) was born out of compromise. While some in Eastern Europe favored immediate extension of full NATO membership, few in the West were supportive of such a dramatic turn. However, as pressure and discussions continued, Washington decided to give the East a taste of what it had been seeking. Partnership for Peace was formally established at NATO's January 1994 summit meeting.

For many in the West, this was as far as the alliance could go in establishing formal relations with the East. Senior officials at the US Department of Defense, including members of the Joint Chiefs of Staff, were highly dubious of creating any new institutions or extending any assurances to Eastern European governments, particularly at a time when the United States was substantially reducing the size of its armed forces.[17]

But for the governments in Budapest, Prague, and even Bucharest and Tallin, PFP was a major step toward their ultimate goal of full NATO membership. While this was a major step, many in Eastern Europe, particularly those in Poland, expressed the view that NATO was moving too slowly and cautiously.

For critics of NATO's decision, Partnership for Peace was derided as 'Partnership for Postponement', 'Partnership for Procrastination', or 'Partnership for Prevarication'.[18] One senior Polish official dismissed PFP with a historical reference to Britain's efforts to appease Germany at the 1938 Munich Conference, stating 'We have gone from Chamberlain's umbrella to Clinton's saxophone.'[19]

With PFP, NATO established institutional mechanisms linking the 16 permanent member-states to the governments of the East. Members of PFP, which would quickly include most of the states of the former Soviet Union and Eastern Europe, were pledged to work with the NATO members on five objectives:

- facilitation of transparency in national defense planning and budgeting processes;
- ensuring democratic control of national defenses;
- maintenance of the capability and readiness to contribute, subject to the constitutional considerations, to operations under the authority of the UN and/or the responsibility of the CSCE;
- the development of cooperative military relations with NATO, for the purpose of joint planning, training, and exercises in order to strengthen the ability of the Central and East European countries to undertake missions in the fields of peacekeeping, search and rescue, humanitarian operations, and others as might subsequently be agreed upon;
- the development, over the longer term, of forces that are better able to operate with those of the members of the North Atlantic Alliance.[20]

Although the PFP protocols did not afford Article 5 protections or identify any state or states that might threaten members of the alliance, some critics argued that the growing integration of permanent members with 'associate' members would lead to the emergence of *de facto* security guarantees. As John Duffield, political scientist at the University of Georgia, concluded, 'the more that NATO is involved with them and the more they restructure their forces and decision-making processes to be compatible with NATO, the harder it will be for NATO to refuse to act as if their security is endangered'.[21]

Indeed, since the inception of PFP, many states have endeavored to become model members of NATO's new club. Beyond participating in numerous PFP conferences, briefings, and training exercises, many PFP states deployed troops to Bosnia, where they participated in NATO's Implementation Force (IFOR) and Stabilization Force (SFOR) operations. Although their involvement in these NATO operations has contributed to the effectiveness of the missions, it is unlikely that the primary motivation for participation was concern about the Bosnia situation *per se*; it was part of their concerted campaigns to move beyond membership in PFP. Their goals were, and remain, full NATO membership with Article 5 security assurances. Indeed, in signing the PFP protocols, the Eastern governments pressured the 16 permanent members to include the following passage:

> We affirm that the Alliance, as provided for in Article 10 of the Washington Treaty, remains open to the membership of the other European states in a position to further the principles of the Treaty and to contribute to the security of the North Atlantic area. We expect and would welcome NATO expansion that would reach democratic states to our East, as part of an evolutionary process, taking into account political and security developments in the whole of Europe.[22]

Those who had hoped that the East would be satisfied with PFP did not adequately appreciate the intense drive of East Europeans, or the power of their Western supporters. For as the train of Partnership for Peace pulled out of the station, the destination was clearly full NATO membership, and waving the train toward that destination was US President Bill Clinton. Indeed, with Clinton's public declarations in autumn of 1996 calling on NATO to admit Poland, Hungary, and the Czech Republic as full members by April 1999, there was virtually no turning back.

EXTENDING FULL MEMBERSHIP

When the original 12 states signed the Washington Treaty in 1949, there was widespread belief that an alliance was necessary to check Soviet power in Europe. Although motivations varied and threat perceptions differed, the North American and West European states concluded that they shared a vital interest in preventing Soviet hegemony over Western Europe. Each of these states possessed other concerns and foreign policy interests, but all agreed to support NATO in its paramount task.

In expanding the alliance in the absence of the Soviet Union, or any state resembling the threat posed by the Soviet Union during the Cold War, NATO was compelled to devise a rationale for retooling the organization. In September 1995, NATO published a study seeking to clarify what the mission and goals of an expanded alliance would be. The major points included:

- encouraging and supporting democratic reforms, including civilian and democratic control over the military;
- fostering in new members of the alliance the patterns and habits of cooperation, consultation and consensus building which characterize relations among current Allies;

- promoting good-neighborly relations, which would benefit all countries in the Euro-Atlantic area, both members and non-members of NATO;
- emphasizing common defense and extending its benefits and increasing the transparency in defense planning and military budgets, thereby reducing the likelihood of instability that might be engendered by an exclusively national approach to defense policies;
- reinforcing the tendency toward integration and cooperation in Europe based on shared democratic values and thereby curbing the countervailing tendency toward disintegration along ethnic and territorial lines;
- strengthening the alliance's ability to contribute to European and international security, including participation in peacekeeping activities under the responsibility of the OSCE and peacekeeping operations under the authority of the UN Security Council as well as other new missions;
- strengthening and broadening the Trans-Atlantic relationship.[23]

In numerous instances, those points simply modified and built upon the functions and goals of PFP noted above. And just as the PFP protocols designated no specific state as a potential threat toward which alliance members could galvanize their policies, this document followed suit, identifying no likely aggressor state.

In July 1997, NATO's permanent members and more than a dozen aspiring member-states gathered in Madrid, to witness the organization's formal invitation of membership to Poland, Hungary, and the Czech Republic. With the understanding that the three nations would comport with the organization's accession requirements, the states would become full members of NATO by April 1999. Throughout the summit, NATO officials were at pains to clarify that the offer to the three Central European states should not be interpreted by other governments as the final chapter in NATO expansion. Indeed, the 'Madrid Declaration' emphatically stated that 'The Alliance expects to extend further invitations in coming years...'[24] To allay the fears and address the disappointment of noninvited governments, the Declaration went on to assert:

> With regard to aspiring members, we recognize with great interest and take account of the positive developments towards democracy and the rule of law in a number of southeastern European countries, especially Romania and Slovenia ... At the same time, we recognize the progress

achieved towards greater stability and cooperation by the states in the Baltic region which are also aspiring members.[25]

In the two years following Madrid, the Central European states worked diligently toward meeting NATO's goal of a signing ceremony to coincide with NATO's 50th anniversary celebrations in Washington. On 12 March 1999 Poland, Hungary, and the Czech Republic formally joined NATO. With great applause, the once-Warsaw Pact nations became full and permanent members of NATO, enjoying the full security guarantees found in Article 5 of the Washington Treaty. In ratifying amendments to the treaty admitting the new member-states, the US Senate declared, 'The invasion of Poland, Hungary, or the Czech Republic, or their destabilization arising from external subversion, would threaten the stability of Europe and jeopardize vital United States national security interests.'[26]

With high hopes, the new 19-member organization went forward. Its charter now called upon members to cooperate on a wide array of endeavors ranging from ameliorating ethnic conflict to promoting economic reforms. Although no specific state-based threat was specified, any one of the 19 members could call upon the entire membership to respond if it perceived a security threat. With threats to national security defined vaguely as 'instabilities', any number of events could trigger requests for support.

As new states have attained membership, attention now shifts to the future. Alain Pellerin, of the Canadian Council for International Peace and Security (CCIPS), quite rightly contends that three possible paths lie in NATO's future:

- stop the enlargement process after the first stage or after a relatively non-controversial second stage that could include Slovenia, Romania, and Austria; or
- expand the alliance to Russia's border to include the Baltic republics and possibly Ukraine; or
- pursue a broad engagement policy, which would include Russia.[27]

Some experts, including former ambassador Jonathan Dean and Yale University political scientists Bruce Russett and Alan Stam, have argued that the circle should be completed, and Russia should be made a member of NATO.[28] That is not a likely possibility.

Others, including this author, maintain that NATO expansion should halt. A third group, dominated by policymakers, contend that while Russian membership is not likely for a great many years, expanding the alliance further east is desirable. The next stage of NATO expansion would include nations from the Baltics and/or the Balkans. Since the first invitations were made in Madrid, some US officials have quietly warned governments in these regions that second-round invitations will move much more slowly than the first round.

However, the Baltic states and some of the Balkan states can point to explicit statements from NATO that expansion into both regions is open and pending. For instance, six months after NATO's Madrid Conference, the presidents of the three Baltic states joined President Clinton in the East Room of the White House and signed the US-Baltic Charter of Partnership. That document devotes considerable attention to nation-building, the rule of law, and free market reforms, but it was also quite explicit on the question of NATO expansion:

> The Partners believe that the enlargement of NATO will enhance the security of the United States, Canada, and all the countries of Europe, including those states not immediately invited to membership or not currently interested in membership ... The United States welcomes the aspirations and supports the efforts of Estonia, Latvia, and Lithuania, to join NATO.[29]

Balkan states have also received assurances that NATO membership remains open. Romania was specifically singled out in the Madrid Declaration as a likely candidate. In February 1998, President Clinton met in Washington with Bulgarian President Petar Stoyanov and signed the US-Bulgarian Partnership. Although that document was primarily an acknowledgement of Bulgaria's continuing reforms, the White House released a statement declaring 'President Clinton reaffirmed America's commitment to NATO's "Open Door" policy and welcomed Bulgaria's aspiration to NATO membership.'[30] With Baltic and Balkan states eager to join NATO, the next round of expansion may result in an additional full NATO member, with Article 5 security protections, bordering Russia. (In granting Poland full NATO membership, the alliance has already extended its eastern presence to Russia's border at Kaliningrad.) To those consequences we now turn.

THE RUSSIAN REACTION

The architects of NATO expansion took a page from the Marshall Plan when considering Russia's likely reaction. Just as participation in the Marshall Plan was offered to the Kremlin in 1947, inclusion in NATO's eastward expansion has been offered to Moscow with each new policy initiative, save an actual invitation formally to join the organization. Although many in the Soviet Union would have welcomed Marshall Plan funds to rebuild the nation, only one voice spoke for the Soviet Union, and Joseph Stalin said no.

Today, there are many voices participating in the political debate within Russia, and while these voices are frequently at odds, on one question the Russians are united: the vast majority of Russian elites oppose NATO expansion. At each stage of NATO's eastward expansion, Russian policymakers have made their objections known. The Russian Duma termed NATO expansion the 'most serious military threat to our country since 1945'.[31] Indeed, the leader of the Communist Party in Russia, Gennady Zyuganov, condemned the May 1997 NATO-Russia Founding Act, which sought to institutionalize NATO-Russian interactions, as a 'complete and unconditional surrender'.[32]

The Russian military has repeatedly demonstrated that it views NATO's new institutions, the NACC, PFP, and even the Founding Act, as empty paternalistic gestures from the West. In 1995, Russia's Defense Minister, General Pavel Grachev, stated that Russia would take military initiatives to counter NATO's expanding membership: 'We might create necessary military groups in the most threatening directions and set up a closer cooperation with the other CIS states.'[33]

Many, if not most, international relations specialists contend that Russian objections to NATO expansion are well founded. Although many Western policymakers discount Russian concerns, the following list delineates possible developments if NATO expansion proceeds:

> A rebirth of Russia's sphere of influence among the now independent states of the former Soviet Union, with particularly negative impact on Ukraine and the Baltic States; a strengthening of the non-democratic opposition, which would undercut those who favor reforms and cooperation with the West; an unwelcome nationalistic influence on internal Russian politics; an intensification of the relationship between Russia and China, to avoid mutual isolation; the annulment of the NATO-Russia Founding Act; encouragement of new militarism in Russia; and a resistance in the Duma to various arms control agreements.[34]

Even as they advocate NATO expansion, US policymakers assure their Russian counterparts that Russia has no legitimate fears of the once-Cold War organization. After all, as NATO's Strategic Concept asserts, the organization's key goal is to promote stability in Europe, and that goal should benefit Russia as well as all other European countries. But it is impossible for Russians to ignore the fact that a primary reason why the East Europeans and Balts seek NATO membership is as a security guarantee against a revanchist Russia.

The United States and its NATO allies are clearly sending Moscow a mixed message. In public statements and in NATO policy directives, Russia has been assured that the organization now functions to promote general European security. Quietly, though, depending on which Western or Eastern policymaker is speaking, NATO is touted as an insurance policy to deal with any future Russian threat to US and European security. As David Yost, Professor of International Relations at the US Naval Postgraduate School, has observed:

> From the perspective of the Russians, NATO's rhetoric is contradictory: If NATO wants to build a relationship of partnership and cooperation with Russia, why are NATO governments extending collective defense commitments to nations that have expressed distrust and antagonism toward Russia?[35]

Just as it would be unwise to poke a stick at a sleeping rattlesnake, it is unwise to prod Russia with NATO expansion. No good can come from either proposition.

OPENING PANDORA'S BOX

It is not difficult to identify the adverse consequences of NATO expansion on Western-Russian relations. However, when one expands the focus to include the impact of NATO expansion on Eurasian security in general, and US interests in particular, the negative ramifications become overwhelming. Nations seeking or discussing NATO membership are remarkably diverse. They include Estonia, Latvia, Lithuania, Ukraine, Slovakia, Slovenia, Romania, and Bulgaria. No matter how skillful NATO's public affairs department may be at arguing that common interests in peace and stability exist among states, the Baltics and Balkans simply do not have fundamentally common security interests. Indeed, in those regions, nations, like nations everywhere, have very particular vital and major interests. Baltic, Balkan, and Central European states are at varying levels of economic, social, military, and political development.

In addition, those nations, like all nations, have particular histories which have been shaped by geography, demographics, religion, language, race, and war. The assertion that the new NATO will be as effective in achieving its goals as the old NATO was in countering the Soviet threat is without historical precedent and defies contemporary logic.

The one interest that aspiring NATO states truly share is their desire to join the alliance and receive its security guarantees. These nations view NATO as the West's most prized, effective, and credible organization. Membership in such an organization would likely yield any number of benefits: economic assistance, political integration, social development, and, of course, a perception of enhanced security. Michael Mandelbaum, Professor of International Relations at Johns Hopkins University, remains a prominent voice in the debate about NATO's future, and notes the understandable quest among non-NATO states to become NATO members:

> It is the political elites in Central Europe who wish to join NATO, for reasons that are rooted in their histories. Theirs are small, weak, vulnerable countries ... The lesson they draw from history is that Europe may once again be divided between or among rival powers, in which case they will be forced to be part of a bloc dominated by those more powerful than they. In those circumstances, they understandably wish to have chosen their affiliation rather than having had it imposed on them, as it was after World War II and so often before.[36]

But simply because the states in the East perceive NATO membership as a major, if not vital, interest does not mean that the current NATO states should share that view. Indeed, NATO expansion is not in the best interest of the West, nor is it really in the interests of the states to the East.

It is difficult to persuade policymakers of Eastern and Central Europe, the Baltics, and the Balkans that NATO expansion is not in their interest. Beyond the issue of needlessly antagonizing Russia, if NATO expands as currently designed, the organization will be required to address security issues that no organization could effectively and successfully manage. Each new NATO state will bring to the organization known and unknown security issues that the organization may become treaty-bound to engage. The list of potential conflicts is myriad: Poland–Belarus, Kaliningrad–Lithuania, Hungary–Slovenia, Romania–Serbia, and Bulgaria–Macedonia, to note but a few. While efforts have been made to ameliorate these issues, many of these are age-old conflicts that rushed treaties designed to placate Brussels will not settle.[37]

New and aspiring NATO states have interests that differ from the organization's charter members and those states that joined during the Cold War. The new and aspiring members want a security guarantee, or a security blanket, that they believe will provide comfort in their present transitions, and afford them lasting security against a large, potentially aggressive Eurasian state. The states of the Cold War-era NATO want the organization to survive well into the new millennium. In that light they have recreated NATO.

Some Western policymakers genuinely believe in NATO's new collective security mission, but others simply want to maintain the alliance as an insurance policy *vis-à-vis* Russia. The new NATO is not focused on a common enemy state but on an enemy concept: instability. However, some would argue that the permanent members of NATO have taken steps to shield themselves from the instabilities emanating from the East. For instance, NATO has assured the Russians that NATO will not deploy sizeable numbers of troops in the new member states and will not deploy any nuclear weapons in the East. Yet for 50 years, NATO's credibility was based on the forward deployment of conventional forces and the deployment of tactical and strategic nuclear forces. Aspiring NATO members are seeking membership in the Cold War NATO. But that NATO no longer exists.

CONCLUSION

With the collapse of the Soviet Union, NATO leaders began the process of gradually transforming the organization for the post-Cold War era. Several options were available. Some argued that the organization was no longer relevant in a world without the Soviet Union, but this remained the position of a distinct minority. Determined to maintain the alliance, policymakers began considering new missions and purposes. Urged on by East European leaders and domestic actors, the Clinton administration proceeded to advocate the expansion of NATO's traditional functions. The first steps at reform were promulgated in policy statements declaring NATO's intent to confront broadly defined instabilities in the emerging era. As time pressed on, the United States initiated structural and institutional changes including NACC, CJTF, PFP, and, ultimately, the extension of full NATO membership to some East European states. Throughout this process, NATO has been transformed from a collective defense organization into an organization that, at least on paper, more closely resembles a collective security organization.

Other options were available to NATO policymakers in the 1990s. Although the Soviet Union no longer existed, one of the reasons for NATO's original creation was still present, and will always be present: the potential threat posed by a large, aggressive Eurasian power. Just as the United States engaged in Europe to confront Germany and the Soviet Union, some argued that the United States should remain in post-Cold War Europe to stem any future threat to European and American security interests. This time-honored position has many champions. In 1982, Hans Morgenthau's study on national interests concluded that the United States has:

> always striven to prevent the development of conditions in Europe which would be conducive to a European nation's interfering in the affairs of the Western Hemisphere or contemplating a direct attack upon the United States. These conditions would be most likely to arise if a European nation, its predominance unchallenged within Europe, could look across the sea for conquest without fear of being menaced at the center of its power; that is, in Europe itself.[38]

In this light, the United States and its NATO allies might have chosen to maintain the alliance, though in the absence of any immediate or medium-range threat, at a substantially reduced scale. During the Cold War, American personnel commitments to NATO reached over 300,000. Currently, the United States maintains a force of approximately 100,000 in Europe. With no serious threat on the horizon, the United States could reduce these numbers even further. Indeed, it could be reasoned that US personnel in Europe should only reach levels necessary to facilitate the rapid deployment of a large-scale American-based force capable of engaging significant military threats that might materialize in the future.

Had that course been selected, there would have been other means available to address the general concerns for post-Cold War European security. For instance, considerable attention and resources could have been devoted to the Organization for Security and Cooperation in Europe.[39] With its large membership and commitments to peacekeeping and other related operations, this institution could have served to advance the goals articulated in NATO's 1991 Strategic Concept without requiring substantial internal reforms to the alliance. A scaled down NATO, whose membership remained closed to newcomers, would have been a NATO held in abeyance. Its function would have been to monitor major shifts and events in Europe and serve as a credible check on any large state or states, seeking to decisively alter the balance of power in Eurasia.

Unfortunately, NATO did not choose that path. Rather, NATO has issued security guarantees to three new states and is poised to continue the process. Baltic and Balkan governments are working diligently within Partnership for Peace and are actively positioning themselves for second-round membership invitations. These nations, however, may find that the new NATO is a hollow shell of its previous incarnation. The Cold War NATO possessed great credibility. There remains little question that the alliance would have responded decisively to a Soviet attack on any of the permanent members. But one wonders how effectively NATO will respond in the future when called upon to address a conflict between two or more new members, or a new member and that nation's neighbor, that does not engage the vital interests of the other states in the organization.

And what of out-of-area operations? The new NATO is not concerning itself solely with issues limited to the old and new membership; NATO is now committed to addressing out-of-area conflicts. The lessons from NATO's experiences in Bosnia and Kosovo are still materializing. If one reads the pages of the *NATO Review* and listens to NATO officials in Brussels, the organization has been highly effective in implementing its role under the Dayton Accords. In Bosnia, the dismal record on refugee relocation and at-large war criminals has not deterred NATO officials from declaring, 'In contrast to the United Nations Protection Force (UNPROFOR) which preceded it, IFOR is a model of military efficiency, and command and control. It has written itself into the history books and textbooks. Only NATO, with its well-established political and military arrangements could have done it.'[40] Time and space do not permit a point-by-point refutation of this statement. Suffice it to say, had NATO truly been that effective in Bosnia, it might have established the necessary credibility to deter Slobodan Milosevic from ravaging Kosovo.

One might trust that the conflict in Kosovo would give policymakers pause as they consider Balkan candidacies for the future rounds of expansion. However, NATO initiatives during the crisis indicated that some in the alliance may be more determined than ever to expand NATO membership into the troubled region. On 24 March 1999, NATO Secretary General Javier Solana wrote to the governments of Albania, Bulgaria, Macedonia, Slovenia, and Romania that the alliance would view as 'unacceptable' any military strikes against the five nations by Serbia. Each of the five countries is a member of Partnership for Peace and all have expressed their desire to become full members of NATO. In his message of 24 March, Solana wrote, 'The alliance has repeatedly made clear that the security of all NATO member states is inseparably linked to that of the partner countries ... Your security is of a direct and material concern to the alliance.'[41]

It could plausibly be argued that this NATO communiqué served as a functional equivalent of an Article 5 security guarantee without corresponding Article 5 obligations having been undertaken by the Balkan states. This communiqué was also issued without the approval of the parliaments or congresses of NATO's existing members. The implications of this action are quite unsettling. In future times of crisis, NATO leaders in Brussels may unilaterally extend guarantees and commitments to states that only NATO governments can legally undertake. Such a development would only serve to widen NATO's sphere of responsibility and require the organization to respond to events that may wholly overtax NATO's interests, resources, and capabilities. Sharing the view that NATO 2000 ill-serves the interests of old or new members, Robert Art has argued that aspiring members 'must be made to understand that their security is better off with a viable NATO that they cannot join than one that is not viable but to which they belong'.[42] NATO has long served the interests of the United States, its allies, and general European security. As NATO enters the new millennium, no state poses a serious threat to the present balance of power in Eurasia. Indeed, it will likely be many years before a possible challenger could materialize. But NATO has a role to play in assuring such a development is checked and confronted. NATO affords the United States considerable flexibility in the manner in which it interacts in European military-security affairs. Through its position in the alliance, the United States can shape and lead policy debates and decision-making.

At this stage in the debate, it will be difficult to reverse the trends of the past decade. But these trends must be questioned and prevented from going further. Senator Richard Lugar (Republican, Indiana) has argued that if NATO does not go out of area, it will go out of business. Some might simply view Bosnia and Kosovo as out-of-area. But to advocates of the 1949 NATO, Poland, Hungary, the Czech Republic, and all aspiring NATO states in the Baltics and the Balkans, are out-of-area as well. In its determination to expand its scope and missions, NATO has set itself on a course that may lead to its collapse. Senator Lugar is incorrect. The phrase should read: 'If NATO goes out-of-area it will go out of business.'

NOTES

1. Donald E. Nuechterlein, *America Recommitted: United States National Interests in a Reconstructed World* (Lexington: UP of Kentucky 1991) p.28.
2. Ibid. pp.20–1.
3. See Hans J. Morgenthau, *Politics Among Nations: The Struggle for Power and Peace*, 3rd ed. (NY: Knopf 1964); Inis L. Claude Jr, *Power and International Relations* (NY: Random House 1962) John Mearsheimer, 'The False Promise of International Institutions', *International Security* 19 (Winter 1994/95), pp.5–49; and Richard Betts, 'Systems for Peace or Causes of War? Collective Security, Arms Control, and the New Europe', *International Security* 17 (Summer 1992) pp.5–43.
4. Charles A. Kupchan and Clifford A. Kupchan, 'Concerts, Collective Security, and the Future of Europe', *International Security* 16/1 (Summer 1991) p.126.
5. Robert Art, 'Creating a Disaster: NATO's Open Door Policy', *Political Science Quarterly* 113/3 (Fall 1998) p.395.
6. Ted Galen Carpenter and Barbara Conry (eds.) *NATO Enlargement: Illusions and Reality* (Washington DC: Cato Institute 1998) p.9.
7. Richard L. Kugler, *Laying the Foundations: The Evolution of NATO in the 1950s* (Santa Monica, CA: RAND 1990) p.22.
8. Robert H. Ferrell, 'The Formation of the Alliance, 1948–49', in Lawrence Kaplan (ed.) *American Historians and the Atlantic Alliance* (Kent State UP 1991) p.14.

176 *NATO Enters the 21st Century*

9. Ibid. p.29.
10. Robert E. Osgood, *NATO: The Entangling Alliance* (U. of Chicago Press 1962) p.29.
11. Marc Trachtenberg, *A Constructed Peace: The Making of the European Settlement, 1945–1963* (Princeton UP 1999) p.85.
12. Ibid. p.96.
13. See 'The Alliance's New Strategic Concept', NATO Document, Rome, Nov. 1991, http://www.nato.int/docu/comm/c911107a.htm.
14. See Trachtenberg (note 11).
15. See 'North Atlantic Cooperation Council Statement on Dialogue, Partnership And Cooperation', Press Communiqué M-NACC-1(91)111, North Atlantic Council, Brussels, 20 Dec. 1991.
16. Cited in David S. Yost, *NATO Transformed: The Alliance's New Roles in International Security* (Washington DC: US Inst. of Peace Press 1998) p.76.
17. Robert Kay, *NATO and the Future of Europe* (Lanham, MD: Rowman & Littlefield 1998) p.69.
18. Yost, *NATO Transformed* (note 16) p.98.
19. See Kay (note 17) p.72.
20. See 'Madrid Declaration on Euro-Atlantic Security and Cooperation', NATO Press Release N-1(97)81, Madrid, 8 July 1997.
21. John S. Duffield, 'Why NATO Persists', in Kenneth W. Thompson (ed.) *NATO and the Changing World Order: An Appraisal by Scholars and Policymakers* (Lanham, MD: UP of America 1996) p.117.
22. See 'Partnership for Peace: Invitation', NATO Press Communiqué M-1(94)2, NATO Headquarters, Brussels, 10–11 Jan. 1994.
23. *Study on NATO Enlargement*, NATO Office of Information and Press, Sept. 1996, p.2.
24. See 'The Madrid Declaration on Euro-Atlantic Security and Cooperation', NATO Press Release M-1 (97)81, Madrid, 8 July 1997.
25. Ibid.
26. 'The Senate Resolution on NATO Expansion', *Arms Control Today* (April 1998) p.14.
27. Alain Pellerin, 'NATO Enlargement – The Way Ahead' (Canadian Council for Int. Peace and Security 14 Feb. 1998) http://www.fas.org/man.eprint/nato-calgary.html.
28. See Jonathan Dean, 'NATO Enlargement: Coping with Act II', in Carpenter and Conry *NATO Enlargement* (note 6) pp.121–8; Bruce Russett and Allan C. Stam, 'Courting Disaster: An Expanded NATO vs. Russia and China', *Political Science Quarterly* 113/3 (Fall 1998) pp.383–403.
29. *A Charter of Partnership Among the United States of America and the Republic of Estonia, Republic of Latvia, and Republic of Lithuania*. Washington, DC (16 Jan. 1998) http://www usia.gov/regional/eur/baltics/tables/gendocs/charter.htm.
30. Rick Marshall, 'Stoyanov Hails US action Plan for Southeast Europe', *USIA*, 11 Feb. 1998, http://www.fas.org/,am/nato/national/98021102_wpo.htm.
31. Susan Eisenhower, 'Starting Cold War II?' *Naval Institute Proceedings* (May 1998) (note 6) http://www.usni.org/Proceedings/Articles98/PRO/eisenhower.htm.
32. Susan Eisenhower, 'Perils of Victory' in Carpenter and Conry, *NATO Enlargement* (note 6) p.113.
33. Cited in Sean Kay, *NATO and the Future of European Security* (Lanham, MD: Rowman & Littlefield 1998) p.95.
34. Pellerin (note 27).
35. Yost (note 18) p.133.
36. Michael Mandelbaum, 'NATO Expansion: A Bridge to the Nineteenth Century', (Washington DC: Center for Political and Strategic Studies, June 1997) http://www.cpss.org/nato/mandel97.htm.
37. William Odom delineates several bilateral agreements among new and aspiring NATO states. See 'Russia's Several Seats at the Table', *International Affairs* 74/4 (Oct. 1998) p.819.
38. Hans J. Morgenthau, *In Defense of the National Interest: A Critical Examination of American Foreign Policy* (Lanham, MD: UP of America 1982) p.5.
39. See Richard E. Rupp and Mary McKenzie, 'The Organization for Security and Cooperation in Europe: Institutional Reform and Political Reality', in Mary McKenzie and Peter Loedel (eds.) *The Promise and Reality of European Security Cooperation: States, Interests, and Institutions* (Westport, CT: Praeger 1998) pp.119–38.
40. Michael Ruhle and Nick Williams, 'View from NATO: Why NATO Will Survive', *International Strategy* 16/1 (1997) p.109.
41. Craig Whitney, 'Conflict in the Balkans: The Alliance', *New York Times*, 25 March 1999, p.25.
42. Art (note 5) p.400.

Abstracts

NATO's New Strategic Concept:
Coherent Blueprint or Conceptual Muddle?
TED GALEN CARPENTER

NATO's new Strategic Concept is a document that attempts to placate competing factions on several major issues. Indeed, the carefully crafted language barely conceals the depth of discord on such matters as NATO's commitment to out-of-area missions or the functional relationship between the alliance and the European Security and Defense Identity. As a political and public relations document, the Strategic Concept has been a solid success in preserving at least the façade of alliance unity. Yet the underlying substantive disagreements continue to roil. Thus, as a coherent strategic blueprint the Concept is not, and likely will not be, terribly relevant.

NATO Burden-Sharing: Promises, Promises
ALAN TONELSON

Securing adequate military burden-sharing has been a major failure of America's NATO policy. The Kosovo War showed that, 50 years after NATO's founding, European alliance members still cannot defeat even a military midget on their own. Continuing transatlantic military imbalances drain from the United States valuable resources, threaten to embroil America in numerous conflicts that do not affect important US interests, and undermine American public support for US-European security cooperation. Only a significantly more detached US approach to European security – reflecting NATO's recent acknowledgement that US and European interests are not always identical – can produce equitable burden-sharing.

US Hegemony and the Perpetuation of NATO
CHRISTOPHER LAYNE

Offensive realist theory explains why – contrary to neorealist predictions – NATO did not unravel after the Cold War. In the wake of the Soviet Union's collapse, Type I offensive realism (which explains why great powers engage in expansionist behavior) predicts that the United States would seek – geographically and ideologically – to extend its influence and control over the European security environment. Type II offensive realism (which explains why great powers seek hegemony) predicts that the United States would seek to prevent both the re-emergence of multipolarity in Europe and the emergence of rival European power centers. US policy – negotiations on German reunification, NATO enlargement, the Bosnia and Kosovo interventions, and the response to the European Security and Defense Policy – confirm these predictions.

The New NATO and Relations with Russia
ALTON FRYE

The promise of constructive NATO-Russia relations remains in jeopardy, prejudiced by friction over the alliance's expansion, its intervention in the Balkans, and Moscow's perception that its interests are being disregarded. On a host of issues, from stability in Europe to the maintenance of effective arms control regimes and management of regional crises beyond the Continent, cooperative working arrangements with Russia are vital. To assure such cooperation NATO should make clear that it is open to Russian membership, priority should go to EU expansion, and the United States should pursue joint defenses with Russia against potential ballistic missile threats.

NATO's 'Fundamental Divergence' over Proliferation
KORI SCHAKE

NATO has been so consumed with managing the Balkans and nascent EU security policies that it has largely ignored the much more serious defense challenge of managing proliferation of weapons of mass destruction. US and European officials have divergent approaches that must be reconciled for the United States to construct a national missile defense in the near term. The means for creating a common approach lie within reach: modifying the

ABM Treaty if possible, including critical allies, assisting European ballistic missile defenses, sustained priority in NATO budgeting and programming, supporting EU strategic intelligence collection and assessment, and building US-EU 'pillar two' links.

The Corruption of NATO: NATO Moves East
AMOS PERLMUTTER

The Cold War ushered the end of political, and especially military, institutions that were designed to deter the Soviet Union and its ambitions on the Central Front. However, the NATO Alliance is unwilling to reform and downsize. In fact, a newly adopted strategic doctrine extended NATO to encompass the newly independent East European states.

The first military exercise of an extended NATO was a response to a humanitarian crisis. American political capital was wasted in the war against Yugoslavia, which was never an American strategic interest, and succeeded in straining relations not only with Russia, but also with China. The Kosovo War, which was designed to demonstrate the political effectiveness of an extended NATO, instead contributed to its corruption.

NATO 1949, NATO 2000:
From Collective Defense toward Collective Security
RICHARD RUPP

During the past ten years, NATO has been gradually transformed from a collective defense organization into one that more closely resembles a collective security organization. The Cold War NATO unified nations that shared a vital interest in confronting a specific threat. The post-Cold War NATO identifies no state as a threat. Rather, managing general Eurasian instability is to serve as the organization's *raison d'être*. Historically, international organizations have failed when called upon to meet similar challenges. If NATO expansion continues, the organization will be required to address a myriad of security challenges and will eventually atrophy and collapse.

About the Contributors

Ted Galen Carpenter is Vice President for Defense and Foreign Policy Studies at the Cato Institute, Washington DC. He is the author or editor of 11 books, including *NATO's Empty Victory: A Postmortem on the Balkan War* (2000), *NATO Enlargement: Illusions and Reality* (1998), *The Future of NATO* (1995), and *Beyond NATO: Staying Out of Europe's Wars* (1994). Carpenter's articles on international affairs have appeared in such journals as *Foreign Policy, Foreign Affairs, and Mediterranean Quarterly* and in newspapers throughout the United States, Europe, and East Asia. Dr Carpenter received his PhD in US diplomatic history from the University of Texas.

Alton Frye is a Presidential Senior Fellow at the Council on Foreign Relations. Previously, he was a strategic analyst at the RAND Corporation and a Visiting Professor of Political Science at Harvard University and UCLA. He is the author of *A Responsible Congress: The Politics of National Security* and the editor of *Toward an International Criminal Court?* His articles have appeared in *Foreign Affairs*, the *New York Times*, the *Washington Post* and many other publications. Dr Frye holds a PhD from Yale University.

Christopher Layne is a MacArthur Foundation Fellow in Global Security and a Visiting Professor at the University of Southern California. Previously, he was a residential fellow at the Center for Science and International Affairs at the Kennedy School of Government, Harvard University. Layne's articles have appeared in numerous journals and newspapers, including *International Security, Foreign Policy*, the *National Interest, Orbis*, the *Atlantic Monthly, New Republic*, the *New*

York Times, the *Washington Post*, the *Wall Street Journal*, and the *Los Angeles Times*. He holds a PhD in political science from the University of California at Berkeley.

Amos Perlmutter is a Professor of Political Science and Sociology at the American University and co-editor of the *Journal of Strategic Studies*. He is the author of numerous books, including *Making the World Safe for Democracy: The Legacy of Wilsonianism and Its Challengers* (1997). Perlmutter's articles have appeared in the *New York Times*, the *Washington Post*, the *Los Angeles Times, Harpers, Foreign Affairs, Foreign Policy, New Republic*, the *Wall Street Journal*, the *National Interest*, and the *International Herald Tribune*.

Richard Rupp received his PhD in political science from the University of California, Santa Barbara, and is currently Visiting Assistant Professor at Purdue University, Indiana. His research focuses on armed conflict in the post-Cold War era. His recent publications center on the Western response to war in the Balkans, where he has spent considerable time. Rupp is currently at work on a book, *Beware the Baltics and the Balkans: The Next Stage of NATO Expansion*.

Kori Schake is a Senior Research Professor at the Institute for National Strategic Studies, National Defense University in Washington DC. She worked previously as a NATO expert on the Joint Staff and as Special Assistant to the Assistant Secretary of Defense for Strategy and Requirements. Dr Schake received her PhD from the University of Maryland and is currently a Visiting Assistant Professor at that institution. Her articles have appeared in *Survival* and other publications.

Alan Tonelson is a Research Fellow at the US Business and Industry Council Educational Foundation, a Washington DC-based institute studying national security, economic, and technology issues. His previous positions include associate editor of *Foreign Policy* and fellow of the Economic Strategy Institute. Tonelson's articles and reviews have appeared in the *Atlantic Monthly, Foreign Affairs*, the *Harvard Business Review*, the *New York Times*, the *Washington Post*, the *Wall Street Journal*, and the *New Republic*, as well as in several anthologies. His book, *The Race to the Bottom: Why a Worldwide Worker Surplus and Uncontrolled Free Trade are Sinking American Living Standards*, will be published later this year by Westview Press.

Index

Note: Figures after the suffix n or nn indicate endnote numbers on the page given before the n.

Books of Related Interest

Twenty-First Century Weapons Proliferation
Are We Ready?

Henry Sokolski, *Executive General of the Non Proliferation Policy Education Center* (Ed)

A decade after Coalition forces targeted Saddam's missile, nuclear, chemical, and biological weapons capabilities, public concern about strategic weapons proliferation has grown. India, Iraq, Iran, North Korea, China and Pakistan have all renewed their efforts to acquire weapons capable of mass destruction. Meanwhile, growing surpluses of weapons-usable materials in the US, Russia, Japan and Europe have raised the specter of nuclear theft and, with the Tokyo sarin attacks of 1995, the most horrific forms of terrorism.

What should we make of these threats? Are the planned responses of the US and its allies sufficient? Will history ultimately end in a more prosperous, democratic and peaceful world or will the accelerating availability of strategic technology be our doom? These questions are the focus of *Next Century Weapons Proliferation: Are We Ready?*

In this book leading national security practitioners from the administrations of Presidents Ford, Carter, Reagan, Bush and Clinton share their insights. Among the authors are two former US assistant secretaries of defense, a former US Nuclear Regulatory Commissioner, a former member of the National Security Council, a former national security director from the White House Office of Science and Technology Policy and a former deputy for nonproliferation policy from the Pentagon. Their analyses along with those of other experts and the editors of two leading journals on terrorism and the Middle East will not only clarify the weapons proliferation threats the US and its friends will face, but suggest what new policies their governments must consider. Teachers of international relations, concerned citizens, and national security analysts interested in learning more about these security challenges will find *Next Century Weapons Proliferation* a useful guide.

192 pages 2001
0 7146 5095 1 cloth
0 7146 8137 7 paper

FRANK CASS PUBLISHERS
Newbury House, 900 Eastern Avenue, Ilford, Essex, IG2 7HH
Tel: +44 (0)20 8599 8866 Fax: +44 (0)20 8599 0984 E-mail: info@frankcass.com
NORTH AMERICA
5824 NE Hassalo Street, Portland, OR 97213 3644, USA
Tel: 800 944 6190 Fax: 503 280 8832 E-mail: cass@isbs.com
Website: www.frankcass.com

The US Military Profession into the Twenty-First Century

War, Peace and Politics

Sam C Sarkesian, *Loyola University* and **Robert E O'Connor Jr**, *Former History Instructor at the US Army Command and General Staff College, Fort Leavenworth, Kansas*

The US military profession in the new security era is faced with a paramount problem: how to reconcile military professional ethos and raison d'etre with the new forces challenging the traditional notion of military professionalism. These new forces can be grouped into two categories: American society and the military; and the utility of military force in the changing international environment. Democratization of the military, the changing domestic landscape and questions about the meaning of American culture pose challenges to the traditional military professional relationship with US society. In addition, the new world order and the new strategic landscape, combined with technological advances and the United States' role as lone superpower – world hegemon – have raised serious doubts about the utility of military power. That is, aside from success in battle, which other uses of US military forces are possible without eroding its effectiveness in battle? The US military therefore faces a dilemma: how to respond to changed domestic and strategic landscapes without diminishing its primary function.

This volume examines this pressing dilemma and proposes that the military profession adopt a policy of constructive political engagement. Although the military profession is not the only actor engaging in shaping and affecting these matters, it is the critical actor. Focusing on the two major categories outlined above, this study looks at a number of elements ranging from the characteristics of the military profession, civilian and military cultures, civil–military relations, to conflict characteristics and US strategy, the operational parameters of military force and the revolution in military affairs. In each chapter the focus is on the need of the military profession to have its voice heard not only within the National Command Authority and Congress, but also by the American people. The authors conclude that without such a political voice, the US military profession will be unable to respond effectively to the domestic and strategic landscapes of the new millennium.

240 pages illus 1999
0 7146 4919 8 cloth
0 7146 4472 2 paper

FRANK CASS PUBLISHERS
Newbury House, 900 Eastern Avenue, Ilford, Essex, IG2 7HH
Tel: +44 (0)20 8599 8866 Fax: +44 (0)20 8599 0984 E-mail: info@frankcass.com
NORTH AMERICA
5824 NE Hassalo Street, Portland, OR 97213 3644, USA
Tel: 800 944 6190 Fax: 503 280 8832 E-mail: cass@isbs.com
Website: www.frankcass.com

US Allies in a Changing World

Barry Rubin, *BESA Center, Bar Ilan University* and
Thomas Keaney, *John Hopkins University* (Eds)

Since the beginning of the Cold War in the 1940s, the United States has become the leader of a far-ranging alliance of system; including countries in Europe, the Middle East, and Asia. The history of these different alliances poses one of the most interesting episodes in modern diplomacy. Many countries or governments saw their relationship to the United States as vital. This link was the source of economic and political aid, strategic backing (sometimes including direct military intervention), intelligence
co-operation, or joint regional efforts. Complicating these relationships were the different objectives of the individual countries and, in some cases, conflicts among the allies themselves. Also present was the tension of divergent interests between the junior and senior partners. At times, only the common need to combat the spread of communist bloc influence bound these partners together.

Several historic changes have forced major adjustments onto these relationships. The Cold War's end removed a fundamental cause of these alliances and perhaps part of the motivation for maintaining them. In its absence, the priority has switched to regional conflicts and other more local issues. For the United States, too, its post-Cold War international role has been challenged by domestic needs. Yet American responsibilities are, if anything, enhanced in an essentially unipolar world. More than ever before-and whether it wants the burden or not-the United States has a capacity for global hegemony.

This book explores the development of America's alliances from the American perspective, as well as that of its most vital allies: Great Britain, Germany, the Gulf States, Israel, Turkey, Australia, Japan, South Korea, and Taiwan. It considers how these relationships have changed in the tumultuous international environment of the past half-century, as well as their present situations, and likely future direction of a country's link to the United States.

256 pages 2000
0 7146 5078 1 cloth

FRANK CASS PUBLISHERS
Newbury House, 900 Eastern Avenue, Ilford, Essex, IG2 7HH
Tel: +44 (0)20 8599 8866 Fax: +44 (0)20 8599 0984 E-mail: info@frankcass.com
NORTH AMERICA
5824 NE Hassalo Street, Portland, OR 97213 3644, USA
Tel: 800 944 6190 Fax: 503 280 8832 E-mail: cass@isbs.com
Website: www.frankcass.com

International Security in a Global Age
Securing the Twenty-First Century

Clive Jones, *University of Leeds*, and
Caroline Kennedy-Pipe, *University of Durham* (Eds)

In the post-Cold War world, debates over security have broadened beyond the realm of traditional military concerns. Resurgent nationalism, mass migration, religious radicalism, economic globalisation and environmental degradation have become increasingly the focus of debate in the field of security studies. International relations theorists in particular have sought to escape the intellectual hegemony of the realist paradigm in favour of a more normative approach to understanding the world in which we live.

Nonetheless, international politics is still trying to cope with the empirical legacy of the Cold War. Nuclear proliferation, the continued search by Russia for security, the attempt by Washington to sustain its dominant position in international affairs, continued concerns in the West over the influence of religious, and in particular Islamic, radicalism, stand as clear examples of themes from the past continuing to inform present debates about international security. This volume examines the new, the changing, and the enduring features of international security in the post-Cold War era. In so doing, it examines the extent to which present state structures and institutions have been able to adapt and accommodate themselves to the diversity of security threats.

Contributors: *Caroline Kennedy-Pipe, Jason Ralph, Deborah Sanders, Neil Winn, Alan Collins, Tamara Duffy, Hugh Dyer, Edward Spiers* and *Clive Jones.*

256 pages 2000
0 7146 5061 7 cloth
0 7146 8111 3 paper

FRANK CASS PUBLISHERS
Newbury House, 900 Eastern Avenue, Ilford, Essex, IG2 7HH
 Tel: +44 (0)20 8599 8866 Fax: +44 (0)20 8599 0984 E-mail: info@frankcass.com
NORTH AMERICA
5824 NE Hassalo Street, Portland, OR 97213 3644, USA
Tel: 800 944 6190 Fax: 503 280 8832 E-mail: cass@isbs.com
Website: www.frankcass.com

Critical Reflections on Security and Change

Stuart Croft and **Terry Terrif**, *both at University of Birmingham* (Eds)

'...an invaluable and stimulating guide to the state of security studies today, demonstrating the rich diversity of approaches.'
Lawrence Freedman, *King's College, London*

'An excellent collection that critically examines current debates, and captures the intellectual ferment in contemporary security studies.
Recommended reading for anyone trying to untangle its threads.'
Keith Krause, *Graduate Institute of International Studies, Geneva*

'Critical Reflections on Security and Change analyzes the issues of the day in a thoughtful and compelling manner. Scholars and policymakers alike will benefit from this study.'
Michael E. Brown, *Georgetown University, Washington, DC*

Security studies has changed drastically over the past twenty years. The transformations that have taken place are remarkable in their scale and scope, and even more impressive is the pace at which they have occurred. But much more striking is that change is continuing. The world seems still to be in a state of flux. The best we may be able to do today, as the various debates about the possible future nature of the international system suggest, is to sketch in some possible broad outlines of how security politics and security studies might evolve and operate.

The contributors to this volume were given a very challenging task: to reflect critically on where we have been over the past twenty years, where we are, and where we might be going, in a select few areas of security studies. In spite of the individuality of approaches and spread of topic areas addressed, the authors set forth observations that are both intriguing and provocative. They conclude that analysts and policy-makers have not been able to respond well to the changes that have occurred and that they must revise their approach to the study of security if they are to meet the challenges of the future.

Contributors: *Stuart Croft, Barry Buzan, Edward A. Kolodziej, Patrick M. Morgan, Steve Smith, John Roper, Craig N. Murphy, Thomas G. Weiss, Colin McInnes, Chris C. Demchak, Darryl Howlett, John Simpson* and *Terry Terriff.*

272 pages 2000
0 7146 4993 7 cloth
0 7146 8061 3 paper
A special issue of the journal Contemporary Security Policy

FRANK CASS PUBLISHERS
Newbury House, 900 Eastern Avenue, Ilford, Essex, IG2 7HH
Tel: +44 (0)20 8599 8866 Fax: +44 (0)20 8599 0984 E-mail: info@frankcass.com
NORTH AMERICA
5824 NE Hassalo Street, Portland, OR 97213 3644, USA
Tel: 800 944 6190 Fax: 503 280 8832 E-mail: cass@isbs.com
Website: www.frankcass.com